High-tech Internet Start-ups in India

Technology entrepreneurship has been receiving growing importance as an effective instrument to promote national economic growth, with empirical researchers and policymakers. India has emerged as the third-largest base for high-tech start-ups in the world. Although there is a surge in start-up creation in India, little is known about the vital factors that are required for these start-ups to survive, sustain, and grow into large enterprises. There is limited exploration on the structure, process, and strategies adopted by high-tech start-ups in existing literature. This has resulted in insufficient understanding of the high-tech start-up life cycle, particularly in emerging economies such as India. This book is an attempt to provide this information based on true facts and verifiable analysis. It reviews the entrepreneurial, firm-specific, and external environment-specific aspects that influence the key life cycle stages of high-tech start-ups and identifies the key factors that influence each milestone. By analysing empirical data, it provides a multidimensional framework to understand the life cycle of high-tech start-ups in India.

H. S. Krishna is a research consultant based in Bengaluru, India. He was previously research associate at the Indian Institute of Science, Bengaluru. His research interests are entrepreneurial ecosystems, high-tech start-ups, transnational entrepreneurship, and entrepreneurial learning.

High-tech Internet Start-ups in India

H. S. Krishna

CAMBRIDGE
UNIVERSITY PRESS

University Printing House, Cambridge CB2 8BS, United Kingdom

One Liberty Plaza, 20th Floor, New York, NY 10006, USA

477 Williamstown Road, Port Melbourne, VIC 3207, Australia

314–321, 3rd Floor, Plot 3, Splendor Forum, Jasola District Centre, New Delhi–110025, India

79 Anson Road, #06–04/06, Singapore 079906

Cambridge University Press is part of the University of Cambridge.

It furthers the University's mission by disseminating knowledge in the pursuit of education, learning and research at the highest international levels of excellence.

www.cambridge.org
Information on this title: www.cambridge.org/9781108485388

First published 2019

Printed in India by Nutech Print Services, New Delhi 110020

A catalogue record for this publication is available from the British Library

Library of Congress Cataloging-in-Publication Data
Names: Krishna, H. S., 1978 - author.
Title: High-tech internet start-ups in India / H.S. Krishna.
Description: Cambridge, United Kingdom ; New York : Cambridge University Press, [2019] | Includes bibliographical references and index.
Identifiers: LCCN 2019016848 | ISBN 9781108485388 (hardback: alk. paper)
Subjects: LCSH: High technology industries–India. | New business enterprises–India. | Electronic commerce–India. | Internet industry–India.
Classification: LCC HC440.H53 K75 2019 | DDC 338.4/760954–dc23
LC record available at https://lccn.loc.gov/2019016848

ISBN 978-1-108-48538-8 Hardback

To Nandini and Anagha

Contents

Tables

Figures

Preface

Start-ups have captured the imagination of people today across the world. Many myths, wrong perceptions, and false notions of success and glory are being propagated and worse – people tend to believe these without verifying. This book is an attempt to state the facts, based on true, verifiable information and analysis of what it takes for an entrepreneur to set up, sustain, and grow new ventures in the digital world today, particularly in the context of India. Although this book is academic in nature, there is enough information for all types of audience to gain value out of it.

For academics, it offers rich insight into how to pursue systematic research and inquiry in the relatively new phenomenon of start-ups and their life cycle. This is meant to be an introductory and exploratory effort in analysing the life cycle of high-tech start-ups in India. The topics dealt with in this book are fairly broad in nature, and each of these topics deserve a much more nuanced examination. This book will be a handy reference for the undergraduate, postgraduate, and doctoral programmes in economics and entrepreneurship. For students and prospective entrepreneurs, this book provides unbiased inputs on the factors that a prospective entrepreneur needs to be equipped with – to pursue the journey of entrepreneurship in the high-tech sector of India.

For practising entrepreneurs, the book will help to reflect on their current state of affairs and help them in taking any required measure in due course. Apart from entrepreneurs, all major stakeholders of the entrepreneurial ecosystem, such as business and technology incubators, accelerators, VC and angel/seed investors, and multinational companies and large enterprises that have corporate development/ mergers and acquisition (M&A) teams and start-up specific programmes/ initiatives, will find the book a handy reference and resourceful input to the various activities that they are pursuing.

For policymakers, the book provides insight into the necessary and sufficient aspects to be taken care of during policy formulation and evaluation, to create regional entrepreneurial hubs, and nurture them. In particular, government institutions, government affiliated entrepreneurship and skill development training institutes, and government-funded R&D institutions and programmes where entrepreneurship is being encouraged will benefit from the dissemination of insights obtained from the systematic study.

The high-level flow of each chapter is as follows:

Chapter 1 provides the context, key concepts, and definitions of start-ups, what they are and what they are not, and their relevance to the economy. Finally, the evolution of policymaking around start-ups across the world and in India, in particular, is discussed.

Chapter 2 would be particularly useful to researchers, academics, and students. One can understand all aspects of the research methodology, starting from binding the scope of the research problem, identification of the research objectives, describing the data sources, research instruments, and definitions of key parameters to be used for the study to providing a brief about the different methods of statistical analysis for the evaluation of proposed hypotheses.

Chapter 3 is a light read relative to the other chapters. It provides an overview of the various characteristics and aspects of the start-ups and entrepreneurs who were contacted for the purposes of the study. Aggregate details such as the distribution of start-ups based on year of incorporation, number of founders, gender of founders, target market segment, location of operations, and entrepreneurial exposure are provided to begin with. Later, some initial statistical analysis is performed to understand how one parameter of the start-up or the founder impacts the other in isolation. For those interested in the micro aspects and interplay of factors affecting the start-ups and their operations, these types of analyses provide them some useful insights.

Chapters 4, 5, 6, and 7 form the core part of this book. Each of these chapters analyses one of the key milestones in the start-up life cycle using a consistent approach. To begin with, the readers are presented with the current state of knowledge about the milestones in the start-up life cycle. Next, the hypotheses that are formulated, based on the literature review, are discussed. This is followed by a section which details how the quantifiable variables and measures are defined to scientifically validate the hypotheses related to the particular milestone of high-tech start-ups life cycle. Later, the results of statistical analyses are discussed. In all these chapters, a visual form of initial analysis is presented for each milestone/set of hypotheses being tested. Post that, the actual results of the statistical analysis are described, followed by the analysis and interpretation of the results – including the implications of the results. Each chapter summarizes the key results and interpretations obtained on account of the analysis of each of the milestones of the high-tech start-up life cycle. For the more statistically inclined, appendices at the end of each chapter provide further details of the statistical test results obtained. The readers need to understand that although the flow of each of these chapters is homogeneous, each chapter deals with different objectives, data sets, and methods of analyses.

Chapter 8 provides the summary of the analyses and their implications to the diverse set of audiences, such as entrepreneurs, students, academics, and policymakers. It also highlights limitations of the scope of study presented in the book and discusses areas for further research and analysis.

This book will meet its intended purpose if any of the readers find value and benefit from the information provided. If any discrepancies or errors inadvertently remain in this book, I am alone responsible for the same.

27 April 2019   H. S. Krishna

Acknowledgements

It is a privilege to get an opportunity to pursue research at the Indian Institute of Science (IISc), Bengaluru. It is equally satisfying to get the key findings of my research published as a book to enable wider dissemination. At this juncture, I would like to take a moment to acknowledge the contributions, support, and guidance of many individuals who were instrumental in enabling me to achieve this goal. To begin with, I would like to express my heartfelt gratitude to my research guide, former Chairman of the Department of Management Studies, Prof. M. H. Bala Subrahmanya. I have been fortunate to work under his supervision. From the time I expressed interest in pursuing research till reviewing the pre-final draft of my thesis and the chapters of this book prior to formal submission, he has steadfastly provided his inputs and feedback, guiding me in each and every aspect of the research work. His dedication and commitment to guiding his students, honesty, integrity, and transparency in his conduct are lessons for life that I will forever remember and practise.

I would like to thank all the faculty members of the Department of Management Studies, IISc, in particular, Prof. Chiranjit Mukhopadyay, Dr Mathirajan, and Dr P. Balachandra, for providing valuable inputs during my PhD days, the outputs of which are now reflected in this book. I learnt the key tenets of research methodology and statistics as part of my research training from these faculty members. I also thank (ret.) Prof. Mathew Manimala from the Indian Institute of Management, Bengaluru, and Prof. N. V. Joshi, Centre for Ecological Studies, IISc, for their useful inputs and review as part of my PhD comprehensive examination. Their inputs helped shape the narrative of the book.

I acknowledge the support and assistance provided by all the office staff at our department, especially Mrs Bhanumathi, Mr Salim, Ms Tharakeshwari, Ms Anitha, Mr Anantha, Mr Umashankar, and Maryamma, for helping me out in all the office administrative aspects related to my tenure at the department.

I am thankful to the help, inputs, guidance, and support provided by Mr Sharad Sharma, Mr Avinash Raghava, Mr Prasanna Krishnamoorthy, Ms Manjula

Sridhar, Mr Ravi Gururaj, Mr Mukund Mohan, Mr Kunal Kashyap, Mr Ashwin, and Mr C. S. Murali; all iKEN, iSPIRT, TiE, and NASSCOM Fellows; and volunteers and entrepreneurs who helped me connect with a vast majority of high-tech start-up founders. Without all your support, my data collection exercise would never have been complete.

I have developed long-lasting relationships with my fellow researchers at IISc, in particular, Kshitija, Deepak, Murali, Ganesh, Vinay, Tarun, Kiranmayi, Sreejith, Sindhuja, Santhosh, Kavita, and Shantanu, who have provided their useful suggestions in shaping this book. I thank them for putting up with me and helping me whenever I needed anything from them.

I would like to thank Anwesha Rana and the Editorial team of Cambridge University Press, particularly Anushruti Ganguly and Tapajyoti Chaudhuri, who have diligently worked on my manuscript and enabled its transformation into this book. I also thank the two blind reviewers of my manuscript – who provided constructive and positive feedback to enable the publication of this book in its current form.

On my family front, I will remain indebted forever to my wife, Nandini, and my daughter, Anagha, who have sacrificed many things over the past several years since I started pursuing active research, put up with my almost eternal absence from home during this period, and helped me gather myself when I faced difficult situations. Further, my parents, my mother-in-law, my brother, and my sister-in-law have always rallied behind me, and have been a constant source of moral and emotional support. I sincerely thank them for encouraging me to pursue my research interests.

1

Introduction

Preamble

New and young businesses, referred to now as 'start-ups', have gained growing relevance and importance among the policy makers and leaders of economies worldwide. In particular, as the developed and developing economies make the transition to knowledge-based economies, the high-technology (high-tech) sector has been the primary engine in enabling this transformation. The promotion of high-tech start-ups helps economies to generate new products, services, and business models that differentiate the nations' output from the rest of the world and enhances the economic progress of these countries (Saxenian 2002).

Therefore, the field of high-tech start-ups has been receiving much importance within the entrepreneurship literature from the 1980s. Gries and Naude (2008) observed that these new, small firms are more likely to grow (Johnson, McMillan, and Woodruff 2000; Lingelbach, de la Vina, and Asel 2005), create new jobs (McMillan and Woodruff 2002; Audretsch, Keilbach, and Lehmann 2006), and promote new and flexible organizational forms (Kim, Aldrich, and Keister 2006). In particular, small high-tech start-ups have been recognized as being the major drivers of job creation and innovation and thus economic growth (Birch 1979; Baumol 2002; Kirchhoff and Spencer 2008).

In the USA, the 1970s and 1980s had the most impact and contribution to employment and economy from high-tech start-ups. The advent of the Internet in the USA and incremental successes in the biotechnology industry disrupted the marketplace through the creation of new start-ups that leveraged these technologies to provide new products and services in ways that were not possible before. At its peak, these entrepreneurial companies contributed 20 per cent of US employment in the 1980s. Despite being in recession, between

March 2009 and March 2010, 394,000 new businesses were formed, creating 2.3 million jobs in the USA (Mutikani 2012).

Even emerging economies have benefited on account of high-tech industry-based growth strategies. Taiwan's contribution to total domestic output from the high-tech sector increased from 9.7 per cent in 1980 to 28.5 per cent in 2003. South Korea's high-tech manufacturing contribution to the total domestic manufacturing output jumped from 9.6 per cent in 1980 to 21.5 per cent in 2003 (Commission on Strategic Development 2007). In India, an average of 400 new technology start-ups were created during 2009–2012 (Microsoft Accelerator India 2012).

The rapid proliferation and use of the Internet across the world have accelerated the process of globalization, aided by disruptive technological changes in just a matter of a decade and half (Startup Genome 2012). Kane (2010) ascertained that in the USA, start-ups were responsible for all the new job creations for 21 out of the past 28 years (75 per cent of the time frame of the study). Some of the leading companies in the technology industry today, such as Apple, Cisco, eBay, Qualcomm, Intel, were incubated as tiny start-ups during their formative years (Barringer, Jones, and Neubaum 2005; Paulraj 2012).

Start-ups have started to contribute in such massive proportions to economies worldwide on account of macroeconomic changes, including the lowering of entry cost for start-ups and the maturing of the institutional finance industry (venture capital [VC] firms, seed and angel investments by firms and high net-worth individuals). Further, the ability to facilitate rapid and global adoption of a new product or service, and better knowhow of how to manage these new and young businesses during their initial years of inception and operations have also paved the way for enhancing the contributions of start-ups to the economies (Startup Genome 2015).

From the Asian perspective, the overall VC investment just for Q2 2015 was over US$10 billion (1 billion = 100 crore), registering a 45 per cent year-on-year growth. Asian Internet and mobile start-ups took about 82 per cent of the worldwide VC funding in Q2 2015, with the Asian region attracting approximately US$33.5 billion VC funding across the past five quarters (Venture Pulse 2015). In India, companies such as Flipkart, MakeMyTrip, and InMobi are making their presence felt in the global marketplace, attracting more than US$1 billion valuations (Nambiar 2011). As of 2015, there were eight home-grown unicorns (start-ups that are valued at US$1 billion or more) operating in India (*The Times of India* 2015).

According to NASSCOM (2014), India has approximately 3,100 start-ups operating in the country, on account of which it has now been recognized as the third-largest base for high-tech start-ups in the world. In the year 2014 itself, about two start-ups were created in India every day – a 100 per cent increase from 2013 – which indicates the momentum building up in this sector in the country.

While the preceding discussion provides a glimpse of the activity around high-tech start-up emergence, we need to understand that these start-ups have a very high mortality rate (Bala Subrahmanya 2010). The contribution to innovation, job creation, and economic growth, as outlined in the preceding discussion, are from those start-ups that are able to brave the uncertainty and come out successful. Storey (1985) concluded that the net job creation was confined to a very tiny population of start-ups that were able to survive the initial hiccups in their operations. He estimated that only about 4 per cent of the small entrepreneurial businesses that started during the previous decade of his study created about 50 per cent of the employment in the economy. This estimation was further supported by Reynolds and Miller (1988), who explored the linkage between new firm formation and their corresponding contribution to employment in Minnesota, USA.

The contributions of these surviving small entrepreneurial firms to the economy can be better understood if we can comprehend the unique set of constraints these firms face along the life cycle. Start-ups have to deal with the liability of newness, because they are trying to create a unique offering that has no precedence (Stinchcombe 1965; Baum 1996; Certo 2003, Bala Subrahmanya 2010). Since this offering is new, there is a considerable degree of uncertainty regarding its future. The degree of uncertainty (market based and technological) and the volatile nature of the environment that they operate in are key factors that can be used to describe high-tech start-up firms (Mohr, Sengupta, and Slater 2011).

More often, these start-ups are created on a small scale and with limited resources. These ventures often face large and experienced competitors, powerful suppliers, sceptical customers, and scarce resources. Therefore, their ability to withstand sustained losses is usually very limited. Given this, researchers have observed that start-ups have a high failure rate relative to established firms (Hannan and Freeman 1984; Stinchcombe 1965; Singh, House, and Tucker 1986; McDougall, Robinson, and DeNiso 1992; Hay, Verdin, and Williamson 1993; Robinson 1998; Bala Subrahmanya 2010).

Financial capitalization is another important factor contributing to the formation of new high-tech start-ups. Cohen and Levin (1989) observed that when capital market imperfections make it difficult for entrepreneurs to secure funding, the chances of emergence of new start-ups are not very likely. Shane and Venkataraman (2000) observed that start-ups emerge when opportunities are more uncertain (Casson 1982), when opportunities do not require complementary assets (Teece 1986), and when opportunities destroy competence (Tushman and Anderson 1986).

Blank (2010) observed that most start-up founders, especially those with prior corporate experience, failed because they tried to apply principles that worked well for them in the context of a large enterprise as they started their new ventures. For example, he explained that most start-ups failed due to the inability to onboard paying customers during the initial stages of operations, and not due to the failure of product development. If a feature or an offering is built on time as per the planned budget with highest quality, good design, and navigation capabilities, but no one from the customer segment is interested in using the offering and paying for it, it just means that start-ups are executing flawlessly on a bad plan.

Despite the high failure rate of high-tech start-ups as illustrated earlier, these firms have played an important role in transforming advanced economies across the world. However, most studies thus far have treated high-tech start-ups synonymously with small businesses (Barringer and Ireland 2008). The unique nature of high-tech start-ups and the key factors that influence their life cycle, particularly in emerging economies like India, have not been examined in detail (Bruton and Rubanik 2002; Song et al. 2008). The present study, therefore, assumes significance in this context.

Key Concepts and Definitions

The study of start-ups provides context to examine and interpret the theories of entrepreneurship. This is primarily because start-ups are a vehicle of the acts of entrepreneurship or institutional arrangements for demonstration of entrepreneurship by an entrepreneur (Shane 1995; Sarasvathy 2004). Prior to understanding the key concepts and definitions that are closely related to high-tech start-ups and their life cycle, it is important that we understand the definition of entrepreneurship in the context of our study. For the purposes of our study, entrepreneurship is defined as the pursuit of opportunity without regard to currently controlled resources (Stevenson and Jarillo 1990).

It is not necessary that every entrepreneurial action always results in the creation of a new firm. The proponents of the opportunity discovery and exploitation theory argued that creation of new firms and sale of opportunities to existing markets constitute two distinct methods of opportunity exploitation (Shane and Venkataraman 2000). There has been a considerable number of studies on the entrepreneurial action and exploitation of business opportunities made by big and established companies. Pinchot (1985) introduced the term *intrapreneurs* to describe the entrepreneurially oriented managers in big companies. Casson (1982) and Amit, Glosten, and Mueller (1993) explained the phenomenon of entrepreneurial occurrence within an existing organization. Barrow (1998) discussed the example of how a large company such as 3M encouraged one of its managers to create and establish a very profitable post-it product by the way of *intrapreneurship*.

Covin and Slevin (1991) coined the term 'corporate entrepreneurship' to explain the entrepreneurial orientation of established firms. Barringer and Bluedorn (1999) defined *entrepreneurial intensity* as a measure of the entrepreneurial activity by an established firm. They explained that firms fall along a continuum that ranges from highly conservative to highly entrepreneurial. The entrepreneurial intensity of the established firm would help in positioning the firm in a particular position along the stated continuum.

While the literature discussed thus far provides a good overview of how the opportunity exploitation occurs in existing markets, it is the former approach of new firm creation which has gained much traction and interest in research circles over the last few years. The increased focus on a particular set of small entrepreneurial firms or start-ups is due to the impact and contributions of these firms to economic growth, job creation, and innovation. Before we delve deeper into discussing the contribution of these small entrepreneurial firms to the economy, it is pertinent to understand the different types of new firms that exist in an economy and their characteristics. The next section accordingly provides insight on the types of small business firms.

Difference between Small Businesses and Start-ups

The terms 'small businesses', 'new ventures', 'new firms', and 'start-ups' have often been interchangeably used in literature. This is primarily because of the context of the earlier studies examining these entities varies significantly from economics to sociology, organizational behaviour, to name a few. It is, therefore, important to clarify and define these terms more precisely for use in this study.

Barringer and Ireland (2008) identified three types of small businesses, namely salary-substitute firms, lifestyle firms, and entrepreneurial firms. According to them, the salary-substitute firms were those small firms that afforded their owner or owners a level of income similar to what they would earn in a conventional job. A new restaurant, a new retail store, and a new hairstyling salon were cited as examples of salary-substitute firms. Further, they observed that a majority of small businesses falls under this category. The Global Entrepreneurship Monitor (GEM) survey (Bygrave et al. 2003) and Furdas and Kohn (2011) pointed out that these firms were to be found mostly in emerging and underdeveloped economies, and that they were a result of necessity-driven entrepreneurship. Barringer and Ireland (2008) noted that these firms offered commonly consumed and undifferentiated products or services to their customers and are not very innovative.

The second type of small businesses identified by Barringer and Ireland (2008) was a category of niche firms called 'lifestyle firms' that provided the owner or owners with the opportunity to pursue a particular lifestyle and earn their living. This type of firms were noted as not being innovative or not being able to grow quickly. Small firms that promote or train people in sports, hobbies, or get their customers indulged in their pastimes were cited as examples of lifestyle firms.

Entrepreneurial firms formed the third type of small businesses as identified by Barringer and Ireland (2008). These firms were those that focused on creating value by offering new products or services to the market by either creating or exploiting entrepreneurial opportunities, regardless of the resources they controlled currently. Innovation and disruption of an existing product offering or service were the norms for these kinds of firms. Companies such as Google and eBay in their formative years were provided as examples of entrepreneurial firms. These entrepreneurial firms were a consequence of opportunity-driven entrepreneurship and were mostly prevalent in developed economies. However, in selected developing countries such as India, this type of firms are beginning to play a significant role in the economy. It is this third type of small businesses which is the focus of the current study.

The word 'start-up' in its current context was first referred to in a *Forbes* magazine article of 1976 wherein it used this word as an alternative to firms that engaged in unfashionable business in the electronic data processing field. The *Oxford Dictionary* (2016) defined start-up as 'a newly established business'. While the U.S. Small Business Administration (2016) does not have a standard definition, it describes a start-up as 'a business that is typically technology oriented and has a high growth potential'. The most accepted definition of a start-up was coined by Blank (2010) who defined a start-up as a temporary organization formed to search for a repeatable and scalable business model. This definition by Blank essentially implies that start-ups are 'entrepreneurial' in nature.

Having understood the key characteristics of start-ups, and the differences between small businesses and start-ups, we will now examine the various definitions of high-tech start-ups that are used across the world.

Definitions of High-tech Start-ups

The first formal attempt to define high-tech start-up firms can be traced to the US Department of Labor (DOL) documents (1999 and 2005) that note that high-tech firms typically use state-of-the-art techniques and in terms of quantifiable resources, devote a 'high' proportion of expenditures to research and development (R&D) and employ a 'high' proportion of scientific, technical, and engineering personnel (Hecker 1999 and 2005).

The US DOL (1999 and 2005) defined three levels of high-tech industry classification. At level 1, it included 14 industries in which the scientific, technical, and engineering occupations contributed to more than 24.7 per cent of the jobs of that sector. At level 2, 12 industries that employed between 14.8 per cent and 24.7 per cent jobs from these occupations have been categorized. At level 3, 20 industries that employed between 9.8 per cent and 14.7 per cent jobs from these occupations have been categorized.

The European Union (EU) and countries allied to EU Free Trade Agreements base their definition of high-tech industry on a way of grouping certain industries together using one of the three different approaches: sector, product, or patent approach (Eurostat 2007 and 2009). The *sector approach* is the grouping of manufacturing industries according to their technological intensity (R&D spending/value added). The *product approach* is devised to complement the sector approach. The product list is based on the calculations of R&D intensity by product groups (R&D spending/total sales). The *patent approach* classifies a firm as high-tech based on whether or not a patent owned by the firm is high-tech. The International Patent Classification (IPC) (World Intellectual Property Organization 2007) is used as the basis to classify if a patent is high-tech or not.

India does not have a formal definition or classification of high-tech industries. However, from an Indian context, to begin with, the National

Industrial Classification (NIC) 2008 would serve as the base to identify the industries that can be classified as high-tech. The EU and the US DOL definitions can be mapped to identify a subset of industry types that can be classified as high-tech.

Mani (2009) has previously used NIC 1998 classification to identify knowledge-intensive manufacturing and services based on Central Statistical Office (CSO) 2008 data. Building on the definition used by Mani and augmenting the presence of newer classifications in the NIC 2008, the following industries may be considered a part of the high-tech sector in India:

High-tech Manufacturing

TABLE 1.1 Classification of high-tech manufacturing industries in India

NIC 2008 industry code	Description of the industry
Division 21	Manufacture of basic pharmaceutical products and pharmaceutical preparations
Division 26	Manufacture of computer, electronic, and optical products
Group 303	Manufacture of air and spacecraft and related machinery

High-tech Knowledge-intensive Services

TABLE 1.2 Classification of high-tech knowledge-intensive services in India

NIC 2008 industry code	Description of the industry
From divisions 59 to 63	Motion picture, video, and television programme productions; sound recording, and music publishing activities; programming and broadcasting activities; telecommunications; computer programming; consultancy and related activities; information service activities
Division 72	Scientific research and development

The NIC 2008 classification is the most recent classification that is available to date for the Indian industry. Now that the precise definitions of high-tech manufacturing and service industries are ascertained, it follows from the earlier definition that any new entrepreneurial firm or business that operates in the aforementioned industry sector constitutes a high-tech start-up in India.

Economic Relevance of High-tech Start-ups

Schumpeter (1934) and many other scholars after him (Solow 1957; Scherer 1984) provided evidence of technological innovation as a source of economic growth. Many studies since 1960 deduced that small entrepreneurial firms were the key drivers of technological innovation in the economy. Till this time, the large firms were being thought of as the dominant contributors to innovation. A series of studies from the 1970s to 1990s focused on comparing the outputs and performances of small entrepreneurial firms against large firms.

Krasner and Dubrow (1979) indicated in their study that large firms would likely be focused on incremental innovations, whereas the small entrepreneurial firms would likely produce new product innovations. Barrow (1998) showed that small entrepreneurial firms were three times more effective at innovating relative to large firms, based on a review of all new inventions produced in the twentieth century. Smollen and Levin (1979: 74) showed that about 48 per cent of the new innovations were developed by small entrepreneurial firms with less than 999 employees, based on a study of about 310 innovations developed over a three-year period from 1973 to 1975.

Storey (1983), through his study, found that more than half of the inventors of that time worked outside the organized research groups of the large firms. A review of patent filing statistics from 1960 through 1980 indicated that independent inventors constituted roughly about 40 per cent of the total patents filed in the USA. Further, about one-third of the patents held by large firms were from employees working outside the corporate laboratories. Kirchoff and Spencer (2008) showed from their study that small entrepreneurial firms were the dominant drivers of radical innovations that defined new fields.

Another interesting fact observed by these studies was that the innovations produced by these small entrepreneurial firms were done at about a quarter of the cost of a mid-sized firm and at about 1/25 of the cost of large firms of that time period (Smollen and Levin 1979: 74). This was further corroborated by Scherer (1980) and Scherer and Ross (1990) who showed that small firms produced disproportionately more innovations than large firms. This ability of firms to innovate at a lower-cost than that of large firms was attributed to a few key factors. The first factor was that small entrepreneurial firms were seen to be providing a less-restrictive environment for their employees who were encouraged to demonstrate initiative (Doctors and Wokutch 1979).

The second factor was that innovation was very much necessary for a small entrepreneurial firm to survive in its early days of operations. Being small and possessing frugal resources, small entrepreneurial firms were forced to seriously consider innovation. These factors made the small entrepreneurial firms more responsive to external market and technological change, in comparison to large firms, leading them to produce innovations that resulted in new products or services (Smollen and Levin 1979: 74).

Acs and Audretsch (1987) studied the linkage between industry structure and innovation in small firms. They found that small firms were more innovative in industries that were less concentrated and had low incidence of unions, where there were very few small firms, and a relatively high innovation rate but a low growth rate. These findings were further amplified by the GEM study (1999) which found that small entrepreneurial firms were responsible for 67 per cent of all innovations in the USA, and that these small entrepreneurial firms were responsible for 95 per cent of radical innovations since World War II (Timmons and Spinelli 1999).

Baumol (2002) noted that most of the revolutionary new ideas from the past two decades were provided by independent innovators (entrepreneurs) who essentially operated small business enterprises. In turn, these innovators, once successful, often established firms of their own, joining or displacing the large enterprises that engage in routine innovation.

Small entrepreneurial firms not only contribute to enhance innovation but are also responsible for large-scale job creation. Birch (1979) showed that small entrepreneurial firms created more jobs than large firms. This study was one of the most comprehensive review of job creation by firms. Birch studied about 5.6 million businesses that operated between 1969 and 1976 in the USA and observed that small entrepreneurial businesses with 20 or fewer employees created 66 per cent of all new jobs. Around the same time, a study by the US Department of Commerce (1980) found that small, young, high-tech businesses created new jobs at a much faster rate than the older and larger businesses. This study was further revalidated by Kirchhoff (1994) who demonstrated that new high-tech firms (start-ups) created a greater percentage of increase to the net new jobs than the other categories of young firms (start-ups). Barringer and Ireland (2008) observed that small entrepreneurial firms were the primary engines of economic activity in the two decades preceding their study. They reasoned that the unique abilities of these small entrepreneurial firms to innovate and focus on specialized tasks helped them to dominate the creation of new jobs during the mentioned period.

Carlsson (1999) provided a comparison of job employment rates between large Fortune 500 companies and the small entrepreneurial firms over a 26-year period. He noted that in 1970, the Fortune 500 companies employed about 20 per cent of the US labour force, whereas by 1996, the same metric drastically came down to about 8.5 per cent. To substantiate this decline in employment by the Fortune 500 companies and the contribution of small entrepreneurial firms to job creation in the USA, Atkinson and Court (1998) noted that between 1993 and 1996, high-growth young companies termed as 'gazelles' created about two-thirds of all new jobs. From the analysis of 1997 Fortune 200 companies, Purrington and Bettcher (2001) found that 197 out of 200 firms in that list could be traced back to one or more entrepreneurial founders, in a list that included companies such as Cisco, Dell, and Microsoft.

Audretsch and Fritsch (1996; 2002) studied the growth trajectories of entrepreneurial small businesses in the USA and Germany during two periods of time. They found out that during the 1980s, while the USA demonstrated a higher growth on account of higher start-up rates, Germany did not show the same characteristic. They explained that this difference in outcomes was due to a lack of innovative activity and the abilities of small, new entrepreneurial firms to disrupt and displace incumbent enterprises in Germany. However, a repeat of similar study of firms during the 1990s in Germany by Audretsch and Fritsch indicated results similar to the ones seen in the USA. When the reasons for this change in Germany were analysed, it came out that during the 1990s, Germany had promoted entrepreneurial firms, shifting away from banking on the established incumbent large firms. This established conclusively that promotion of high-tech entrepreneurship drove broad-based economic growth in developed economies.

Holtz-Eiken and Kao (2003) examined the impact of high-tech entrepreneurship on economic growth in the USA, and concluded that entrepreneurship had a positive impact on productivity growth. Similar results were demonstrated by Hart and Hanvey (1995) in a UK-based study of small entrepreneurial businesses. Callejon and Segarra (1999) studied start-up birth and death rates of Spanish manufacturing industries during 1980–1992 and concluded that both the start-up birth and death rates contributed positively to the growth of total factor productivity of the industry, sector, and region.

In summary, all the aforementioned research studies enabled the recognition of high-tech start-ups as being the major drivers of job creation and innovation and thus, economic growth.

Evolution of Start-up Policies in Developed Economies

Policy making related to small businesses and more recently on high-tech start-ups across the world has evolved with time, reflecting the enhanced understanding of the contribution of knowledge and technology in the economy. Neoclassical economic theory that relied on capital and labour being the drivers of economic growth (Solow 1956) guided the policymaking for almost six decades of the twentieth century. From the 1980s onwards, neoclassical economists recognized *knowledge* as the key factor in spurring economic growth (Romer 1986). In the next two decades, it was established that entrepreneurship was one of the key ways in which knowledge was converted into *economic knowledge,* which in turn helped drive economic growth (Audretsch and Keilbach 2004). High-tech start-ups emerged primarily out of the USA. Only in the past few decades have other high-tech start-up clusters outside the USA emerged (Startup Genome 2015). Therefore, most of the policy evolution related to high-tech start-ups are discussed in the context of the USA.

Gilbert, Audretsch, and McDougall (2004) reviewed the business policymaking shifts in the USA and noted that a definite shift towards promoting entrepreneurship occurred during the decades of the 1980s and 1990s. They noted that since 1800, the public policymaking in the USA was dictated by the need to harness the market power of large established organizations by way of policy interventions, such as regulation, government ownership, and antitrust laws. However, during the 1980s and further, the US government made a series of changes in its policymaking stance. First, it tried to minimize government intervention in the operations of the firms. Second, instead of constraining the firms by way of regulations and laws, the policy changes promoted new, small entrepreneurial firms. Last, unlike earlier times, these entrepreneurial promotion policies were implemented at all levels of governance – at the federal, state, region, and local county levels.

The reasons for the change in government policymaking stance can be explained as follows. During the middle of the nineteenth century, production and output emanated primarily out of small-scale, informal, family-owned establishments in the USA. However, by the beginning of the twentieth century, large-scale production from big firms replaced these small-scale informal units on account of superior efficiency and output (Chandler 1977). Gilbert, Audretsch, and McDougall (2004) observed that the advent of large corporations and the accompanying managerial revolution ensured that the small-scale family-owned enterprises became unviable. The production efficiency gains created by these large firms posed a problem for policymakers. These policymakers needed to ensure that negative implications coming out of the presence of the large enterprises were sufficiently controlled. Hence, they adopted modes of regulation, antitrust laws, and public ownership as tenets of policymaking during the early twentieth century in the USA (Gilbert, Audretsch, and McDougall 2004).

The advent of large enterprises, however, did not completely wipe out the small businesses in the USA. Political and social reasons ensured that small businesses, even though they were inefficient, were protected. The Robinson–Patman Act was one of the first policy interventions by the USA to protect small businesses during the 1950s. Gilbert, Audretsch, and McDougall (2004) observed that these protectionist measures were further continued by the creation of the US Small Business Administration by way of an Act passed by Congress in 1953 to aid, counsel, assist, and protect the interests of small business concerns.

The two decades of the 1970s and 1980s brought about disruptive changes in the US economy on account of globalization and the rapid pace of technological adoption by the economy. In the early years of these decades, researchers studied the impact of globalization on small businesses and concluded that globalization would further hurt the interests and survival of small businesses (Vernon 1970). The predominant view was that globalization would cause additional costs to be incurred by small businesses, and therefore, any globalizing activity was best performed by large established firms (Horst 1972; Chandler 1990). However, Gilbert, Audretsch, and McDougall (2004) noted that both large and small firms gained on account of increased globalization. In particular, they noted that entrepreneurial activity started to boom in the mid-1970s, precisely at the time when globalization was accepted as a disruptive instrument affecting the economies.

The reason for the growth of entrepreneurial activity, as evidenced by the growth of small entrepreneurial firms since 1970 in the USA, was primarily on account of an increase in knowledge workers who were able to master new technologies that emerged during this period (Bartlett and Ghoshal 1999). Berman, Bound, and Machin (1998) showed that demand for less skilled workers decreased dramatically in comparison to the demand for highly skilled workers, which was shown to have had an exponential increase. The number of patent applications post the 1970s also indicated the increase of knowledge-driven activities in the USA (Kortum and Lerner 1998). Many scholars during the late 1990s and early 2000s provided empirical evidence that entrepreneurial activity by small firms created employment growth in the regions of their study, and therefore, also influenced major portions of economic activity during that time (Reynolds 1999; Thurik 1999).

On account of these structural changes in the economy, since the 1990s policymakers in the USA shifted focus from controlling large firms to promoting entrepreneurial small firms. It also resulted in a fundamental change in the role of government from that of an overseer of business, constraining the freedom of firms to contract, to that of a partner in business, enabling and fostering the development of new small firms. This shift in policy emphasis as a response to the changing source of competitiveness from the traditional factors of capital and labour to the emerging factor of knowledge is depicted in Figure 1.1. This shows that when competitiveness was generated from capital and labour, the policy response towards large enterprises was restricted in nature, while small business was the target of preservationist policy. By contrast, when knowledge is the source of competitiveness in emerging markets, policy shifted towards enabling the start-ups and growth of new enterprises, or what can be termed as entrepreneurship policy (Gilbert, Audretsch, and McDougall 2004).

As a direct consequence of these structural changes, policy interventions were carried out since the 1990s in the USA across all levels to promote and enable entrepreneurship via small firms. Sternberg (1996) documented a few local-level policy initiatives that helped spur entrepreneurship in different

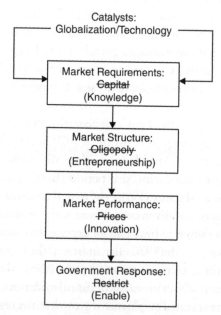

FIGURE 1.1 Change in US policymaking during the twentieth century

SOURCE: Reproduced from Gilbert, Audretsch, and McDougall (2004).

regions of the USA, notably that of economic growth of the Austin, Texas, region. Lugar (2001) described the implications of regional entrepreneurship policies to the economic growth of North Carolina. He described the success and role of the Research Triangle Park in North Carolina that was responsible for one-quarter of all the jobs created in the region from 1959 to 1990.

Carlsson and Brunerhjelm (1999) explained the contribution of the Edison Biotechnology Institute in Ohio state which was successful in developing a model of technology transfer from universities and government institutes to new technology start-ups. Cooper (2003) documented the contribution and success of the Small Business Innovation Research (SBIR) programme that was implemented across the USA. He noted that due to the SBIR programme, all the major R&D agencies in the USA were made to allocate a share of research budget to innovative small firms, which resulted in employment growth.

In Germany, the government, aiming to promote start-ups in high-tech sectors, announced the Existenzgründungen aus Hochschulen (EXIST) programme that was targeted at encouraging start-ups from universities and government research laboratories (German Ministry of Economics and Technology 1999). Kim and Nugent (1999) documented the shift in South Korea's policy that previously promoted *chaebol*s (large enterprises) till the 1970s to the existing policies during the 1980s and 1990s that promoted small businesses and start-ups. They explained that a slew of policy interventions by South Korea by way of provision of tax breaks to start-ups, creation of credit funds to ensure VC availability for start-ups, and technology transfer and upgrade schemes from universities to new small entrepreneurial firms resulted in the creation of world-leading technology-based enterprises in South Korea.

Start-up Policy Evolution and Related Activities in India

India's policymaking towards small businesses, and most recently on start-ups, has evolved over time to address a variety of issues. Bala Subrahmanya (2015) explained that the evolution of Indian policymaking towards small businesses could be viewed under three distinct phases since Independence. He described that the first phase (1947–1991) was characterized by the building up of both protective and promotion measures for small scale industries (SSI). The second phase (1991–2006) was characterized by the dilution of protective measures and the strengthening of measures to enhance the competitiveness of SSI, whereas the third phase (2006 onwards) focused more on developing the micro, small, and medium enterprises (MSME) sector as a whole and its integration with the large domestic and multinational enterprises, while giving scope for the exit of inefficient ones.

During the last decade, the government has particularly focused on promoting and supporting technology and knowledge-intensive entrepreneurial small firms. The government tried to provide a mechanism to support individual technology-based entrepreneurs through the Technopreneur Promotion Programme (TePP), anchored by the Ministry of Science and Technology (MoST), Department of Scientific and Industrial Research (DSIR) (2014), Government of India. The formation of technology business incubators (TBI) by the National Institute of Science and Technology Entrepreneurship Development Board (NSTEDB), Department of Science and Technology (DST), and the Council for Scientific and Industrial Research (CSIR), through National Chemical Laboratory (NCL), Pune, was another important step in promoting technology-driven entrepreneurship in India (Bala Subrahmanya 2015).

The introduction of Promoting Innovations in Individuals, Startups and MSME (PRISM) scheme in the Twelfth Five Year Plan is another policy intervention by the government to support knowledge-intensive entrepreneurship in India. PRISM is open to any Indian citizen with an innovative idea or public-funded institutions or organizations engaged in the promotion of innovation. Furthermore, the PRISM scheme can also be availed by the aforementioned entities to translate their idea into working prototypes/models/processes (DSIR 2014).

From 2013 onwards, the Government of India has created policies that have allowed companies to invest in technology incubators (of academic institutions approved by the central government) as a part of their corporate social responsibility (CSR) initiatives under the Companies Act 2013. This is aimed at increasing the financial capital availability to the early-stage high-tech start-ups operating out of India. Further, the policy recommendations of the Inter-Ministerial Committee for MSME (Ministry of MSME 2013) identified key areas including financial support to high-tech start-ups as one of the primary areas of focus. Following these recommendations, the market regulator Securities Exchange Bureau of India (SEBI 2015) has introduced new policies targeted at registered angel investors and VCs to allow for ease of investing in start-ups.

The Government of India has further introduced new funding programmes from 2014 to support and promote technology- and knowledge-driven entrepreneurship. The India Aspiration Fund was launched by the Ministry of

Finance, Government of India, in 2015, with an initial corpus of ₹2,000 crore to finance and promote start-ups in the technology-intensive sector. Further, in the union budget of 2015, the government announced another programme called the Self-Employment and Talent Utilisation (SETU) programme with an initial corpus of ₹1,000 crore to act as a techno-financial incubation programme to support start-ups and technology-intensive entrepreneurial small business. The SETU programme was mandated to be executed by the National Institution for Transforming India (NITI) Aayog.

To promote innovation in the country, the union budget of 2015 announced a new programme called Atal Innovation Mission (AIM) under the NITI Aayog. The AIM programme was conceived to be the innovation platform for the nation, involving academics, entrepreneurs, and researchers, which would facilitate the discussion of national and international experiences and result in fostering a culture of innovation and R&D in India. An initial budget of ₹150 crore was earmarked in the union budget of 2015 for the AIM programme. These are concrete examples of how government action has recognized the importance of supporting knowledge-intensive high-tech start-ups in the country.

During the 2015 Independence Day speech, the Prime Minister of India announced the 'Startup India' initiative, which would encourage entrepreneurship among the youth of India, with an aim to create 1.25 lakh entrepreneurs in India. Further, in subsequent visits to other nations, particularly the USA, the Prime Minister has engaged with prominent start-up leaders of the ecosystem to understand the modalities of how Silicon Valley became the best example for a thriving start-up ecosystem. The Department of Industrial Policy and Promotion (DIPP) held more than 40 consultation meetings with all players of the start-up ecosystem across the world to understand the high-tech start-up ecosystem aspects, and announced a comprehensive action plan in 2016.

The primary aim of the Startup India Action Plan (2016) is to accelerate the spread of the start-up movement in India from digital/technology sector to others, such as agriculture, manufacturing, social, healthcare, education, and so on. Second, the action plan has specific initiatives and plans to accelerate the start-up movement from existing tier 1 cities to tier 2 and tier 3 cities including semi-urban and rural areas. A variety of schemes and incentives were announced as part of the launch of this action plan. The action plan has been divided into three areas: simplification of regulatory procedures and handholding for start-ups, funding support and incentives, and industry–academia partnership and incubation.

Under the simplification of regulatory procedures, the main aim of the policy is to reduce the regulatory burden on start-ups and lower the compliance costs as well. A scheme for self-certification of compliance by the start-up with about nine labour and environment laws, and no inspection from regulatory officials during the first three years of formal operation of start-ups are a few of the policy changes to existing laws that are mentioned under this area. Further, a single point of contact for knowledge exchange and access to funding for start-ups, by provision of a start-up portal accessible to all stakeholders of the ecosystem, has been created in 2016.

Recognizing that intellectual property rights (IPR) as a strategic business tool for start-ups, particularly to those in the knowledge-intensive sector, a system for fast-tracking the patent application examination process, as well as a rebate in fees for start-up-filed patent applications has been proposed. Another important area where regulation has been relaxed in favour of start-ups is under the public procurement norms from the government. From 1 April 2015, all central government, state government, and public sector units have to mandatorily procure at least 20 per cent of their orders from MSME. Further, for all manufacturing-sector start-ups, the 'prior experience/turnover' clause would be exempted, allowing them to participate in tenders. Also, to ensure that start-ups can wind up operations easily, in case of a business failure, provisions for voluntary closure or fast-tracking of business has been introduced in the Insolvency and Bankruptcy Bill (IBB) tabled in the Lok Sabha (the lower house of the Indian bicameral Parliament) in 2015.

Among the last set of measures to ease regulatory hurdles and provide incentives to start-ups, income tax exemption for a period of three years of formal incorporation has been promulgated. Further, to encourage seed capital investments, tax exemption has been provided for any excess consideration of valuation above the fair market value (FMV) of shares of the start-ups.

In addition to the Government of India's Startup India Action Plan, a few states also have come up with their state-level start-up policies. During 2015 and 2016, states such as Rajasthan, Karnataka, Kerala, Uttar Pradesh, Uttarakhand, Madhya Pradesh, Andhra Pradesh, Telangana, and Jharkhand have unveiled their state-specific start-up policies and have announced sector-specific incentives based on their regional and locational advantages. The state government of Karnataka has aimed at creation of 20,000 technology-based start-ups by 2020. It has aimed to create about 6 lakh direct and 12 lakh indirect employment opportunities based on the promotion of this sector. To achieve these goals, it has earmarked about ₹2,000 crore from the state budget to help fund and incentivize the start-ups in Karnataka (Government of Karnataka 2015).

The start-up policy of Rajasthan (Government of Rajasthan 2015) aims at supporting 500 start-ups, to begin with, via 50 incubators and has provided for a budget of ₹500 crore to pursue the aforementioned objectives. It intends to promote social sector- and tourism-related start-ups based on the inherent strengths of the people of its state. Andhra Pradesh's start-up and innovation policy (Government of Andhra Pradesh 2014) aims to promote about 5,000 start-ups incubated across 100 accelerators spanning 9 identified sectors, such as Internet of things (IoT); social, mobile, analytics and cloud (SMAC); animation and gaming; visual effects; health and fitness; automotive; and a couple more. Kerala's technology start-up policy (Government of Kerala 2014) aims at achieving similar goals by 2020. It has provisioned about ₹2,500 crore to support this initiative and expects to incubate and facilitate at least 10,000 start-ups.

As can be observed from the national- and state-level policies, the government is laying emphasis on enabling access to capital to these high-tech start-ups – since this has been viewed as one of the most significant causes of failure for start-ups. Given this extra emphasis from the state and central governments, it is prudent to review some of the key financial support schemes available to start-ups in detail. The funds provided by these schemes could be used at all stages of the high-tech start-up life cycle, starting from the idea validation stage to the full-scale commercialization stage. Magesh, Vibhor, and Premnath (2009) provided a detailed overview of the funding schemes made available to the entrepreneurs by the government. They noted that needs at each stage of technology commercialization and new-venture development were to be understood before one could fully exploit the funding landscape and funding opportunities offered by the government. The graphic presented in Figure 1.2 provides a brief outline of the various stages involved in starting and growing a technology start-up.

The government funding can be categorized into six different types with each type supporting the different phases of the venture creation process. Technology development funds are aimed at supporting early-stage technology-related works, such as development of proof of concept, using a niche technology. Usually these activities are carried out by entrepreneurs during the pre-emergence stage of their venture. Various government organizations under the MoST, such as DSIR and CSIR, have schemes that fund these initiatives. The funds are given out as grants or soft loans and the funding support ranges from ₹75,000 to ₹10 crore.

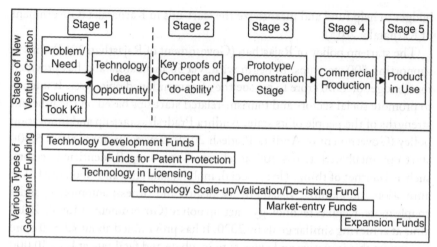

Figure 1.2 New Venture creation and technology commercialization process flow chart

Source: Reproduced from Magesh, Vibhor, and Premnath (2009).

Further, there are multiple schemes by different government departments that aid the entrepreneurs to avail protection for their intellectual property. In India, entrepreneurs face many roadblocks as they embark on the process of applying for a patent and obtaining it. Therefore, before filing a patent, an entrepreneur in India needs to weigh the cost and benefit aspects of paying for patent-filing cost and its maintenance costs, particularly if intellectual property protection is being sought in foreign countries as well. Without patents, the start-up venture risks losing its competitive edge. In view of this, multiple government organizations, such as DSIR, CSIR, and the ministries of MSME and Communications and IT of Government of India, have created schemes that disburse funds to help entrepreneurs file for patent protection. The funding support available for patent protection or intellectual property (IP) licensing varies from ₹25,000 to ₹45 lakh.

For the purposes of scaling up the operations of a start-up, or for de-risking against the technology or market risks, various institutions in the government, such as DSIR, National Research Development Centre (NRDC), and government-owned financial institutions, such as Small Industries Development Bank of India (SIDBI), provide funding assistance. The magnitude of this assistance ranges from ₹10 lakh to ₹25 crore for start-ups that work on high-risk and nationally important areas.

There are also funding schemes available to start-ups and entrepreneurs for purposes of supporting market entry and expansion into new geographies and segments. From a life cycle of high-tech start-ups perspective, this is a stage where significant risks for the start-up are already mitigated. The ministries of MSME and Science and Technology, SIDBI, and a host of other state-based VC funds provide assistance to start-ups in this phase. The financial support extended ranges from ₹10 lakh to ₹5 crore, against divestment of equity from the start-up (Magesh, Vibhor, and Premnath 2009).

Finally, for a start-up that has demonstrated product-market fit and has arrived at a scalable operating model, funds are available from the government as well as from the VC community to support its growth and expansion. It is in this stage that a start-up ceases to be a small entrepreneurial business and transitions to a large firm. SIDBI and state-VC funds are the key players supporting the entrepreneurs at this phase. There are many VCs in India who invest heavily in start-ups of this stage (NASSCOM 2014). The usual deal sizes are above ₹25 crore. While the existence of these government-backed funds is laudable, it is observed that not many entrepreneurs have used these effectively as of date (NASSCOM 2018).

In summary, the policymaking in India with respect to promotion of knowledge-intensive firms and start-ups has primarily been focused on making the right amount of capital allocations through various schemes and programmes. However, since the response from the entrepreneurial community was tepid for these capital allocation-related policies, suitable policy changes were initiated to attend to other core issues of IPR management and reducing regulatory barriers to conduct business and supporting technology upgradation among others. These policy actions from both the central and state governments indicate that the administration recognizes the need to promote knowledge-intensive entrepreneurship in the country. However, the lack of knowledge of factors that contribute to the life cycle of these high-tech firms have created barriers in decision-making, resulting in slower than expected response in policymaking and implementation. It is in this context and background that the present study assumes significance.

With these backgrounds and contexts about high-tech start-ups, their characteristics, and the various policy initiatives that are currently present to support this sector, we now move on to provide a brief orientation towards the need to study high-tech start-ups in India.

Motivation for the Study

This chapter brought out the importance and uniqueness of high-tech start-ups for the economy. While the changes brought about by the advent of globalization and rapid technological change have been well understood and responded to in the developed economies, the same is not the case with respect to the emerging economies like India. To begin with, the uniqueness of high-tech start-ups and their contribution to the economy have not been adequately studied in the context of emerging economies.

Song et al. (2008) have observed that there has been limited investigation of high-tech start-ups in emerging economies. Further, the distinction between entrepreneurially oriented high-tech start-ups and small businesses emerged only in recent years, about a decade back (Barringer and Ireland 2008). The limited understanding of the unique characteristics of high-tech start-ups as well as the unique features of the ecosystem which supports these start-ups have led to small businesses and high-tech start-ups being treated on the same scale.

Bala Subrahmanya (2015) noted that the new-generation start-ups emerging in India represent the third wave in the evolution of small businesses in India. He reasoned that these new start-ups were essentially technology/knowledge-based and emerged largely due to the information and communication technology (ICT) revolution and globalization. He further observed that there was limited knowledge among policymakers and entrepreneurs about the unique aspects of these new start-ups. He argued that these ICT-based start-ups were very different from the older generation MSME based on a variety of parameters.

Most importantly, the entrepreneurial backgrounds of these new start-ups were different to that of the previous generation MSME. The ecosystem of TBI and accelerators that has started to grow in India to support these new ICT start-ups is very different from the traditional support systems provided to the MSME. Furthermore, the mode of financing for these new start-ups (by angel investors, VCs) is also different to the traditional funding institutions. Bala Subrahmanya further remarked that very little is known about the life cycle events of these ICT start-ups. This study, therefore, tries to address some of these knowledge gaps. Since most new-generation start-ups are ICT based, this study focuses on studying the life cycle of high-tech start-ups in the ICT sector.

These discussions bring out the fact that there are very few studies in this domain which have examined the factors that impact the different life cycle stages of start-ups in the context of emerging economies like India. Although there is a surge in the creation of start-ups in India, very little is known about the vital factors that are required for these start-ups to survive, sustain, and grow into large enterprises. Further, very little is known about the start-up ecosystem that is developing alongside these start-ups. This limited exploration on the structure, process, and strategies adopted by high-tech start-ups has resulted in insufficient understanding of the high-tech start-up life cycle in emerging economies in general, and with respect to India in particular. This study, therefore, attempts to fill these gaps.

2

Objectives, Scope, and Methodology

Introduction

In this chapter, we present the research objectives, the conceptual framework, the scope, and the research methodology adopted for the study. The research methodology will provide the sources of data and the definitions of key variables used in this study. It will also describe the research instrument and the method of analysis that are employed to analyse the research objectives.

Objectives

The overarching research objective of this study is to investigate the dynamics involved in the life cycle of high-tech start-ups in the context of India. The knowledge about the factors that enable the sustenance of start-ups and that act as barriers, hindering the creation, survival, and success of the firms, will help in the creation of suitable policies that promote high-tech entrepreneurship in India. The outcomes of this study will help in achieving the larger objective of higher economic growth bolstered by new jobs and wealth creation due to the promotion of high-tech start-ups.

To be able to realize these, the following research objectives are outlined:

1. To determine the entrepreneurial, firm-specific, and external environmental factors that influence the *creation* of high-tech start-ups in India;
2. To understand the entrepreneurial, firm-specific, and external environmental factors that are critical to ensure the *survival* of high-tech start-ups in India;
3. To understand and determine the entrepreneurial, firm-specific, and external environmental factors that ensure the *growth* of high-tech start-ups in India;

4. To understand and determine the factors (entrepreneurial, firm-specific, and external environmental specific) that have an impact across the entire *life cycle* of high-tech start-ups in India; and

5. To derive policy implications for the entrepreneurs, start-up ecosystem partners, and policymakers, based on the analysis of our study.

Scope of the Study

This study will be confined to ICT start-ups operating in India. To ensure homogeneity of data, only the high-tech start-ups that are offering products and cloud-based solutions in the ICT sector are considered. This implies that start-ups that have their established headquarters in India and have majority of investments or R&D personnel in India (in cases where the start-ups have multiple global offices) will also qualify.

Further, we restrict our study to cover start-ups that started operations after 2005. This restriction allows us to get a good spread of start-ups that initiated operations over the ten-year period between 2005 and 2015. It also provides sufficient room to analyse the end-to-end life cycle of high-tech start-ups across the three key milestones of start-ups – creation, survival, and growth.

Methodology

We detail the sources of data that are used in the study, the research instruments that enabled the examination of the objectives, and the methods of statistical analysis used.

Data Sources

As indicated earlier, the scope of the study is restricted to ICT high-tech start-ups, who have their registered headquarters in India. Since there is no single credible database of start-ups, operating out of India, industry associations – National Association for Software and Services Companies (NASSCOM) and Indian Software Product Industry Round Table (iSPIRT) – were contacted to identify the start-ups. Using the data obtained from the database of these associations, a consolidated database of start-ups was thus created. This consolidated database has data of 1,567 start-ups.

Using the contacts of the start-ups in the consolidated database, a request for participation in the study was sent to the founders of these start-ups by email between March 2014 and June 2014. After three rounds of subsequent follow ups and in person meetings in some cases, finally, about 547 respondents confirmed their participation in the study. The data collection is performed using multiple methods that comprised in-person meetings, telephonic interviews, and by soliciting responses via online survey websites. The analysis of responses yielded a final set of 275 start-ups for the purposes of our study.

The unit of analysis in our study has been the start-up, represented by the founder. We understand that most start-ups in the high-tech fields start with multiple co-founders. However, in most cases, there would be one founder who would have the most context about the start-up and its operations. We have fairly successfully targeted such founders in our study.

To ensure that our data is representative of the population, we obtained the demographic distribution of start-ups data from the *iSPIRT Product Industry Monitor* report of 2014, which is considered a benchmark for authentic information on Indian start-ups, and compared it with our data. We find that our sample is representative on all dimensions that we could assess: industry demographics, such as location and age of the start-up; market sector; and founder profiles, such as education, experience, and external funding status. For example, about 36 per cent of our sample consists of start-ups from the North Zone of India, similar to about 40 per cent of the sample of the iSPIRT report (2014). About 23 per cent of our sample had start-ups with single founder, similar to about 25 per cent of the iSPIRT report. Further, 67 per cent of the founders in our sample had prior start-up experience, similar to 69 per cent as per the iSPIRT report. In terms of education pedigree, our sample and the iSPIRT report conveyed that all start-ups surveyed for both reports had a graduation degree and above for their founders. Based on the similarities of the descriptive statistics of the iSPIRT report with our data sample, we conclude that our sample is representative of the population.

Most of the data used in our study are collected using our research instrument – the questionnaire. The secondary data are collected primarily to obtain the profiles of the entrepreneurs. This information is obtained from public and professional websites, such as LinkedIn, Angel List, Facebook, and similar ones. We resorted to secondary data collection for the entrepreneur profile, so that we could optimize the time during our interview to focus on the core objectives of the study.

Research Instruments

With respect to the instrument used in the study, a questionnaire has been developed to collect the primary data and validate the objectives of the study. To be able to accurately develop the questionnaire, selective case analysis of about six high-tech start-ups has been carried out in the first stage. While selecting the six start-ups, we have ensured the following:

1. Two start-ups are identified for each of the three phases of the start-up life cycle.
2. All the selected start-ups belonged to the same industry sector (Internet start-ups).

Among the set of start-ups that satisfied the aforementioned criteria, the start-up with the most indicative of the operating phase in consideration and the most representative of the population is identified.

To begin with, a semi-structured schedule is created and used for the study. The schedule primarily consists of the following sections:

1. Background of the start-ups and the founders, including the circumstances that led to the creation of the start-up;
2. The entrepreneurial path taken to creation and/or survival and/or growth of the corresponding start-up; and
3. Outcome and learnings of the transnational entrepreneurs, as they set these start-ups in their country of origin relative to that of local entrepreneurs.

Based on the responses received and an in-depth study of these start-ups by following the way of the case study methods, the final questionnaire is designed to collect basic profile-related information about the founder and the start-up, as well as to collect information related to the development and sales capabilities, funding status of the start-up, and the time, taken for the start-up to reach the key milestone in the start-up life cycle. The data on the development and sales capabilities are standardized to ensure comparison across the samples.

Description of the Questionnaire

The questionnaire is created to capture all the data points necessary to conduct the present study. It has four sections. The first section captures the basic profile of the founder and the start-up. These include details such as the month and year of formal incorporation of the start-up (if incorporated), the type of the firm during incorporation (with options of proprietorship, partnership, limited liability partnership, private limited, public company, and others), and the number of founders at the time of inception. Profile information of the founders has questions that helped capture the details, such as the name of the founder(s), their previous industry and start-up experiences, performed roles in previous industry or start-ups, if any; gender; educational details; information on whether the founders knew each other prior to incorporation; and if yes, how and how long they knew each other. It also captures information about what motivated the founders to start the company.

The second section captures all the details related to the milestone of creation of the start-up. Details such as whether the start-up has been formally incorporated or not; time taken in months to formally incorporate the company from the time of initial idea of the start-up; and the firm-specific resources, such as development, sales, and financial capabilities of the start-up at the time of formal incorporation, are captured in this section.

The third section captures the details that are relevant to the milestone of survival of the start-up. Details such as the month and year when the start-up obtained the product-market fit (if applicable) and the firm-specific resources at the time of achieving the milestone, such as the development capabilities, number of product offerings, revenue-generated financial support from external sources in the form of seed/angel/VC investments (if applicable), are captured. Further, any changes in the founding team is also captured to study comprehensively the entrepreneurial and firm-specific attributes of the start-up at this milestone.

The fourth section captures the details that are relevant to the milestone of growth of the start-up (if applicable). Details such as the month and year since the start-up started to clock, sustained increase in revenue and the firm resources at that point of time (where applicable).

Key Parameters and Definitions Used in the Study

Since the research objectives of this study are to analyse the entire life cycle of high-tech start-ups, it is imperative that we explicitly define the three key milestones (emergence, survival, and growth). Further, for all the three milestones, additional analyses will be performed based on three distinct segments, namely, (a) market segment being targeted by the start-ups (B2B versus B2C), (b) location of operations (North Zone versus South Zone), and (c) entrepreneurial exposure (local versus transnational entrepreneurial background). Accordingly, the definitions of each of these aspects are provided in this section.

Emergence of High-tech Start-ups

For the purposes of this study, the date of formal incorporation of the start-up (month and year) under the government laws at the Registrar of Companies office in India is considered the milestone of start-up emergence. Firms or entrepreneurs that operate informally are considered as 'not yet created' for the purposes of this study.

Survival of High-tech Start-ups

A start-up that has been formally incorporated and has achieved product-market fit with its offerings is considered to have achieved the survival milestone in its journey. This milestone indicates that the start-up has been able to achieve repeatable sales with a standardized offering, and that it has now a formidable set of initial customers that have validated the offering and are paying for the offering.

Growth of High-tech Start-ups

A start-up that has achieved the survival milestone and received external valuation of more than ₹5 crore if they are services-based, or more than ₹10 crore if they are a manufacturing-based start-up, is considered to be operating in the growth phase.

Definitions of Parameters Used in Our Study

For the purpose of this study, the high-tech start-ups in our sample have been analysed based on three distinct segments of comparison, namely, (a) B2B versus B2C start-ups, (b) start-ups based out of North Zone versus those based out of South Zone, and (c) start-ups created by transnational entrepreneurs versus those created by local entrepreneurs. The analysis of these segments will yield useful interpretations and will help drive the policy initiatives more effectively.

The B2B versus B2C start-ups segmentation is prepared primarily to understand the nuances of start-ups catering to different market segments. For example, the sales cycle in a B2B start-up is expected to be much longer in comparison to the sales cycle for a B2C start-up. However, the revenue generated per customer will be higher in B2B start-up in comparison with the B2C start-up. Segmenting the start-ups along the lines of the targeted customer market will help us identify specific factors that impact the 'time to survival' and growth in an effective manner (Mahadevan 2000; Fish 2009; Andersen 2009: 274; Osterwalder and Pigneur 2010).

In our study, we have analysed the start-ups by differentiating them on the basis of the location of their operations. We have divided the regions in our country into two zones – North Zone and South Zone. Start-ups operating out of NCR, Mumbai, Kolkata, Ahmedabad, Surat, and Nagpur among others fall under the North Zone classification and start-ups operating out of Bengaluru, Cochin, Chennai, Coimbatore, and Hyderabad among others are categorized under the South Zone. This categorization of start-ups based on zones is necessitated for the following reasons. An assessment of the macroeconomic parameters of the states of our country revealed that the southern states have consistently registered higher economic growth in comparison to the national average during the period of the study. First, we noticed that the GDP per capita values (at constant prices) of all the southern states and union territory of India, namely, Karnataka, Andhra Pradesh, Telangana, Tamil Nadu, Kerala, and Pondicherry, have consistently been higher than the national GDP per capita value (at constant prices) for the period of our study (Ministry of Finance 2016). Second, we observed that these southern states performed better in comparison to the northern states when evaluated against human development indicators (such as, life expectancy at birth and infant mortality rates) and socio-economic indicators (health, education, and income) (Ministry of Finance 2016). Third, four out of these five states came out with their state-specific start-up action plans during 2014 and 2015, indicating the willingness of these state governments to promote high-tech start-ups. These aspects seem to indicate that southern states of the country are perhaps the best region that may provide support to a robust start-up ecosystem. However, to the best of our knowledge, there has been no empirical examination of these aspects. Hence, we chose to bifurcate the region of the country into two zones. The analysis of start-ups operating in these two zones will help us understand the extent of proliferation of high-tech economic activity across the country. Second, it will help us analyse the different factors that may come to play in impacting start-ups purely based on the location of operations.

Last, we have analysed the start-ups based on the entrepreneurial background and experience, in particular, and whether they are local or transnational. Prior research has suggested that transnational entrepreneurs and their communities enable diffusion of knowledge and creation or upgrading of local capabilities. Saxenian and Li (2003) noted that transnational entrepreneurs built specialization and innovation by simultaneously maintaining connections with their host country and country of origin. They observed that this mechanism helped them to monitor and respond to changes in markets and technology. Given this background, this study investigates whether transnational entrepreneurs who create and operate high-tech start-ups in India are more likely to survive and sustain in comparison with local entrepreneurs. For the purposes of this study, transnational entrepreneurs are those entrepreneurs who have either worked or studied in a country other than that of their birth for a period of at least one year continuously (Drori, Honig, and Wright 2009). Entrepreneurs who have visited other countries and stayed in other countries during their visits do not qualify to be transnational entrepreneurs.

Proposed Methods of Analysis

We use multiple statistical techniques for the analysis of our data set. The choice of method is based on the characteristics of the data fields (type of variables) and the purpose of the analysis. While each of these will be discussed in much detail in the respective chapters, we provide a brief overview of the methods here.

Objective 1 analyses the factors that impact and influence the emergence of high-tech start-ups in India. To be able to analyse this objective, we consider whether the start-up under study has been formally incorporated or not as the dependent variable. The entrepreneurial and firm-specific factors such as age and education of the primary founder; prior industry and start-up experience of the primary founder; and the development, sales, and financial capabilities present with the start-up at the time of inception form the independent variables for this analysis. The external environmental factors such as SDP growth, number of VC firms in the region and the number of VC-funded deals in the region are considered independent variables for the analysis.

We use binary logistic regression technique for building and analysing the model. These analyses are carried out under three segments, namely, (a) target market being addressed by the start-ups (B2B versus B2C), (b) location of operation of the start-ups (North Zone versus South Zone), and (c) exposure of the entrepreneurs (local versus transnational). In all, a total of six logistic regression analyses models will be executed and results and conclusions will be drawn from these analyses. Finally, an overall model is built to understand the factors that are significant for the emergence of high-tech start-ups in India. Statistical techniques such as one-way analysis of variance (ANOVA) and chi-square tests of independence are used as part of preliminary analysis on each of the variables involved in this study.

Objective 2 examines the factors that influence the survival of high-tech start-ups in India. To analyse this objective, we use statistical techniques of survival analysis or time to event analysis. This technique provides us the advantage of being able to incorporate information about start-ups that have not yet achieved this milestone in the study. This inclusion will help us to understand the factors that impact survival of high-tech start-ups more accurately.

We perform survival analysis on the data set, wherein the time in months of operation of the start-up and whether the start-up has achieved survival or not, taken together, form the dependent variable. The entrepreneurial and firm-specific variables that are captured as part of the questionnaire form the independent variables for this analysis. The external environmental factors such as SDP growth, number of VC firms in the region, and the number of VC-funded deals in the region are included as independent variables for the analysis. We also examine the data using survival analysis against our three segments, namely, (a) target market being addressed by the start-ups (B2B versus B2C), (b) location of operation of the start-ups (North Zone versus South Zone), and (c) exposure of the entrepreneurs (local versus transnational) to obtain a deeper understanding of the factors that influence survival of high-tech start-ups in India. Statistical techniques such as one-way ANOVA and chi-square tests of independence will be used as part of preliminary analysis on each of the variables involved in this study.

Objective 3 examines the factors that influence the growth of high-tech start-ups in India. To understand what factors contribute to the growth of the start-ups, we have chosen the measure of valuation of the start-up by an external entity to the firm, in the year of our study (2015), as the proxy to indicate growth. Using the valuation status of the start-ups in our study, we categorize them into two distinct groups. The first category of start-ups consists of those start-ups that have no reported external valuation, have valuation less than ₹5 crore if they are services-based, or less than ₹10 crore if they are manufacturing-based start-ups. These start-ups are classified under the category of start-ups that have achieved product-market fit but have not yet found their growth trajectory. The second category of start-ups consists of start-ups that have received external valuation of more than ₹5 crore if they are services-based, or more than ₹10 crore if they are manufacturing-based start-ups. The second category start-ups are classified as growth-oriented start-ups. We postulate that higher valuation of the start-up indicates higher growth and vice versa. The entrepreneurial, firm-specific, and external environment-specific factors constitute the independent factors that are examined for impact and influence.

We use logistic regression techniques to analyse the results of this examination. We execute six regression models, two each respectively to understand better the aspects of variance in market segment, location of operations, and the background of the entrepreneurs. An overall model is then built to understand the factors that influence the survival of high-tech start-ups in India. Statistical techniques such as one-way ANOVA and chi-square tests of independence are used as part of the preliminary analysis on each of the variables involved in this study.

Objective 4 analyses the factors that are relevant and impactful across the entire life cycle of high-tech start-ups. To analyse the objective, we create a categorical variable as the dependent variable that indicates the current life cycle milestone of the start-up. This variable takes values among '0' (emerged-only), '1' (emerged and survived), and '2' (emerged, survived, and grown start-ups). We then conduct multivariate analysis of variance (MANOVA) using this categorical variable as the baseline to understand the entrepreneurial, firm-specific, and external environment-specific variables that can help explain the differences prevailing in these three categories. Further, the multinomial logistic regression technique is adopted to understand and statistically validate which of the factors have an influence on the entire start-up life cycle.

Based on the findings of the four objectives, we derive suitable implications to the entrepreneurs, start-up ecosystem partners, and policymakers, with a view to enable them to overcome the key impediments across the high-tech start-up life cycle.

Description of Methods of Analysis

Logistic regression is used as the method of analysis of the first and the third objectives to examine the emergence and growth of high-tech start-ups. Survival analysis models are used to analyse the second objective (survival of high-tech start-ups). Multinomial regression technique is used to analyse the fourth objective, namely, the determination of factors that are impactful across the entire life cycle of high-tech start-ups. Further, MANOVA is also carried out as part of the analysis of the fourth research objective. The description of these methods are presented hereafter.

Logistic Regression

Logistic regression has been used for analysis when the dependent (or outcome) variable is discrete in nature (taking two or more possible values). When there is a need to explore the relationship between this type of discrete dependent variable and one or more independent variables, logistic regression has been established as the standard method of analysis (Hosmer and Lemeshow 2000).

Although the broad principles of analysis using logistic regression is similar to that of linear regression, we must note that there are two key differences between these two methods. The first difference is with the nature of the relationship modelled between the dependent and the independent variables. In any problem using linear regression, the key variable analysed is the mean value of the dependent variable, given the values of independent variables. In other words, the dependent variable is modelled as the *conditional mean*, expressed as '$E(Y \mid x)$' where Y denotes the dependent variable and x denotes the value of the independent variable. The quantity $E(Y \mid x)$ denotes the expected value of Y, given the value x. Hence, the equation formulation of this will be

$$E(Y \mid x) = \beta_0 + \beta_1 x \qquad (2.1)$$

where $E(Y \mid x)$ can take on any values, since x ranges between $-\infty$ and $+\infty$.

In case of the dependent variable with dichotomous or binary values, the aforementioned cannot be used for analysis, since the dependent variable follows a logistic distribution. Hence, we model the dichotomous dependent variable as follows:

To start with, we express the probability of occurrence of the event i in the following manner:

$$Pi = 1/1 + e^{-(\beta_1 + \beta_2 Xi)} \qquad (2.2)$$

The above can be written alternatively as

$$P_i = 1/(1 + e^{Zi}) = e^{Z_i}/(1 + e^{Zi}) \qquad (2.3)$$

where $Z_i = \beta_1 + \beta_2 Xi$.

Equation 2.3 represents the logistic distribution function. As Z_i ranges from $-\infty$ to $+\infty$, Pi ranges from 0 to 1, and Pi is non-linearly related to Z_i (X_i). However, it can be observed that equation 2.3 is highly non-linear, not only in terms of X_i but also βs. Hence, we need to first linearize equation 2.3 and then estimate its coefficients. For doing so, we need to undertake the steps given below.

If P_i refers to the probability of an event, then $(1-P_i)$ refers to the probability of non-event.

$$1 - P_i = 1/1 + e^{Zi} \qquad (2.4)$$

Therefore, we can write

$$(Pi/1-Pi) = 1 + e^{Zi}/1 + e^{-Zi} = e^{Zi} \qquad (2.5)$$

$(Pi/1-Pi)$ is known as the odds ratio of the event.

Now if we take the natural log of Equation 2.5, we obtain

$$L_i = ln\ (Pi/1-Pi) = Z_i = \beta_1 + \beta_2 Xi \qquad (2.6)$$

L_i is the log of odds ratio – it is not only linear in X but also in parameters. It can be observed that as P_i goes from 0 to 1, the logit L varies from $-\infty$ to $+\infty$. It can be observed that, although the probabilities lie between 0 and 1, the logit is not so bounded. Also, while L is linear in X, the probabilities are not.

Thus, with the logit value, we now have a metric variable that can have both positive and negative values but that can always be transformed back to a probability value between 0 and 1. This value is now the dependent variable in the logistic regression model.

Survival Analysis

In this study, we use survival analysis as the method to understand the key factors that impact survival of high-tech start-ups in India. Survival analysis deals with analysing the time to event related data. The model built for survival analysis takes in to account the time elapsed till the point of data collection, even for the units of observation for which the event under observation has not occurred (Aalen, Borgan, and Gjessing 2008). In our study, if a start-up did not yet achieve the product-market fit at the end of the observation phase, then this start-up would be censored 'on the right' that is, we know that this particular start-up's survival time exceeds the time duration between its formal creation and the closure of observation. This censored data provides additional information for statistical analysis, which is the reason why survival analysis is used.

The statistical approach of studying the probability of some event occurring as a function of the elapsed time is known as *survival analysis* or *duration analysis*. In survival analysis, the times at which certain events occur are assumed to be realizations of some random process (Allison 1995). Therefore T, the time for an event to occur for a particular observation, is a random variable having a certain probability distribution. Different methods are used to model survival data, depending on the kind of distributions that the survival time T follows.

The survival function which represents the unconditional probability of surviving longer than 't'time units, has the following general form: $S(t) = $ Probability$(T > t) = 1 - F(t)$, where $F(t)$ is the cumulative distribution function of the random variable T, denoting time to failure (Chatterjee 2010). A standard estimator of the survival function in the presence of censoring is the Kaplan–Meier (KM) product limit estimator. This is a non-parametric method of estimation. Plots of the KM estimates of the survival function against time provide a visual understanding of the survival function (Chatterjee 2010). The focus of the survival analysis would be used to model the hazard rate h(t), which is defined as $h(t) = f(t)/S(t)$.

There are semi-parametric and parametric models to use with survival data. The Cox proportional hazards model (Cox 1972) is popular because it does not require one to make an assumption about the exact parametric form of the underlying distribution of survival time. Also, in this model, hazards for two individuals are proportional with a proportionality constant that is independent of time.

Techniques for initial analysis and modelling survival data

The statistical analysis of survival data can be categorized as on the basis of three distinct set of tasks, namely, (a) initial analysis of survival data using non-parametric estimators, (b) semi- parametric model building and validation of assumptions, and (c) building accelerated failure time models, which are parametric models to analyse the survival data when the assumptions of semi-parametric models are not met.

Two prominent estimators have been used in past studies to perform the initial analysis of the survival data. These are KM estimator and Nelson–Aalen estimator, respectively. Both of these estimators estimate the survival function S (t) in the presence of censored data. The KM estimator can also be used to estimate the cumulative hazard H (t). They are particularly useful when comparing the survival probabilities among different groups with discrete levels of one independent variable (for example, when comparing the effect of treatment with a particular drug). Another way of estimating the cumulative hazards, non-parametrically, is by using the Nelson – Aalen estimator. The Nelson – Aalen estimator has better performance for small samples (Klein and Moeschberger 1997).

The Cox proportional hazards model is a widely used semi-parametric model for modelling survival data, especially for estimating the effect of continuous covariates. The goal is now to predict the probability of survival until time T, given a vector of covariates. The Cox proportional hazards model is popular because it does not require one to make an assumption about the exact parametric form of the underlying distribution of survival time. For the Cox proportional hazards model, the most important assumption that needs to be checked is that of proportionality. Several formal statistical tests have been proposed for the assessment of proportionality of hazards. Scaled Schoenfeld residuals are often used to check proportionality. If the element-wise plots of the scaled Schoenfeld residuals are sufficiently flat, then it can be concluded that the beta estimates do not vary with time, and hence the proportional hazards assumption is acceptable (Chatterjee 2010).

Once the proportional hazards assumption is met, the next step is to check the extent to which the model can explain the data. Cox–Snell residuals are used to check the overall goodness of fit of the model. If the graph of the cumulative hazard corresponding to these residuals forms a straight line passing through the origin with a slope of 45 degree, then we can conclude that the model specification is correct. If not, the converse is true.

MANOVA

MANOVA is a technique for comparing multivariate sample means. As a multivariate technique, it is used when there are two or more dependent variables, and is typically followed by significance tests involving individual dependent variables separately (Warne 2014). It helps to answer whether the changes in the independent variable(s) have significant effects on the dependent variables, or to ascertain the relationships among the dependent and independent variables (Stevens 2002).

MANOVA can be viewed as the generalized form of univariate ANOVA. The one-way MANOVAis used to determine whether there are any differences between independent groups on more than one continuous dependent variable. In this regard, it differs from a one-way ANOVA, which only measures one dependent variable. MANOVA uses the covariance between outcome variables in testing the statistical significance of the mean differences. There are two major situations in which MANOVA is used: first, whenthere are several correlated dependent variables, and the researcher desires a single, overall statistical test on this set of variables, instead of performing multiple individual tests; and second, in some cases, the more important purpose is to explore how independent variables influence some patterning of response on the dependent variables (Carey 1998).

It is important to understand that one-way MANOVA is an omnibus test statistic and cannot reveal to us which specific groups are significantly different from each other; it is able to test that at least two groups are different. Since in our study design, we have three to four groups that need to be compared, determining which of these groups differ from each other is important. There are established post hoc MANOVA that help us converge on the aforementioned aspects.

As with any statistical technique, prior to usage of MANOVA for comparison of groups, we need to check if the assumptions that are made on the data are amenable for usage of this technique. There are many assumptions that need to be met for carrying out the MANOVA. The first assumption, to be validated, is that there should be two or more dependent variables to carry out MANOVA. Second, the independent variables for the study should consist of two or more categorical, independent groups. Further, for carrying out the MANOVA, the observations (data points) should be statistically independent of each other, should not possess any significant outlier data points, and the data should meet the conditions of multivariate normality. The data sample to be subjected for MANOVA should also possess a linear relationship between each pair of dependent variables against each group of independent variables. Last, MANOVA requires homogeneity of the variance–covariance matrices and absence of multicollinearity. There are suitable tests to examine each of the assumptions.

Multinomial Regression Analysis

Multinomial logistic regression (often just called 'multinomial regression') is used to predict a multinomial dependent variable with one or more independent variables. It can be considered an extension of binomial logistic regression. As with other types of regression, multinomial regression can also use interactions between independent variables to predict the dependent variable.

For a nominal dependent variable with k categories, the multinomial regression model estimates k-1 logit equations. For a given outcome variable Y (multinomial dependent variable), assuming that there are three categories (k = 3) of the outcome variable which are coded as 0, 1, and 2, two (k-1) logit equations will need to be developed for the analysis. Usually, the category Y = 0 is used as the referent or baseline outcome and logit equations Y = 1 and Y = 2 are compared against this baseline outcome. For modelling the objective that has p covariates and a constant term, denoted by the vector $\mathbf{x}$, of length p + 1 where $x_0 = 1$, the two logit functions are denoted as

$$f_1(x) = \ln \left[P(Y = 1 \mid x) / P(Y = 0 \mid x) \right]$$

$$= \beta_{10} + \beta_{11}x_1 + \beta_{12}x_2 + \dots + \beta_{1p}x_p = \mathbf{x'\beta 1} \qquad (2.7)$$

and $\qquad f_2(x) = \ln \left[P(Y = 2 \mid x) / P(Y = 0 \mid x) \right]$

$$= \beta_{20} + \beta_{21}x_1 + \beta_{22}x_2 + \dots + \beta_{2p}x_p = \mathbf{x'\beta 2} \qquad (2.8)$$

Based on these models, the likelihood functions are constructed and parameter estimates are derived. By carrying out multinomial regression, we will be able to determine which of the independent variables (if any) have a statistically significant effect on the dependent variable. For categorical independent variables, we will be able to interpret the odds that one group has a higher or lower value on the dependent variable compared to the second group. For continuous independent variables, we will be able to interpret how a single unit increases or decreases in that variable (for example, a one-year increase or decrease in founder's age) would be associated with the odds of the dependent variable having a higher or lower value. As with other forms of regression models, we will also be able to determine how well our multinomial regression model predicts the dependent variable.

The assumptions that need to be met before conducting the multinomial regression analysis are that there should be only one dependent variable, which is measured at the multinomial scale. All the observations made to capture the values of the variables should be independent of each other and the dependent variable in this case must have mutually exclusive and exhaustive categories. There must exist at least one or more independent variables that can be continuous, ordinal, or categorical in nature. Further, there should be no multicollinearity (absence of high correlation between two or more independent variables) amongst the variables considered for the study. Last, there should be a linear relationship between any continuous independent variables and the logit transformation of the dependent variable.

Analysis Plan

This section lays out the broad plan for analysing each of the objectives. It outlines the conceptual framework that would be used to examine the objectives as well as the hypotheses that would be tested in order to analyse the stated objectives. Figure 2.1 presents the overall approach and the conceptual framework that will be used to evaluate the research objectives.

Figure 2.2 outlines the conceptual framework that will be used to understand the differences in impact of the entrepreneurial, firm-specific, and external environment-specific factors across the three segments of (a) target market segment of start-ups (B2B versus B2C), (b) location of operations (North Zone versus South Zone), and (c) entrepreneurial exposure (local entrepreneurs versus transnational entrepreneurs).

The chapter will further describe the appropriate hypotheses that would be validated in order to analyse the objectives of this study.

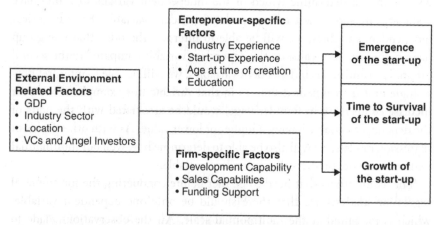

FIGURE 2.1 Overall conceptual framework to analyse the life cycle of high-tech start-ups
SOURCE: Author.

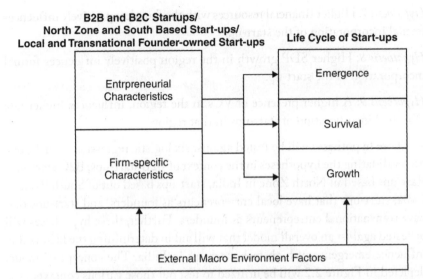

FIGURE 2.2 Overall conceptual framework to analyse differences across market segment, location of operations, and entrepreneurial exposure

SOURCE: Author.

Analysis of Factors Impacting Emergence

Based on the conceptual framework presented in Figure 2.1, the following set of hypotheses will be tested as part of the analysis of the first research objective.

Hypothesis 1: Prior industry experience of the primary founder positively influences formal incorporation of the start-up.

Hypothesis 2: Prior start-up experience of the primary founder positively influences formal incorporation of the start-up.

Hypothesis 3: Primary founders of higher age are more likely to formally incorporate the start-up earlier than the founders of lesser age.

Hypothesis 4: Higher educational pedigree positively influences formal incorporation of the start-up.

Hypothesis 5: Higher R&D resources with the founders positively influences formal incorporation of the start-up.

Hypothesis 6: Higher sales capabilities with the founders positively influences formal incorporation of the start-up.

Hypothesis 7: Higher financial resources with the founders positively influences formal incorporation of the start-up.

Hypothesis 8: Higher SDP growth in the region positively influences formal incorporation of the start-up.

Hypothesis 9: A higher presence of VCs in the region, influences higher rate of formal incorporation of start-ups in that region.

These hypotheses will be tested against six logistic regression models, one each validating the hypotheses in the context of B2B start-ups, B2C start-ups, start-ups based in North Zone in India, start-ups based out of South Zone in India, start-ups that have local entrepreneurs as founders, and start-ups that have transnational entrepreneurs as founders. Further, these hypotheses will be tested against an overall model that will aid in determining the factors that influence emergence of high-tech start-ups in India. The conceptual model depicted in Figure 2.2 will be utilized to test out those various contexts.

Analysis of Factors Impacting Survival

Based on the conceptual framework presented in Figure 2.1, the following set of hypotheses will be tested as part of the analysis of the second research objective.

Hypothesis 1: Prior industry experience of the primary founder positively influences the time to survival of the start-up.

Hypothesis 2: Prior start-up experience of the primary founder positively influences the time to survival of the start-up.

Hypothesis 3: Primary founders of higher age are more likely to achieve survival of their start-ups earlier than the founders of lesser age.

Hypothesis 4: Higher educational pedigree positively influences the time to survival of the start-up.

Hypothesis 5: Higher R&D resources with the founders' start-up positively influences the time to survival of the start-up.

Hypothesis 6: Higher sales capabilities with the founders' start-up positively influences the time to survival of the start-up.

Hypothesis 7: Higher financial resources with the founders' start-up positively influences the time to survival of the start-up.

Hypothesis 8: Higher SDP growth in the region where the start-up is located positively influences the time to survival of the start-up.

Hypothesis 9: The higher the presence of VCs in the region, the faster the start-ups will be able to achieve survival.

These hypotheses will be tested using six survival analysis models, one each validating these hypotheses in the context of B2B start-ups, B2C start-ups, start-ups based in North Zone in India, start-ups based out of South Zone in India, start-ups that have local entrepreneurs as founders, and start-ups that have transnational entrepreneurs as founders. Further, these hypotheses will be tested against an overall model that will aid in determining the factors that influence survival of high-tech start-ups in India. The conceptual model depicted in Figure 2.2 will be utilized to test out those various contexts.

Analysis of Factors Impacting Growth

Based on the conceptual framework presented in Figure 2.1, the following set of hypotheses will be tested as part of analysis of the third research objective.

Hypothesis 1: Prior industry experience of the primary founder positively influences the growth of the start-up.

Hypothesis 2: Prior start-up experience of the primary founder positively influences the growth of the start-up.

Hypothesis 3: Primary founders of higher age are more likely to influence growth of the start-up than the founders of lesser age.

Hypothesis 4: Higher educational pedigree of the founder positively influences the growth of the start-up.

Hypothesis 5: Higher development resources with the firm positively influences the growth of the start-up.

Hypothesis 6: Higher number of customers acquired since inception of the firm positively influences the growth of the start-up.

Hypothesis 7: Higher financial resources at the disposal of the firm positively influences the growth of the start-up.

Hypothesis 8: Higher SDP growth in the region positively influences the growth of the start-up.

Hypothesis 9: A higher presence of VCs in the region influences higher rate of growth of start-ups in that region.

Hypothesis 10: A higher number of funded-VC deals in the region influences higher rate of growth of start-ups in that region.

These hypotheses will be tested using six logistic regression models, one each validating these hypotheses in the context of B2B start-ups, B2C start-ups, start-ups based in North Zone in India, start-ups based out of South Zone in India, start-ups that have local entrepreneurs as founders, and start-ups that have transnational entrepreneurs as founders. Further, these hypotheses will be tested against an overall model that will aid in determining the factors that influence growth of high-tech start-ups in India. The conceptual model depicted in Figure 2.2 will be utilized to test out those various contexts.

Analysis of Factors Impacting the Entire Start-up Life Cycle

Based on the conceptual framework, presented in Figure 2.1, the following set of hypotheses will be tested as part of analysis of the fourth research objective.

Hypothesis 1: Prior industry experience of the primary founder positively influences all the three key life cycle milestones of emergence, survival, and growth of the start-up.

Hypothesis 2: Prior start-up experience of the primary founder positively influences all the three key life cycle milestones of emergence, survival, and growth of the start-up.

Hypothesis 3: Age of the founder positively influences all the three key life cycle milestones of emergence, survival, and growth of the start-up.

Hypothesis 4: Higher educational pedigree of the founder positively influences all the three key life cycle milestones of emergence, survival, and growth of the start-up.

Hypothesis 5: Higher development resources with the firm positively influences all the three key life cycle milestones of emergence, survival, and growth of the start-up.

Hypothesis 6: Higher number of customers acquired since inception of the firm positively influences all the three key life cycle milestones of emergence, survival, and growth of the start-up.

Hypothesis 7: Higher financial resources at the disposal of the firm positively influences all the three key life cycle milestones of emergence, survival, and growth of the start-up.

Hypothesis 8: Higher SDP growth in the region positively influences all the three key life cycle milestones of emergence, survival, and growth of the start-up.

Hypothesis 9: A higher presence of VCs in the region influences all the three key life cycle milestones of emergence, survival, and growth of the start-ups in that region.

Hypothesis 10: A higher number of VC-funded deals in the region influences all the three key life cycle milestones of emergence, survival, and growth of the start-ups in that region.

These hypotheses will be tested by subjecting the data of high-tech start-ups to multinomial logistic regression analysis. Prior to the regression analysis, the data of the high-tech start-ups would be classified under three categories, namely, (a) start-ups that have emerged but not survived ('emerged-only start-ups' category), (b) start-ups that have survived but not grown ('survived-only start-ups' category), and (c) start-ups that have experienced growth ('growth-only start-ups' category) based on the responses the start-up founders provided to us as part of the survey. A statistical comparison of these three groups using MANOVA and two-way ANOVA is carried out, using the grouping variables – life cycle status of the start-up, the target market segment, location of operations, and entrepreneurial exposure as baseline of comparison. These comparisons will reveal the key entrepreneur-specific, firm-specific, and external environment-specific factors that differentiate the three phases of life cycle of the start-ups. With this tentative insight, we perform the multinomial regression analysis, which will help us statistically identify the key factors that influence the entire life cycle of high-tech start-ups in each of the aforementioned categories.

Summary

In this chapter, we lay down the research objectives of this study. The focus of these research objectives is twofold. First, we seek to understand the key factors that impact and influence the three milestones (emergence, survival, and growth) of high-tech start-up life cycle which form the first three research objectives. Second, we intend to analyse the contribution of these factors across the entire life cycle of high-tech start-ups, which forms the fourth research objective. Using the lens of target market (B2B versus B2C start-ups), location of operations (North Zone versus South Zone), and background of founders (local versus transnational entrepreneurs), we will be able to derive additional insights that aid in meaningful interpretation of the analyses. The findings that emerge from the analyses of the first four objectives will enable us to derive inferences and policy implications for researchers, entrepreneurs, financiers, and policymakers in large.

Further, we defined the scope of the study in the context of the stated research objectives. This is followed by a detailed description of the research methodology, which includes the description of sources of data, definitions, methodology, and the statistical methods of analysis. Towards the end of the chapter we laid out a detailed plan for analysing each of the research objectives.

3

High-tech Start-ups in India

Profile and Characteristics

Introduction

This chapter describes the profiles and characteristics of the high-tech start-ups in our sample. To start with, we analyse the univariate profiles of the start-ups with respect to their characteristics, such as year of incorporation, number of founders at the time of creation, gender distribution of primary founders, number of founders who knew each other prior to the starting of the enterprise, and the location of operations of the start-ups.

Further, univariate and bivariate analyses of the characteristics are carried out based on the market segment that these start-ups are catering to (B2B versus B2C), the location of operations of the start-ups (North Zone versus South Zone), and the entrepreneurial background of the founders (local entrepreneurs versus transnational entrepreneurs). There are 275 start-ups that constitute our sample for the study. Out of these, 100 start-ups are informally active (not emerged), 88 of them have emerged but have not survived, 38 of them have survived but have not yet grown, and 49 of them have grown. The rest of this chapter is organized as follows. The next section discusses the results from univariate analysis. The following section analyses the bivariate relationships of the characteristics and the last section summarizes the major observations based on the univariate and bivariate analyses carried out.

Profile of the Start-ups: Univariate Analysis

The profiles of the high-tech start-ups in our sample are analysed with respect to the characteristics mentioned earlier. Each of these characteristics has been discussed in detail here.

Year of Incorporation

Figure 3.1 presents the distribution of high-tech start-ups, based on their years of incorporation. The figure indicates that there has been more or less a steady increase in formal incorporation of the start-ups post the 2008 financial crisis. In particular, the rate of inceptions of the start-ups in our sample has doubled in the past two years – consistent with the observations made by NASSCOM (2015).

Number of Founders at Inception

Figure 3.2 presents the distribution of high-tech start-ups, based on the number of founders present at the time of creation of the start-up. About 50 per cent has start-ups with two co-founders. For most of these start-ups, one of the founders focused on the technological aspect of the start-up, while the other co-founder focused on the business aspects of the start-up. Further, we observe that majority of the start-ups in our sample have more than one founder, indicating that entrepreneurs are better prepared to face challenges during the initial phases of the start-up life cycle.

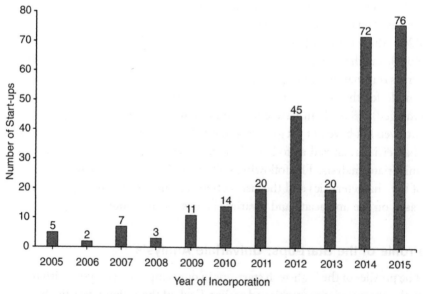

FIGURE 3.1 Distribution of high-tech start-ups based on the year of incorporation

SOURCE: Author.

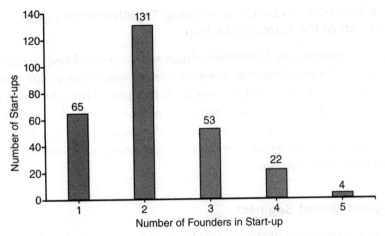

FIGURE 3.2 Distribution of high-tech start-ups based on the number of founders

SOURCE: Author.

Gender Distribution in the Founding Team

Figure 3.3 presents the distribution of high-tech start-ups based on the gender of the founding team members. The figure clearly indicates the lack of female participation in the start-up ecosystem. Only about 6 per cent of our sample has female founders while 94 per cent of the founders are male. This observation of the overall gender distribution is on similar lines as observed in the NASSCOM (2015).

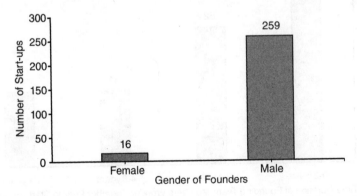

FIGURE 3.3 Distribution of high-tech start-ups based on the gender of the founders

SOURCE: Author.

Time Duration of Founders Working Together Prior to the Inception of the Current Start-up

Figure 3.4 presents the distribution of high-tech start-ups, based on the time duration of the founding team members working together as a team prior to the inception of their current start-up. It can be observed from the figure that about 70 per cent of the founding team members knew each other and worked with each other for more than two years. We interpret that this long-term association of the co-founders with each other increases the odds of success or survival of the start-ups.

Targeted Market Segment

Figure 3.5 presents the distribution of high-tech start-ups, based on the targeted market segment (B2B versus B2C). The B2C start-ups are slightly more in number (about 55 per cent of the sample) than the B2B start-ups (45 per cent of the sample). The B2B sector-focused start-ups target large enterprises as their potential customers. Typically, they start working with prospective customers of one sector and then expand their business operations if their offering is viable and usable by enterprises across multiple industry sectors. On account of this, B2B sector-focused start-ups have a niche or segmented

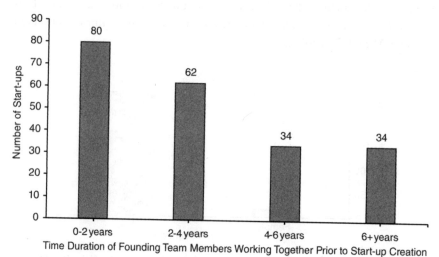

Figure 3.4 Distribution of high-tech start-ups based on the time durations of the founding team members working together prior to the inceptions of the current start-ups

Source: Author.

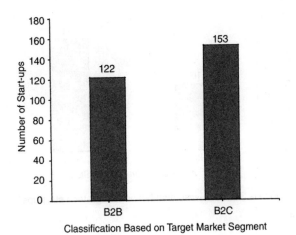

Classification Based on Target Market Segment

FIGURE 3.5 Distribution of high-tech start-ups based on targeted market segments

SOURCE: Author.

target customer audience to reach out to. In contrast, start-ups targeting the B2C sector will need to cater to the needs of individual customers. Hence, their offerings need to serve a very diverse and distributed customer segment (Mahadevan 2000; Andersen 2009: 274). The presence of start-ups catering to these markets will help us derive more meaningful insights, as we evaluate the research objectives in the subsequent chapters.

Location of Operations

Figure 3.6 presents the distribution of high-tech start-ups, based on the location of their operations (North Zone versus South Zone). We observe that South Zone has more number of start-ups (about 63 per cent), thus tentatively justifying our motivation to classify start-ups across these two zones. Figure 3.7 presents the distribution of high-tech start-ups in our sample, classified across metro and non-metro cities. Delhi, Mumbai, Bengaluru, Chennai, Kolkata, Hyderabad, and Pune are classified as metro cities, and all other cities in our sample are classified as non-metro cities. We can observe that the presence of high-tech start-ups is very highly skewed in favour of metro cities, with about 88 per cent of high-tech start-ups operating out of metro cities. This heavily skewed presence of high-tech start-ups in metro cities seems to indicate that start-ups get established in regions where there is better access to skills, capital, and an addressable market that has higher spending power.

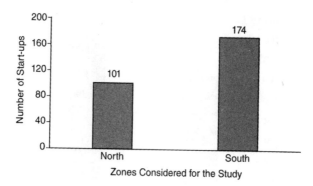

FIGURE 3.6 Zone-wise distribution of high-tech start-ups

SOURCE: Author.

Entrepreneurial Exposure

Figure 3.8 presents the distribution of high-tech start-ups based on the exposure of the founder to foreign markets. About 152 entrepreneurs or 55 per cent of the sample are local entrepreneurs, whereas our sample consists of 123 transnational entrepreneurs, accounting for 45 per cent of the sample. The presence of transnational entrepreneurs in almost equal proportion indicates that these entrepreneurs perceive good returns from pursuing entrepreneurial opportunities in their country of origin. This can also be interpreted as the market in India being attractive and conducive for entrepreneurs in high-tech sector to try and offer new products and services.

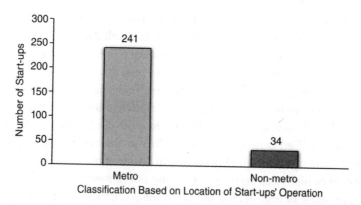

FIGURE 3.7 Distribution of start-ups based on metro versus non-metro cities

SOURCE: Author.

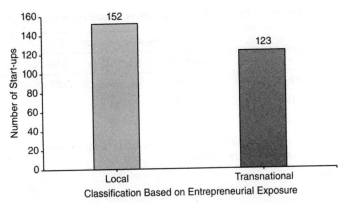

FIGURE 3.8 Distribution of high-tech start-ups based on entrepreneurial exposure

SOURCE: Author.

Profiles of the Start-ups in Our Sample: Bivariate Analysis

The high-tech start-ups have been classified and studied under three segments – by the market segment that they address (B2B and B2C), by the location of their operations in India (North Zone and South Zone), and by the background of the primary founder (local entrepreneur and transnational entrepreneur).

The bivariate profile for each of the three segments has been analysed with respect to the following variables – founder's prior industry experience; founder's prior start-up experience; age of the founder at the time of creation of the start-up; and sales, development and funding capabilities of the start-up at the time of inception. Bivariate techniques such as chi-square test of independence and one-way ANOVA are used to derive these results. Chi-square test of independence is used when both the variables under consideration are discrete in nature; one-way ANOVA is used when one of the variables is continuous (dependent variable) while the other is discrete (Gujarati 2012; Hair et al. 2015).

Chi-square tests of independence statistically ascertain if the two variables are distributed independently of each other. According to the null hypothesis, 'the two variables are independently distributed', and in the alternate hypothesis, 'the two variables are not independently distributed'. The rejection of the null hypothesis (that is, a small p-value) would imply that the two variables are not independently distributed and there exists a discernable pattern between the two.

TABLE 3.1 Bivariate profile of market segments versus location of operations of start-ups

Market segments	Zone-wise allocation		
	North Zone	South Zone	Total
B2B	32	90	122
B2C	69	84	153
Total	101	174	275

Chi-square test of independence: Pearson chi-square test value 10.399; **p-value 0.001**

SOURCE: Author.

One-way ANOVA statistically determine whether the mean values of the dependent variable are statistically different across subgroups. The null hypothesis proposes that 'the mean values are not significantly different across sub-groups'. And in the alternative hypothesis, 'the mean value of at least one of the sub-groups is significantly different from the others'. The rejection of the null hypothesis (that is, a small p-value) would imply that the mean values are indeed different across subgroups, and there exists a relationship between the dependent and the independent variables.

Bivariate Profiles: Market Segment versus Operating Location

This section presents the results obtained from the chi-square tests carried out to analyse the bivariate relationships among the three categories of segmentation variables. In particular, we analyse the relationship between targeted market segment and operating location of the start-ups (Table 3.1 and Figure 3.9).

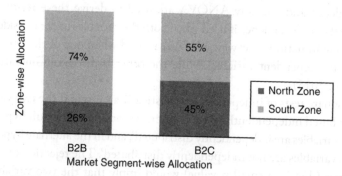

FIGURE 3.9 Distribution of market segment versus location of operations of start-ups

SOURCE: Author.

TABLE 3.2 Bivariate profile of market segments versus entrepreneurial exposure of start-ups

Entrepreneurial exposure	Market segment		
	B2B	B2C	Total
Local	59	93	152
Transnational	63	60	123
Total	122	153	275

Chi-square test of independence: Pearson chi-square test value 4.238; **p-value 0.040**

SOURCE: Author.

The small p-value (0.001) of the results as presented in Table 3.1 indicates that there exists significant dependence between the start-ups' location of operations and the targeted market segment. From Figure 3.9, we can deduce that majority of the start-ups in the B2B and B2C sectors (74 per cent and 55 per cent, respectively) are located in South Zone, as against 26 per cent and 45 per cent, respectively for B2B and B2C sector start-ups located in the North Zone. This concentration of start-ups in South Zone seems to indicate that southern states may be relatively a better location of choice for high-tech start-ups.

Bivariate Profiles: Market Segments versus Entrepreneurial Exposure

This section presents the results obtained from the chi-square tests that analyses the relationship between targeted market segments and entrepreneurial exposure of the start-ups (Table 3.2 and Figure 3.10).

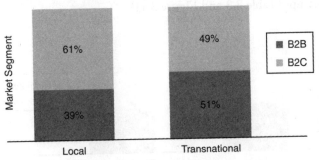

FIGURE 3.10 Distribution of market segment versus entrepreneurial exposure of start-ups
SOURCE: Author.

TABLE 3.3 Bivariate profile of location of operations versus entrepreneurial exposure

Entrepreneurial exposure	Zone-wise allocation		
	North Zone	South Zone	Total
Local	60	92	152
Transnational	41	82	123
Total	101	174	275

Chi-square test of independence: Pearson chi-square test value 1.103;
p-value 0.294

SOURCE: Author.

The low p-value from the chi-square test indicates that there is a statistically significant dependence between entrepreneurial exposure and targeted market segments of the start-ups. From Figure 3.10, it can be observed that majority of the local entrepreneurs (about 61 per cent of the sample) opt for starting up B2C ventures, whereas transnational entrepreneurs can be found not showing too much bias to a particular market segment to start their new ventures. One of the possible reasons for local entrepreneurs looking to start B2C ventures in greater proportion could be that they are aware of the local market needs much better and hence feel more confident of the viability of market acceptance of their new offerings.

Bivariate Profiles: Entrepreneurial Exposure versus Location of Operations

Here, we present the results obtained from chi-square test of independence between the location of operations of start-ups and entrepreneurial exposure of the start-ups (Table 3.3 and Figure 3.11).

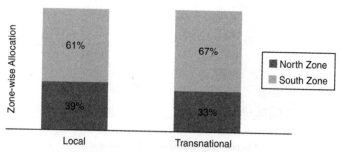

FIGURE 3.11 Distribution of location of operations versus entrepreneurial exposure
SOURCE: Author.

From Figure 3.11, it appears that South Zone dominates the choice of both local and transnational entrepreneurs, with 61 per cent of local entrepreneurs and 67 per cent of transnational entrepreneurs opting to locate their start-up operations. However, the chi-square test results indicate that there is no statistically significant relationship between the entrepreneurial exposure (local or transnational) and the location of operations for their start-ups.

Bivariate Profile of the Founder's Age

The results from the one-way ANOVA between the average age of the founder at the time of inception of the start-up vis-à-vis the market segment targeted, the location of operations, and entrepreneur exposure have been presented in Table 3.4.

From Table 3.4, it can be seen that although the average age of the founders across different zones of operations in India and across different targeted market segments, rangeing from 29 years to 34 years, there are significant statistical differences across these groups. The average age of founders in North Zone is about 30 years, whereas the average age of founders in South Zone is two years higher, at 32 years. Similarly, while the average age of founders concentrating

TABLE 3.4 Profile of founder's age at the inception of the start-up

Location of operations		ANOVA results		
North Zone	South Zone	Computed F-values	p-value	Homogeneity of variances
30	32	5.117	**0.024**	Yes
Market segment				
B2B	B2C	13.806	**0.000**	Yes
32.98	29.87			
Entrepreneurial exposure				
Local	International	26.143	**0.000**	Yes
29.36	33.57			

SOURCE: Author.

NOTE: The test for equality of means was preceded by the test for equality of variances. In case the variances are equal, the regular F-statistic values have been reported; otherwise, Welch-F-statistic values have been reported. p-values of significant results are in **bold**.

on serving the B2B market is about 33 years, the founders concentrating on serving the B2C market have an average age of 30 years in our sample. Further, the average age of local entrepreneurs is about 30 years, whereas the average age of the transnational entrepreneurs who are setting their venture in India is at a higher side of about 34 years.

Considering the lesser average age in B2C start-ups, it can be explained by the fact that B2C start-ups have relatively lesser barriers to customer acquisition, in comparison with their B2B counterparts. Hence, B2B start-ups usually require some prior experience or deeper skills – which explains the observation that B2B start-ups have founders with a higher average age (Fish 2009). The same argument can be made of transnational entrepreneurs starting their ventures at an average age higher than those of the local entrepreneurs. In case of the transnational entrepreneurs, usually, after their primary graduation in India, they would have spent time in developed countries either on account of further studies or on account of working overseas (Saxenian 2003). Further, the founder age being relatively higher in South Zone seems to indicate that entrepreneurs in this region would focus on getting the right skills (business and technical), prior to starting up. They may choose to work at a corporate job, or at another start-up as an employee to obtain the requisite skills prior to starting their own venture.

Bivariate Profile of R&D Capabilities of the Start-ups

The results from the one-way ANOVA between the R&D capabilities of the start-up at the time of inception of the start-up vis-à-vis the targeted market segments, the location of operations, and entrepreneurial exposure have been presented in Table 3.5.

In this case, for the purposes of this analysis, the number of R&D personnel in a start-up at the time of formal initiation is considered the proxy for the R&D capabilities of the start-up. From Table 3.5, it can be seen that the average R&D capabilities of the start-up at the time of inception does not vary significantly across different zones of operation in India and across different targeted market segments. The average R&D capabilities of the start-ups in North Zone is about 6 people, whereas the average R&D capabilities of the start-ups in South Zone is about 8 people. Similarly, while the average R&D capabilities of the start-ups concentrating on serving the B2B market is about eight people, the R&D capabilities of the start-ups serving the B2C market have an average of seven people in our sample. From the perspective

TABLE 3.5 Profile of R&D capabilities of the start-ups at time of inception

Zone		ANOVA results		
North Zone	South Zone	Computed F-values	p-value	Homogeneity of variances
6.50	7.72	1.04	**0.309**	Yes
Market segment				
B2B	B2C	0.007	**0.932**	Yes
7.33	7.23			
Entrepreneurial exposure				
Local	Transnational	0.147	**0.702**	Yes
7.47	7.03			

SOURCE: Author.

NOTE: The test for equality of means was preceded by the test for equality of variances. In case the variances are equal, the regular F-statistic values have been reported; otherwise, Welch-F-statistic values have been reported. p-values of significant results are in **bold**.

of entrepreneurial backgrounds, it is seen that both local and transnational entrepreneurs employ about seven people in their R&D team as they start their operations. Since the aforementioned result indicates that there are no statistically significant differences, and we do not further interpret or analyse these outcomes.

Bivariate Profile of Sales Capabilities of the Start-ups

The results from the ANOVA between the sales capabilities of the start-up at the time of inception vis-à-vis the targeted market segment, the location of operations, and entrepreneurial exposure have been presented in Table 3.6. In this case, for the purposes of this analysis, the revenue as reported by the founders (in INR, lakhs) from time of inception till the day of data collection for their start-ups has been considered the proxy for the R&D capabilities of the start-up. The results from Table 3.6 indicate that there are no statistically significant differences between the groups, and hence we do not further interpret the results. Further, the data for this analysis comes entirely from a subset of start-ups that are generating revenue, and hence the data set for this analysis is skewed and is not representative the entire population.

TABLE 3.6 Profile of sales capabilities of the start-ups at time of inception

Zone		ANOVA results		
North Zone	South Zone	Computed F-values	p-value	Homogeneity of variances
45.18	75.22	1.084	**0.299**	No
Market segment				
B2B	B2C	2.177	**0.141**	Yes
87.12	45.90			
Entrepreneurial exposure				
Local	Transnational	0.002	**0.966**	Yes
63.65	64.85			

SOURCE: Author.

NOTE: The test for equality of means was preceded by the test for equality of variances. In case the variances are equal, the regular F-statistic values have been reported; otherwise, Welch-F-tatistic values have been reported. p-values of significant results are in **bold**.

Bivariate Profile of Founder's Industry Experience

The bivariate profile of the primary founder's industry experience with the targeted market segment is presented in Table 3.7 and Figure 3.12. The graphs provide us further insights on explaining the significant differences of founder's industry experience variation across the B2B and B2C sectors. We can understand that B2C sector attracts more entrepreneurs, irrespective of their prior industry experience. This is explainable based on the increasing purchasing power of the individuals in India between 2005 and 2015, which is creating the market for start-ups. In contrast, given the inherent entry barriers for new companies to sell to established enterprises, it is natural that many entrepreneurs choose to set up ventures targeting B2C segment.

Chi-square test of independence indicates that prior industry experience of the founder of the start-up varies significantly across the B2B and B2C target market segments. The low p-value indicates that there is a distinct and different pattern of how industry experience of the founder varies across these segments. This implies that prior industry experience of the entrepreneurs would impact the choice of target market selection for their start-ups.

TABLE 3.7 Bivariate profile of founder's industry experience versus market segment

Industry experience	Market segment		
	B2B	B2C	Total
0	6	26	32
1	116	127	243
Total	122	153	275

Chi-square test of independence: Pearson chi-square test value 9.626; **p-value 0.002**

Source: Author.

The bivariate profile of the primary founders' industry experience with the location of operations is presented in Table 3.8 and Figure 3.13. The graphs presented in Figure 3.13 indicate that South Zone dominates in the number of start-ups set-up, irrespective of the background of the founder's prior industry experience. However, chi-square test of independence indicates that prior industry experience of the start-up's founder does not influence the locations of setting up of operations of the start-up.

The bivariate profile of the primary founder's industry experience with the entrepreneurial exposure is presented in Table 3.9 and Figure 3.14. The graphs presented in Figure 3.14 indicate that local entrepreneurs seem to be the ones who are embarking on new venture creation without prior industry experience, relative to the transnational entrepreneurs. Further, chi-square test of independence indicates that there is dependence between prior industry experience of the entrepreneur and entrepreneur exposure.

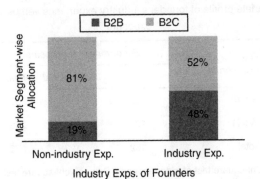

FIGURE 3.12 Distribution of founder's industry experience versus market segment

Source: Author.

TABLE 3.8 Bivariate profile of founder's industry experience versus location of operations

Industry experience	Zone allocation		
	North Zone	South Zone	Total
0	15	17	32
1	86	157	243
Total	101	174	275

Chi-square test of independence: Pearson chi-square test value 1.605; **p-value 0.205**

SOURCE: Author.

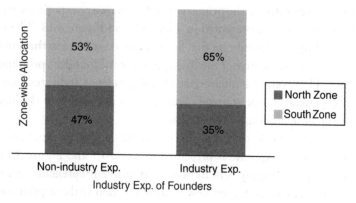

FIGURE 3.13 Distribution of founder's industry experience versus location of operations

SOURCE: Author.

TABLE 3.9 Bivariate profile of founder's industry experience versus entrepreneurial exposure

Founder's industry experience	Entrepreneurial exposure		
	Local	Transnational	Total
No (0)	25	7	32
Yes (1)	127	116	243
Total	152	123	275

Chi-square test of independence: Pearson chi-square test value 7.650; **p-value 0.006**

SOURCE: Author.

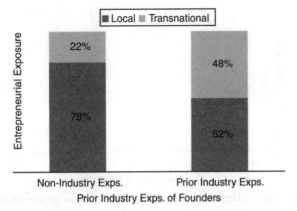

FIGURE 3.14 Distribution of founder's industry experience versus entrepreneurial exposure

SOURCE: Author.

Bivariate Profile of Founder's Start-up Experience

The bivariate profile of the primary founder's start-up experience with the targeted market segment is presented in Table 3.10 and Figure 3.15. Among the entrepreneurs with prior start-up experience, about 59 per cent of them have created new ventures targeting the B2C market segment and about 41 per cent of them are focusing on the B2B market segment. Among the set of entrepreneurs with no prior start-up experience, the opposite pattern is observed. About 49 per cent of the sample of novice entrepreneurs target the B2C market, as against 51 per cent who target the B2B market. The chi-square test of independence indicates that the founder's prior start-up experience does not influence the target market segments chosen by the entrepreneurs.

TABLE 3.10 Bivariate profile of founder's start-up experience versus market segment

Start-up experience	Market segment		
	B2B	B2C	Total
0	45	44	89
1	77	109	186
Total	122	153	275

Chi-square test of independence: Pearson chi-square test value 2.048; **p-value 0.152**

SOURCE: Author.

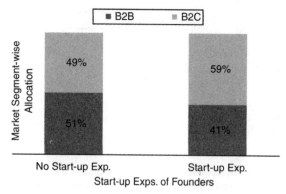

FIGURE 3.15 Distribution of founder's start-up experience versus targeted market segment
SOURCE: Author.

The bivariate profile of the primary founder's start-up experience with the location of operations is presented in Table 3.11 and Figure 3.16. We observe that about two thirds of start-up entrepreneurs with prior start-up experience in our sample have located their start-ups in South Zone. This indicates that entrepreneurs in the South Zone understand and value the need to possess skills prior to starting their new ventures. From a location of operations perspective, we observe that South Zone hosts entrepreneurs with and without prior start-up experience in similar proportions (62 per cent of entrepreneurs with prior start-up experience and 66 per cent of entrepreneurs without prior start-up experience). Given this observation, we can postulate that prior start-up experience of entrepreneurs may not have a statistically significant influence on the location of operations of the start-ups. The chi-square test of independence (Table 3.11) confirms that the founder's prior start-up experience does not influence the location from where the start-ups operate.

TABLE 3.11 Bivariate profile of founder's start-up experience versus location of operations

Start-up experience	Zone allocation		
	North Zone	South Zone	Total
0	30	59	89
1	71	115	186
Total	101	174	275

Chi-square test of independence: Pearson chi-square test
value 0.516; **p-value 0.472**

SOURCE: Author.

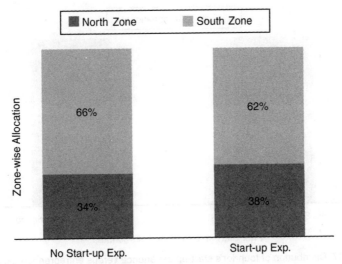

FIGURE 3.16 Distribution of founder's start-up experience versus location of operations

SOURCE: Author.

The bivariate profile of the primary founder's start-up experience with entrepreneurial exposure is presented in Table 3.12 and Figure 3.17. From Figure 3.17, we can observe that the distribution of start-ups across these two groups are pretty similar. Further, the chi-square test results presented in Table 3.12 also confirm the lack of dependence of prior start-up experience on the entrepreneurial exposure.

TABLE 3.12 Bivariate profile of founder's start-up experience versus entrepreneurial exposure

Start-up experience	Entrepreneurial exposure		
	Local	Transnational	Total
No (0)	50	39	89
Yes (1)	102	84	186
Total	152	123	275

Chi-square test of independence: Pearson chi-square test value 0.44; p-**value 0.834**

SOURCE: Author.

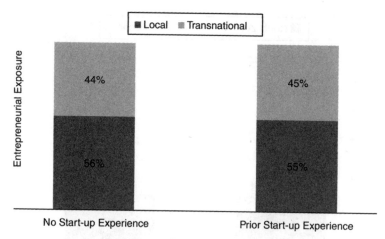

FIGURE 3.17 Distribution of founder's start-up experience versus entrepreneurial exposure
SOURCE: Author.

Bivariate Profile of Founder's Education Status

The bivariate profile of the founder's education with the targeted market segment is presented in Table 3.13 and Figure 3.18. From Figure 3.18, it appears that in the segment of entrepreneurs who do not possess an engineering degree, the entrepreneurs choose to set up B2C ventures. For the other two categories of founders' education, there does not appear to be much difference of choice of market segments chosen by the entrepreneurs. A statistical verification by chi-square test results points out that the founder's education and the target market chosen by these founders are independent.

TABLE 3.13 Bivariate profile of founder's education versus market segment

Market segment	Founder's education			
	Non-engineering degree	Engineering degree	Master's degree and above	Total
B2B	38	71	13	122
B2C	66	75	12	153
Total	104	146	25	275

Chi-square test of independence: Pearson chi-square test value 4.247; **p-value 0.120**

SOURCE: Author.

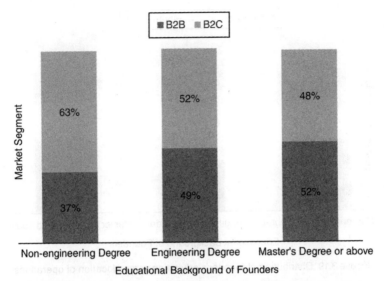

FIGURE 3.18 Distribution of founder's education versus targeted market segment

Source: Author.

The bivariate profile of the founders' education with the location of operations is presented in Table 3.14 and Figure 3.19. From Figure 3.19, it appears that the segment of entrepreneurs who possess an engineering degree seem to prefer South Zone as their location of operations for their start-ups, whereas we do not observe the same in the other two categories of education backgrounds of entrepreneurs. To confirm if there is any statistical dependence between these two variables, chi-square tests are conducted. The results point out that the founder's education and the choice of locations for operations for start-ups are dependent on each other.

TABLE 3.14 Bivariate profile of founder's education versus location of operations

| Location of operations | Founder's education | | | |
	Non-engineering degree	Engineering degree	Master's degree and above	Total
North Zone	45	45	11	101
South Zone	59	101	14	174
Total	104	146	25	275

Chi-square test of independence: Pearson chi-square test value 4.675; **p-value 0.097**

Source: Author.

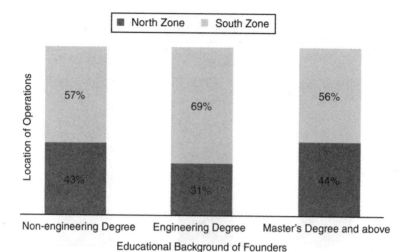

Figure 3.19 Distribution of founder's education versus location of operations

Source: Author.

The bivariate profile of the founder's education with entrepreneurial exposure is presented in Table 3.15 and Figure 3.20. From Figure 3.20, we can observe that more number of transnational entrepreneurs have a technical degree or higher educational qualifications in comparison to the local entrepreneurs. We conduct chi-square tests to examine if there is any dependency between the two variables. The results point out that the founder's education and the entrepreneurial exposure are dependent on each other. The very low p-value establishes the dependency between the two variables.

TABLE 3.15 Bivariate profile of founder's education versus entrepreneurial exposure

Entrepreneurial exposure	Founder's education			
	Non-engineering degree	Engineering degree	Master's degree and above	Total
Local	77	69	6	152
Transnational	27	77	19	123
Total	104	146	25	275

Chi-square test of independence: Pearson chi-square test value 28.496; **p-value 0.000**

Source: Author.

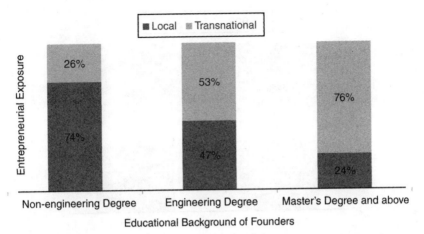

F<small>IGURE</small> 3.20 Distribution of founder's education versus entrepreneurial exposure

S<small>OURCE</small>: Author.

Bivariate Profile of Start-ups' Funding Status

The bivariate profile of the start-ups' funding status at inceptions with the targeted market segments is presented in Table 3.16 and Figure 3.21. We observe that B2C start-ups are getting funded in higher proportion (at about 59 per cent) in comparison to the B2B start-ups that constitute the remaining 41 per cent of the funded start-ups in our sample. Chi-square test of independence indicates that there is no statistically significant relationship between the choice of target markets for the start-ups and its funding status at the time of inceptions.

T<small>ABLE</small> 3.16 Bivariate profile of start-ups' funding status versus targeted market segments

Funding status	Market segment		
	B2B	B2C	Total
0	90	106	196
1	32	47	79
Total	122	153	275

Chi-square test of independence: Pearson chi-square test value 0.668; **p-value 0.414**

S<small>OURCE</small>: Author.

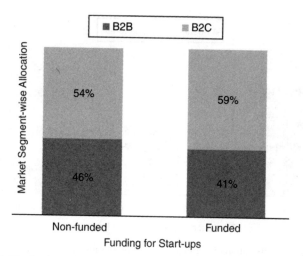

F<small>IGURE</small> 3.21 Distribution of start-ups' funding status versus targeted market segments
S<small>OURCE</small>: Author.

The bivariate profile of the start-ups' funding status at inception with the location of operations is presented in Table 3.17 and Figure 3.22. We observe that about two-thirds of the funded start-ups are located in South Zone, with the remainder one-third of the start-ups based in North Zone. We notice that South Zone has the most number of start-ups in comparison to the North Zone. Chi-square test of independence indicates that location of operations does not have a statistically significant influence on the funding status of the start-up at the time of inception. High p-value for the location of operations against the funding status of the start-ups at inception indicate that there are no discernable patterns that can be inferred from these analyses.

T<small>ABLE</small> 3.17 Bivariate profile of start-ups' funding status versus location of operations

Funded	Zone allocation		
	North Zone	South Zone	Total
0	74	122	196
1	27	52	79
Total	101	174	275

Chi-square test of independence: Pearson chi-square test value 0.310; **p-value 0.578**

S<small>OURCE</small>: Author.

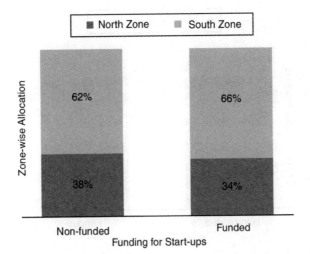

FIGURE 3.22 Distribution of start-ups' funding status versus location of operations

SOURCE: Author.

The bivariate profile of the start-ups' funding status at inception with entrepreneurial exposure is presented in Table 3.18 and Figure 3.23. From Figure 3.23, we can understand that there does not seem to be too much difference in patterns of funding when it is categorized based on the entrepreneurial exposure. To verify if the same is true statistically, we conduct chi-square test of independence. The results as tabulated in Table 3.18 indicate that entrepreneurial exposure does not have a statistically significant influence on the funding status of the start-up at the time of inception. High p-value for the entrepreneurial exposure against the funding status of the start-up at inception indicates that there are no discernable patterns that can be inferred from these analyses.

TABLE 3.18 Bivariate profile of start-ups' funding status versus entrepreneurial exposure

Funded	Entrepreneurial exposure		
	Local	Transnational	Total
0	110	86	196
1	42	37	79
Total	152	123	275

Chi-square test of independence: Pearson chi-square test value 0.199; **p-value 0.655**

SOURCE: Author.

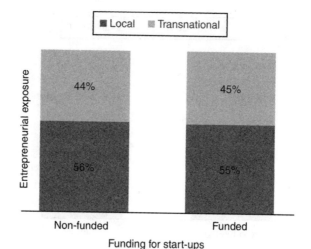

Summary

To summarize, in this chapter an attempt has been made to describe the profile of the high-tech start-ups of our sample. To start with, we perform a univariate analysis on the characteristics of these high-tech start-ups. We find that the majority of the high-tech start-ups in our sample are relatively young in terms of their years of operation in India – about 95 per cent of them have been established in the post-2008 recession period. In particular, there has been a considerable increase in the number of start-ups incorporated from 2013 onwards – reflecting the trend in the Indian economy. Further, we observe that the gender-wise distribution of founders is heavily skewed towards the male founders. The male founders constitute about 96 per cent of the population, in line with the trends observed across the country from other industry reports.

An analysis of start-ups based on their location of operations reveals that the majority of the start-ups have operations in metro cities. This implies that start-up emergence and operations are primarily a metro cities-based phenomenon. In our sample, about 88 per cent of the start-ups reported to be operating out of metro cities, and the remainder from non-metro cities. In terms of cities where start-ups are located, Bengaluru has a major share with about 49 per cent of the overall sample, followed by start-ups in the NCR. However, in order to obtain a better perspective on the spread of start-ups across the country, we have categorized and analysed the start-ups as falling under two zones—North and South. Start-ups operating out of NCR, Mumbai, Kolkata, Ahmedabad, Surat, and Nagpur among others fall under the North Zone classification. Start-ups operating out of Bengaluru, Cochin, Chennai, Coimbatore, and Hyderabad among others are categorized under South Zone in our sample.

From a targeted market segment perspective, our sample is spread across the B2B and B2C sectors, with B2B start-ups constituting about 44 per cent of the sample, and B2C start-ups constituting about 56 per cent of the sample. A similar spread can be observed from our sample if we view it with the lens of the entrepreneurs' exposure. In our sample, about 56 per cent of the founders are local entrepreneurs, and about 44 per cent of the sample are transnational entrepreneurs. The higher percentage of transnational entrepreneurs in our sample indicates the opportunities for trade in the country, as well as the perception of exploitable opportunities by these transnational entrepreneurs.

Further, we perform bivariate tests to understand the similarities and differences of these different segments of our sample. Tests for independence across the three segments, namely, (a) targeted market segment (B2B versus B2C), (b) location of operations (North Zone versus South Zone), and (c) entrepreneur's exposure (local versus transnational) reveal that there are indeed differences in characteristics across these segments.

The bivariate tests conducted on the three continuous variables of entrepreneur's age, the sales and R&D capabilities of the start-ups against these three segments indicate that entrepreneur's age vary significantly across these three segments, whereas the firm-specific attribute of R&D and sales capabilities of the start-ups do not show any marked deviation statistically across these three segments.

Similarly, the bivariate tests conducted on the three discrete variables of founder's prior start-up experience and founder's prior industry experience, founder's education, and the funding status of the start-up at the time of inception across these three segments revealed identical results. The founder's industry experience was found to be varying significantly across the three segments of targeted market segment, location of operations, and entrepreneur's exposure, whereas the other two variables, namely, prior start-up experience of the founder and funding status of the start-up at the time of inception, did not show any variation between the three segments. Further, the founder's education was found to influence the choice of location of operations and indicate a dependency on entrepreneur's exposure.

While these results appear to be counter-intuitive and contrary to established knowledge, it must be noted that this chapter provides only an initial descriptive analysis of the sample under study. A more detailed examination of these influences on specific milestones of the start-up life cycle and between these segments are presented in subsequent chapters.

4

Emergence of High-tech Start-ups

Introduction

In this chapter, we discuss in detail the factors that lead to the emergence of high-tech start-ups in India. The emergence of high-tech start-ups has been studied under different theoretical approaches. Notable among them are approaches related to economics (Brenner 1987), psychology (Katz 1992), and population ecology (Aldrich 1990). The 1990s also saw a few empirical contributions that attempted to explain the phenomenon of high-tech start-up emergence. Bhave (1994), Reynolds and Miller (1992), and Carter, Gartner, and Reynolds (1996) made useful contributions to enhance the existing knowledge on start-up emergence in this regard. However, the major criticism of all the initial contributions was that researchers examined high-tech start-up emergence as a linear process, with a sequential set of steps that entrepreneurs carried out to achieve the milestone of formal creation of a new venture.

To address these criticisms, the next decade of contributions to the study of start-up emergence primarily focused on modelling start-up emergence as a process. During this period, many terms associated with the emergence of high-tech start-ups were coined, as part of examination of the phenomenon. Firm gestation (Reynolds and Miller 1992), organizational emergence (Gartner, Bird, and Starr 1992), pre-organization (Katz and Gartner 1988), and start-up (Vesper 1990) were the key constructs under which the emergence of new ventures was discussed.

Katz and Gartner (1988) suggested four emerging properties that indicate that an organization is in the process of coming into existence. These properties include the intention to gather information for the creation of an organization; boundary-establishment activities that distinguish the venture from the rest of the world (such as incorporation, partnership/management agreements, the establishment of physical offices, and a phone line), the acquisition of financial resources needed to operate an entity (including payments for rent, a phone bill, and equipment), and finally, exchanges with external suppliers and customers, culminating with initial sales and/or initial hiring.

In the context of this study, the boundary-establishment activity pursued by entrepreneurs is the focus of examination and analysis. This act of formal incorporation of the start-up by its founders serves as a signal to interpret many different phenomena related to start-up emergence that simultaneously are at play.

In emerging economies, plagued by insufficient infrastructure and institutional voids, many start-ups do not formally register themselves with the government due to the overheads of time and effort associated with pursuing such actions. Instead, they tend to operate informally till such time that it requires them to register formally to continue their exploitation of opportunities. This trigger to formally register may come as a result of the need to show legitimacy (pressure by customers or by government rules and regulations), confidence of the founding team members about the viability of business, and other reasons.

Given all these aspects, we model the act of formal incorporation as an important milestone of the high-tech start-up's journey for the purposes of analysis in this chapter. We further probe the key dimensions (entrepreneurial, firm-specific, and external environment related) that lead to formal incorporation of a high-tech start-up.

Factors Influencing Emergence of High-tech Start-ups

The emergence of high-tech start-ups can be viewed as being influenced by three dimensions – entrepreneurial, firm-specific, and external environment related factors. There is a body of literature that deals extensively with the events across these dimensions leading up to the formal emergence of the firm.

Katz and Gartner (1988) and Van de Ven, Hudson, and Schroeder (1984) formulated the concept of pre-organizations to explain the different sets of events unfolding till the formal firm creation. Their studies illustrated the complexity involved in the creation of new high-tech start-ups. Bygrave (1989) stated that every firm's start-up process is a disjointed, discontinuous, and unique event. Continuing on that thought, Roininen and Ylinenpää (2009) explained that the process of creating a new venture could be viewed as a system of coexisting activities undertaken during different phases, where one event could affect others, resulting in complexity, disorder, and even chaos sometimes.

Vesper (1980) was one of the first researchers to propose a model to understand the dynamics of new firm creation. He argued that knowledge, idea, connections, resources, and implementation are the fundamental constructs that impact new firm creation. Gartner (1985) aggregated the previous works and identified personality of the entrepreneur, environment, the firm (organization), and implementation as the primary tenets contributing to new firm creation. Bygrave (1989) further extended the theoretical understanding by identifying 'the triggering event' as one more construct contributing to a new firm creation. Mazzarol et al. (1999) added the parameters such as personal characteristics/traits and influence of social, political, and economic contextual factors in analysing the dynamics of high-tech start-up creation. These studies enabled the recognition of start-up emergence as an important milestone to be examined.

Further, the review of literature on factors impacting start-up emergence revealed that the entrepreneurial factors that influence the phenomenon of start-up emergence are age and education of the founder and prior industry experience and prior start-up experience of the founder (Storey 1982; Ronstadt 1988). Similarly, the firm-specific factors that influence the start-up emergence are the functional resources of a start-up at the time of creation, such as human capital, financial capabilities, and sales and marketing capabilities of the start-up (Kim, Aldrich, and Keister 2006; Munshi 2007).

From these contributions, it is evident that the knowledge on high-tech start-up emergence incrementally evolved by examining multiple dimensions and factors over time. Based on the aforementioned topic and the survey of literature, we arrive at the following hypotheses regarding the emergence of high-tech start-ups.

Hypothesis 1: Prior industry experience of the primary founder positively influences formal incorporation of the start-up.

Hypothesis 2: Prior start-up experience of the primary founder positively influences formal incorporation of the start-up.

Hypothesis 3: Primary founders of higher age are more likely to formally incorporate the start-up earlier than the founders of lesser age.

Hypothesis 4: Higher educational pedigree positively influences formal incorporation of the start-up.

Hypothesis 5: Higher R&D resources with the founders positively influences formal incorporation of the start-up.

Hypothesis 6: Higher sales capabilities with the founders positively influences formal incorporation of the start-up.

Hypothesis 7: Higher financial resources with the founders positively influences formal incorporation of the start-up.

Hypothesis 8: Higher SDP growth in the region positively influences formal incorporation of the start-up.

Hypothesis 9: A higher presence of VCs in the region influences higher rate of formal incorporation of start-ups in that region.

These hypotheses will be tested against six logistic regression models, one each validating the hypotheses in the context of B2B start-ups, B2C start-ups, start-ups based in North Zone regions of India, start-ups based in South Zone regions in India, start-ups that have local entrepreneurs as founders, and start-ups that have transnational entrepreneurs as founders. Finally, an overall model will be fitted to understand the factors that are significant for the emergence of high-tech start-ups in India.

Key Semantics of the Data

For the purposes of this study, the date of formal incorporation of the start-up (month and year) under the government laws, at the Registrar of Companies office in India, is considered the milestone of start-up emergence. Firms or entrepreneurs that operate informally are considered not yet created for the purposes of this study. Most of the data used in the study are collected using our research instrument – the questionnaire. The secondary data are collected primarily to obtain the entrepreneur's profile. The unit of analysis in our study has been the start-up, represented by the founder. Logistic regression is used as the method for analysis of this objective. Chapter 2 provides a more detailed overview of the theory and motivation for the usage of this method. We used a total of 275 start-ups-related data for analysis of this objective. Among these, 175 were formally incorporated, whereas the remainder 100 start-ups were informally active. The statistical tool 'SPSS' was used for the analysis of this research objective.

Variables and Measures

Dependent variable

The dependent variable for analysis is *formal incorporation*, a discrete dichotomous variable. This variable takes the value of 1 for every start-up in the sample that has been formally incorporated with the Registrar of Companies

(ROC). A value of 0 indicates that the start-up is not formally registered as a company with the ROC. This variable is labelled in SPSS as *logitcreat* for the purposes of analysis.

Independent variables

The entrepreneurial and firm-specific factors such as age and education of the primary founder; the industry and start-up experience of the primary founder before working with the current start-up; and the development, sales, and financial capabilities present with the start-up at the time of inception form the independent variables for this analysis. The external environmental factors such as SDP growth, number of VC firms in the region, and the number of VC-funded deals in the region are considered independent variables for the analysis.

Relevant industry experience: A discrete dichotomous variable which indicates whether or not the founder has previous industry experience. This variable takes the value of 1 for every start-up founder who has industry experience prior to founding the current start-up considered for the study. A value of 0 for this variable indicates that the founder of the start-up does not possess any previous industry-working experience. This variable is labelled in SPSS as *fiexp* for the analysis.

Prior start-up experience: A discrete dichotomous variable which indicates whether or not the founder has prior start-up experience. This variable takes the value of 1 for every start-up founder who has experience working in a start-up either as an employee or as a founder, prior to founding the current start-up considered for the study. A value of 0 for this variable indicates that the founder of the start-up does not possess any previous start-up experience. This variable is labelled in SPSS as *fsexp* for the analysis.

Age of the entrepreneur: The age of the entrepreneur in years at the time of founding the current start-up. This variable is labelled in SPSS as *fage* for the analysis.

Education of the entrepreneur: The education of the entrepreneur is categorized using two dummy variables. The base reference variable indicates graduate education without an engineering degree (degree in science, arts, and others), the first dummy variable indicates graduate education with a technical (engineering) degree, and the second dummy variable indicates education with a technical master's degree or above. This variable is labelled in SPSS as *fedn* for the analysis. The base reference variable takes the value of 1 for every founder of the start-up, who has a non-engineering degree. A value of 0 for the base reference variable indicates the absence of a non-engineering degree of the founder. The first dummy variable *fedn(1)* takes the value of 1 for every start-up founder who has a technical (engineering) degree as his/her educational credentials. A value of 0 for this variable indicates the absence of a technical (engineering) degree of the founder. The second dummy variable *fedn(2)* takes the value of 1 for every start-up founder who has education credentials of a technical (engineering) master's degree or above. A value of 0 for this variable indicates the absence of a technical master's degree or a higher technical qualification (for example, PhD) of the founder.

Sales capabilities of the start-up at the time of initiating operations: The sales capabilities of the start-up at the time of initiating operations are measured as a categorical value with 3 levels. This variable is labelled as *csales* in SPSS for the analysis. A value of 1 for the base reference variable indicates that the start-up does not possess any sales capabilities. This means, either the founders do not have the sales background, or they have not yet formalized a co-founder with sales background or that the start-up has not yet obtained initial customers and started sales. A value of 0 for the base reference variable indicates the converse. The first dummy variable *csales(1)* takes the value of 1 for every start-up that has sales capabilities, but no revenue is yet generated. This value is assigned to all start-ups that either have a co-founder focusing on sales or hired employees who have prior selling experience, but no revenue has been accrued on account of selling the offerings of the start-up. A value of 0 for this dummy variable indicates the absence of the capabilities as indicated in the preceding sentence. A value of 1 for the second dummy variable *csales(2)* indicates that the start-up has already clocked some revenue by selling to initial customers. A value of 0 for this variable indicates the converse.

R&D capabilities of the start-up at the time of initiating operations: The R&D capabilities of the start-up at the time of initiating operations are measured as a categorical variable with 3 levels. This variable is labelled as *cdev* in SPSS for the analysis. A value of 1 for the base reference variable indicates that the start-up does not possess any R&D capabilities. This means either the founders do not have a technology background or they have not yet formalized a co-founder with the technology background. A value of 0 for the base reference variable indicates the converse. A value of 1 for the first dummy variable *cdev(1)* indicates that the start-up has R&D capabilities, but no viable product prototype has been built yet. This level is assigned to all start-ups that have a founder or a co-founder with a technology background or has hired employees with technical capabilities. However, as an entity, this team has not yet produced an initial prototype that could be demonstrated to its prospective customers. A value of 0 for this dummy variable indicates the absence of the capabilities as indicated in the preceding sentence. A value of 1 for the second dummy variable *cdev(2)* indicates the presence of a working and demonstrable initial product or service offering at the time of beginning the operations. A value of 0 for this variable indicates the converse.

Financial capability of the start-up: Measured by a discrete dichotomous variable which indicates whether or not the start-up obtained funding external to its founder's and his family's funds. This variable is labelled as *fin* in SPSS for the analysis. A value of 1 for this variable indicates that the start-up was funded from external sources, and conversely, a value of 0 for this variable indicates that the start-up under consideration is not funded from external sources.

SDP: This variable is used as a proxy for the macroeconomic environment prevalent in the state in which the start-up is located. This variable provides the percentage of change in the SDP in comparison to its previous year (at constant prices). This variable is labelled as *sdp* in SPSS for the analysis.

Number of funded deals: This variable is used to indicate the number of early stage VC deals that happened for a given year and a given geography. This measure is a proxy to measure the maturity of the start-up ecosystem for the given year and geography. This variable is labelled as *deals* in SPSS for the analysis.

Number of VC funds: This variable indicates the presence of the active VC funds for a given year and a given geography. This variable is a proxy to measure and understand the availability of external funding options for a particular region and year. This variable is labelled as *vc* in SPSS for the analysis.

Control variables

Target market segment: This variable is a dummy variable with two levels. A value of 0 indicates that the target market segment of the start-up is B2B sector, whereas the value of 1 indicates that the target market segment of the start-up is B2C sector. This variable is labelled as *market_segment* in SPSS for the analysis.

Location of operations: This variable is a dummy variable with two levels. A value of 0 indicates that the start-up is located in northern part of the country, whereas the value of 1 indicates that the start-up is located in the southern part of India. This variable is labelled as *zone* in SPSS for the analysis.

Entrepreneurial background: This variable is a dummy variable with two levels. A value of 0 indicates that the entrepreneur is a local entrepreneur, whereas the value of 1 indicates that the entrepreneur is transnational (which indicates that the entrepreneur has exposure to working or studying in more than one country, other than the country of his/her origin, for a period of at least one year). This variable is labelled as *te* in SPSS for the analysis.

With this background about the semantics of the data, variables and measures, the method of analysis, and modes of data collection, we now proceed to discuss and interpret the results of the first research objective.

Discussion of Results

We present the results of the analysis of the key factors that impact the emergence of high-tech start-ups in India. We begin by describing the relationships of the independent variables (entrepreneur-specific, firm-specific, and external environment-specific) with the dependent variable (formal incorporation). Next, we present the results of the logistic regression models that were analysed based on the three segments, namely, (a) target market being addressed by the start-ups (B2B [122 start-ups] versus B2C [153 start-ups]), (b) location of operations of the start-ups (North Zone [101 start-ups] versus South Zone [174 start-ups]), and (c) exposure of the entrepreneurs (local [152 start-ups] versus transnational [123 start-ups]). We end with the presentation and interpretation of results of the overall model that contained data of 275 start-ups.

Initial Analysis of Data

To begin with, the visual inspection of the dependent variable with the three segments of market, location, and entrepreneurial background are presented, followed by presentation and analysis of the relationship of the dependent variable with the independent variables. The distribution of high-tech start-ups based on their status of incorporation is presented in Figure 4.1.

We observe that about 36 per cent of the start-ups in our study have not formally incorporated their start-up, but have initiated operations. About 64 per cent of the start-ups in our study have formally registered their start-up

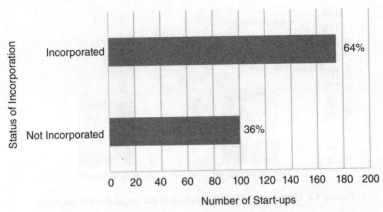

FIGURE 4.1 Distribution of start-ups based on status of incorporation

SOURCE: Author.

with the Registrar of Companies of the corresponding region. The high percentage of formal incorporation indicates that most of the founders of the start-ups are confident of their business idea. Hence, they have gone ahead and registered their firms with the appropriate government authorities. Further, formal incorporation is an important prerequisite for the entrepreneur and the firm to gain legitimacy and engage in transactions external to the firm, such as to acquire customers, raise funds, and so on.

If we further analyse the incorporation status of start-ups in our study, based on the three dimensions of target market segment, location of operations, and entrepreneurial background, these sets of analyses will provide us with further insights. Figures 4.2–4.4 respectively present the analysis based on these dimensions.

The distribution of start-ups based on target market segment is presented in Figure 4.2. We can observe that the pattern of incorporation varies based on the target market segment to which the start-up caters to. We can observe that a higher percentage of B2B start-ups (about 51 per cent) are incorporated. Also, among the start-ups that are not incorporated, a smaller proportion of them (about 33 per cent) are B2B start-ups. This behaviour of preference to incorporation by B2B start-ups can be explained by the fact that B2B start-ups need to show legitimacy (Higgins and Gulati 2006) to prospective customers and suppliers. Hence, the act of formal incorporation will serve as one of the modes of establishing legitimacy and genuineness, and this acts as a signal to all external entities with whom the B2B start-up needs to interact in its initial days of operations.

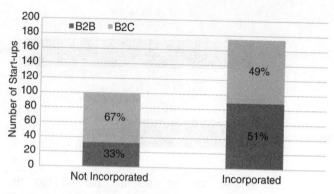

FIGURE 4.2 Distribution of start-ups based on target market segment

SOURCE: Author.

The distribution of start-ups based on the location of operations is presented in Figure 4.3. We observe different patterns of incorporation across the two zones, based on the information presented in Figure 4.3. The start-ups based in the North Zone show a bias towards incorporation, whereas the start-ups based in the South Zone indicate a bias towards informally initiating the start-up operations.

Figure 4.3 helps us understand that, overall, there are more number of start-ups that are informally and formally operating in the South Zone. This inference is on expected lines, given that most of the high-tech activities are centred in Bengaluru, which is kown as the Silicon Valley of India (Startup Genome 2015). Further, all the southern states (Karnataka, Tamil Nadu,

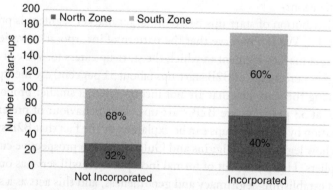

FIGURE 4.3 Distribution of start-ups based on location of operations

SOURCE: Author.

Andhra Pradesh, Telangana, and Kerala) are highly progressive states with high literacy and per capita income. These states offer favourable ecosystem for entrepreneurship, through policies geared towards start-up incubation and promotion. Further, the availability of highly talented workforce and the presence of other enabling agents, such as investors and prospective customers that are very essential during the initial days of start-up operations, encourage nascent entrepreneurs to locate their start-up in the South Zone of the country.

Figure 4.3 also points to a very high level of informal activities in the South Zone of the country. This can be attributed to the nature of nascent entrepreneurial activity, when the entrepreneur is just trying to establish the viability of the business idea. A nascent entrepreneur is someone who is in the process of establishing a business venture by exploring the viability of an opportunity (Reynolds and White 1997; Casson 1982). The exploitation of this opportunity might result in introduction of new products or services and creation of new markets or enhancements of existing methods of production (Shane and Venkataraman 2000). But before such a venture is actually established, the opportunity is just a venture idea (Davidsson 2006; Dimov 2007). The value of this venture idea cannot be established at the time of it's inception. However, over time, the exact economic value of this idea will emerge, based on the different set of entrepreneurial activities performed by the nascent entrepreneur (Davidsson 2003; Dimov 2007; Sarasvathy 2001).

It is not possible for every venture idea to result in the emergence of a new firm. After pursuing a few entrepreneurial activities to implement the idea, it is also possible that the nascent entrepreneur deems this idea to be no longer attractive or feasible. On the other hand, the outcomes of the initial entrepreneurial activities, carried out to implement the venture idea, might result in the emergence of a viable business. In this sense, over time, the nascent venture can move towards being discontinued or towards emerging successfully as an operating entity (Dimov 2010). Hence, a combination of factors such as the ambiguity in determining the viability of the business idea, low entry costs to engage in pre-organization activities of a high-tech start-up idea, and the reliance of the nascent entrepreneur on the external ecosystem resources would have contributed to the high degree of informality in pre-organization start-up activities.

Figure 4.4 presents the distribution of start-ups based on entrepreneurial background. We observe differences across the incorporation status among the local and transnational entrepreneurs. From Figure 4.4, we observe that

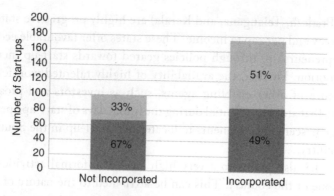

FIGURE 4.4 Distribution of start-ups based on entrepreneurial background
SOURCE: Author.

transnational entrepreneurs exhibit a clear bias towards incorporation as they start their operations, whereas majority of the the local entrepreneurs prefer to not formally incorporate their start-ups, even as they begin their operations. This is because local entrepreneurs lack the resources, know-how, and the intent to pursue an entrepreneurial opportunity in comparison with the transnational entrepreneurs (Saxenian 2003). However, on the other side, the local entrepreneurs are better aware than the transnational entrepreneurs about the challenges that exist on the ground during the initial days of operation. Given all these factors, the local entrepreneurs might prefer not to take the overhead of incorporation of their start-up, despite beginning to work on their business idea in the initial stages.

On the other hand, transnational entrepreneurs might prefer formal incorporation to signal their intent and enhance their resources to take their business idea forward. Further, their arrival to the host country, leaving behind their country of current residence, to explore entrepreneurial opportunity indicates a stronger entrepreneurial intent and orientation in comparison with the local entrepreneurs. The transnational entrepreneurs might come with a strong (international) social network to take advantage for their business operations, which might induce them to incorporate earlier than later. Hence, we see these differences in approach between the local and the transnational entrepreneurs.

With this background about the semantics of the data, variables and measures, modes of data collection, and proposed hypotheses for validation, we now discuss and interpret the results of the study.

Results and Discussion of Findings

Table 4.1 provides a summary of the hypotheses that were accepted and rejected across the seven regression models. An entry A in the table indicates acceptance. The sign in the brackets indicates the direction of the influence of the variable. A '+' sign indicates positive influence, whereas a '−' sign indicates a negative influence. The detailed results of each of the regression models are presented in the chapter-end Appendix (Tables 4A.1–4A.7).

The two logistic regression models based on the target market segment focused by the start-ups in our study bring about interesting results. Across the two models, the *funding capabilities* of the start-up, irrespective of whether it focuses on B2B or B2C market, has been established as the single most factor that influences the emergence of the start-up. In both the cases, the lack of funding capabilities is likely to enhance the emergence of the high-tech start-up.

Prior literature has studied the need for capitalization and the availability of funds at the time of formal incorporation of the firm. Freear, Sohl, and Wetzel (2002) noted that entrepreneurial venture creation is a dynamic process undertaken by entrepreneurs founding high-growth technology-based ventures. They observed that these technology-based ventures are defined less by absolute size and more by growth and the potential for future returns. In the

TABLE 4.1 Summary of results of the study

	Prior industry experience	Prior start-up experience	Age of the founder	Education of the founder	Sales capabilities	R&D capabilities	Funding capabilities	SDP growth	Number of funded deals	Number of VCs
B2B	A (+)					A	A (−)			
B2C						A (−)	A (−)			
North Zone		A (+)		A (+)			A (−)	A (−)	**A (−)**	
South Zone	A (+)					A (−)	A (−)			
Local entrepreneur						A (−)	A (−)			
Transnational entrepreneur					A (+)		A (−)			
Overall model	A (+)					A (−)	A (−)			

SOURCE: Author.

NOTE: All the empty cells in the table indicate the rejection of the hypotheses.

high-tech sector, entrepreneurial ventures with high growth potential require funding far beyond than what is being supplied by the founders. Therefore, these ventures must seek funding from other sources. If the requirements of initial capital go beyond that of the ability of the entrepreneur to raise it from his/her family and friends, then finance markets provide a means of bringing together investors and entrepreneurs – at a price. Hence entrepreneurs may tend to formally incorporate their new venture in order to raise external funding.

R&D capabilities of the start-up at the time of incorporation is another factor that has been found to be significant in both B2B and B2C sector-based results. The result from Tables 4A.1 and 4A.2 (presented in the chapter-end Appendix) indicates that the overall variable R&D capabilities of a firm is statistically significant in influencing the emergence of high-tech start-ups in the B2B sector. However, the two dummy variables that represent presence of R&D capabilities and presence of a prototype/offering respectively at the time of incorporation of the new venture are not significant in influencing the emergence of high-tech start-ups in the B2B sector. Since the overall variable is significant, we can infer that the presence of R&D capabilities, relative to absence of R&D capabilities (base reference level), would seem to enhance the likelihood of the emergence of high-tech start-ups, whereas presence of a working prototype/offering right at the time of formal incorporation relative to absence of R&D capabilities could in fact hinder the emergence of high-tech start-ups in the B2B sector.

In the case of B2C-related start-ups, the result indicates that the overall variable, capturing R&D capabilities of the start-up at the time of incorporation, is statistically significant, and the second dummy variable of R&D capabilities – indicating the presence of prototype/offering at the time of incorporation of new venture – would negatively impact the likelihood of emergence of high-tech start-ups. This result indicates that entrepreneurs targeting the B2C sector may not be willing to invest too early in augmenting R&D resources, at such an early stage of the life cycle.

The results from the logistic regression models from the North Zone and South Zone respectively provide important implications. Across the two models, the *funding capabilities* of the start-up has been established as the single most factor that influences the emergence of the start-up, irrespective of whether it is located in North or South Zone. In both cases, the lack of funding capabilities is likely to enhance the emergence of the high-tech start-up. As discussed earlier, entrepreneurial ideas in the high-tech sector will need the cushion and comfort of financial capitalization to be able to hire knowledge workers, spend on sales and market creation of their new product or service offering, and so on. Based on the size of the target market, appropriate resources should be raised by the entrepreneur during the pre-organization phase of the entrepreneurial venture. Prior literature has indicated that friends and family of the entrepreneur are the first set of providers of finance, followed by external providers, such as angel investors and VCs (Freear, Sohl, and Wetzel 1995; Gompers and Lerner 1999). These results indicate that entrepreneurs who have external funding are likely to go slow on formally incorporating their new venture, or conversely, entrepreneurs who have not raised external funding are likely to formally incorporate their start-ups.

For start-ups operating in the North Zone, results indicate that higher the age of the entrepreneur, the greater the odds of formal incorporation of the start-up. The influence of the age of the entrepreneur in setting up a new venture, in particular, ventures in the high-tech sector, has been studied in the past, with divergent results emerging out of these examinations. For example, Arabsheibani et al. (2000) and Forbes (2005) showed that overconfidence, dispositional optimism, and over-optimism in prediction are associated with an entrepreneur's age. Further, Gimeno et al. (1997) indicated that age affects switching costs, with older entrepreneurs more likely to continue involvement in new businesses with marginal performance. In general, all these studies indicate that higher age of the entrepreneur is associated negatively with growth and performance of new ventures.

In contrary to the aforementioned observations, research, based on the resource-based view (RBV), states that resources in the form of human capital will increase with age (Wennberg and Lindqvist 2010). Coleman, Cotei, and Farhat (2013) indicated that resources in the form of maturity, problem-solving ability, life experiences, and contacts increase as the entrepreneur ages. However, in our case, since our focus is on whether the entrepreneur's age matters at the time of inception, we find that age contributes positively to formal incorporation of the new high-tech ventures, strengthening the arguments based on the RBV theory.

The results from Tables 4A.3 and 4A.4 also indicate that in the North Zone when external environmental parameters such as SDP growth and the number of VC deals in a year show a negative growth (year-on-year), the likelihood of emergence of high-tech start-ups increases.

The analysis of results from Table 4A.4 indicates that in the South Zone, entrepreneurs who have prior start-up experience are more likely to formally incorporate their start-ups, even when they do not have a ready prototype and are not funded externally. South Zone in India has been known to have the highest concentration of skilled workforce and addressable market. Bengaluru, in particular, has been identified as the leader among many urban clusters that are demonstrating higher start-up activity (NASSCOM 2015). Further, these results seem to indicate that entrepreneurs who have relevant start-up experience would prefer to formally start operations without seeking external funding and without investing too much on R&D at the time of starting operations.

The logistic regression models based on entrepreneurial background reveal that the decision to formally incorporate the start-up is primarily guided by the availability of *funding resources*, irrespective of whether the venture is promoted by local or transnational entrepreneurs. Further, the results point out that local entrepreneurs do not invest heavily on R&D capabilities at the time of starting the new high-tech venture.

The start-up emergence from local entrepreneurs can be explained based on the personal motivations and capabilities of these entrepreneurs as well. We need to recollect that all founders in our study have good education and technical skills to begin with. In the high-tech sector, technology changes over the past decade have accelerated exponentially. Therefore, when a technically qualified person comes up with a new and unique innovation, or a new product idea or offering, the next immediate step taken by that person is to go for formal incorporation of the new venture. Given with exponential technological advancements, the entrepreneur will be motivated to introduce his/her new idea or offering to the market as quickly as possible to avoid the risks of obsolescence of the new innovative idea. South Zone in India presents a good initial addressable market. At the same time, tacit knowledge among the local entrepreneurs would enable them to not go overboard with the investments into a new venture, and hence we can see from the results that the likelihood of start-up emergence increases when there is no external funding and no investments on R&D capabilities at the time of starting up.

Results from Tables 4A.5 and 4A.6 help us understand that when transnational entrepreneurs see market traction in terms of revenue trickling in for their intended entrepreneurial venture, they will likely go ahead for formal incorporation in India. Literature on transnational entrepreneurs has shown that they have better resources relative to the local entrepreneurs. Further, they would start entrepreneurial activities when they sense opportunities of profit based on the specialized knowledge they possess, on account of exposure to multiple economies. However, the results seem to indicate that as they start their operations in their country of origin, it is likely that unless they see market traction, they may not formally incorporate their new venture. Further, they may not be well apprised of the local difficulties in formal incorporation of their venture. Hence, one of the possibilities could be that they may decide to wait till they get market traction and then pursue incorporation-related activities if things pan out positively for them.

The results from the execution of the overall model indicate that the variables, modelling for the *prior start-up experience of the founders* and *the R&D and financial capabilities* of the start-ups at the time of initiation of operations, are the key significant factors influencing the emergence of high-tech start-ups in India. From Table 4A.7, we can infer that prior start-up experience of the entrepreneur and absence of R&D and financial capabilities increase the likelihood of high-tech start-up emergence. In addition to these, the logistic regression model results also indicate that high-tech start-up emergence is likely to be from *local* entrepreneurs, focusing on *B2C markets* and who have operations in *South Zone* of the country.

Our results across the six models as well as with the overall model did not find evidence of entrepreneur-specific factors, *previous industry experience,* and *education of the founder* at the time of initiation of operations, influencing the decision to formally incorporate a start-up when it begins its operations.

The findings of prior start-up experience of entrepreneurs influencing the decision to formally incorporate the start-up as they begin operations revalidate and provide additional support to existing prior literature in this domain (Westhead et al. 2005; Politis 2008). This is explainable, specifically in the context of emerging economies. The entrepreneur would need to deal with an increased degree of liabilities of newness, given the underdeveloped infrastructure and environment support system that exist in the region of operation. Having prior experience of starting up and dealing with uncertainty adds to the bundle of knowledge and, therefore, when the entrepreneur embarks on the second venture, he or she would be more prepared to overcome the liabilities of newness in comparison to another individual who may have industry and domain knowledge but venturing to start up for the first time.

The factor of *funding* has long been researched and established as a key factor that contributes to the life cycle of the start-up. Cassar (2004) observed that start-ups can be affected by market access, in that their newness and scale make some financing options inaccessible. New firms are also more likely to be subject to idiosyncratic forces, in particular, the influence of the entrepreneur upon the financing and capital structure choices. Further, given their limited operating history, start-ups are arguably the most informationally opaque firms in the economy. Consequently, it is generally believed that start-ups, due to potential difficulties in obtaining intermediated external finance, are heavily dependent on initial insider finance (Berger and Udell 1998). This explains the reason for entrepreneurs not availing external funding as they formally incorporate their new venture.

As regards the factor of education not appearing significant in any of the models, it has to be noted that all the entrepreneurs in this study had the basic level of education, a degree at least. In the context of our study, all of these individuals would already have had the necessary and sufficient basic skills to pursue an entrepreneurial opportunity. Further, the technology maturity occurred only a couple of decades back and clearly, the current generation of entrepreneurs can be expected to be more responsive and dynamic in responding to an entrepreneurial opportunity. Hence, these results indicate that given the minimum education, these individuals are more likely to exploit entrepreneurial opportunities.

It is important to elaborate why local entrepreneurs fare well in comparison to transnational entrepreneurs of emerging economies. Local entrepreneurs have better local networks and tacit knowledge, as well as have a better realization of the addressable demand for the proposed new venture idea. Hence, although they are resource-constrained in comparison to transnational entrepreneurs, given their knowledge of the local conditions, they relatively are likely to set up new high-tech ventures.

Summary and Conclusions

In this study, we have tried to ascertain the key enablers and barriers that influence and impact the emergence of high-tech start-ups in India. We developed a conceptual framework to examine the objectives of the study, based on review of prior literature. Further, choosing India as the region of study and ICT sector, we modelled the status of *formal incorporation* of every high-tech start-up in our data set as the dependent variable for evaluating this objective. Since this variable was dichotomous in nature, we utilized logistic regression to execute the tests. In total, we built seven logistic regression models to analyse the emergence of high-tech start-ups under different contexts. Each one of the models helped us in validating the formulated hypotheses in the context of B2B start-ups, B2C start-ups, start-ups based in north Indian cities, start-ups based out of south Indian cities, start-ups that have local entrepreneurs as founders, and start-ups that have transnational entrepreneurs as founders. Finally, a model fitted based on all the data collected across the country revealed the key entrepreneurial and firm-specific factors that affect the start-up emergence.

Overall, the results from the execution of these models indicate that prior start-up experience of the entrepreneur, absence of R&D and financial capabilities increase the likelihood of high-tech start-up emergence. In addition to these, the logistic regression model results also indicate that high-tech start-up emergence is likely from *local* entrepreneurs, focusing on *B2C markets* and who have operations in *South Zone* of the country.

The results from our analysis of factors impacting the emergence of high-tech start-ups indicated that entrepreneurs who do not have prior start-up experience take more time to incorporate their new venture formally. Second, hiring too many technical people prior to formal incorporation will further delay the founding of the firm. On similar lines, possession of external funding delays the chances of incorporation of the start-up. None of the external environmental factors seemed to impact the emergence of the high-tech start-ups.

These results on factors influencing emergence of high-tech start-ups provide insights that will be helpful to entrepreneurs, policymakers, and external start-up ecosystem partners. From the results, we understand that entrepreneurs with prior start-up experience will be the ones who would more likely incorporate their start-up, irrespective of whether they have the right resources to further sustain their start-up. In contrast, those entrepreneurs who do not have prior start-up experience would take time to formally set up their new venture. The results indicate that knowledge, learning, and entrepreneurial judgement gained from the past stints would allow the entrepreneur to make a start with larger/bigger scope of the entrepreneurial idea, whereas the uncertainty of outcomes in the pre-entrepreneurial phase might constrain the founders with no prior start-up experience to go slowly on formal incorporation.

We also have been able to gain useful insights on which firm-specific factors impact the emergence of high-tech start-ups in India and how these influences play out. The results from our analysis indicated that obtaining initial financial capitalization prior to starting up delayed the emergence of a high-tech start-up. In the early stages of start-up life cycle, it is usually the self-funding routes or funds lent by family and friends towards commercializing an entrepreneurial idea that contribute to capitalizing the firm to be incorporated. The outcome of having sufficient funds to initiate the initial activities of the start-up operations would lead the entrepreneur to focus on key activities of building the product/service. Since the entrepreneur no longer needs to raise funds immediately this may cause delay in the emergence of a start-up. Further, as an alert to what sort of firm-specific resources might be harmful in the pre-emergence phase, our results indicated that having too much of R&D personnel at the pre-emergence stage would actually hinder the process of emergence of high-tech start-ups in India. This result indicates that hiring high-skilled R&D team members at a stage when even initial market acceptance is not proven will create unnecessary distractions and drain on pre-start-up finances.

Our results on start-up emergence also provided new insights, such as in which type of market we might expect start-ups to emerge faster, and in which location in the country, and whether it is led by a transnational entrepreneur or not makes any difference on the emergence of high-tech start-ups. From our results, we observe that any start-up idea concentrating on the B2C market will emerge quickly. This is explainable from the fact that any entrepreneurial idea in the B2C market segment would perhaps provide rapid feedback on product development, initial customer segments to be targeted, and other strategies since the target audience is not any particular subset of customers and that they can easily be tapped for initial feedback collection.

In a similar manner, our results indicated that start-ups having ideas would take relatively less time to emerge in south India. The external ecosystem knowledge present in the south Indian region will ensure that entrepreneurs in this region prepared well prior to formal incorporation of their start-up. Further, our results indicated that local entrepreneurs show a bias to quickly set up their new venture in their country of origin. This result also is understandable, since most often, local entrepreneurs have better insight on the market requirements of the entrepreneurial idea that they wish to pursue. This aspect would spur them to begin the operations.

While the analysis of objectives of this study provide meaningful insights, there is further scope to enhance the knowledge in this area by further investigating on a couple of areas. First, addition of a few more variables in the study would have enhanced our know-how on the emergence of the high-tech start-ups. For example, we could not collect data on all the co-founders of the start-ups studied. If we obtained this data, we could have further provided deeper insight on how the leadership team acts would influence emergence of high-tech start-ups. Second, most variables considered in this study are binary in nature, which limits the ability to derive correlations and hence limits the ability to statistically infer with a higher degree of confidence. Despite these known limitations, we believe that this study offers initial insights on the high-tech entrepreneurship aspects of one of the largest and fastest growing economies.

Appendix: Results of Logistic Regression Models

This section contains the results of the statistical analysis performed on the data, for all the seven models. To begin with, Tables 4A.1 and 4A.2 present the results of the tests carried out for the B2B and B2C sectors. Then, Tables 4A.3 and 4A.4 provide the results of the tests carried out with the location of operations (north India and south India) as the variable differentiator. Last, Tables 4A.5 and 4A.6 provide the results of tests that were carried out with data which are grouped based on entrepreneur exposure.

TABLE 4A.1 Results of logistic regression model of start-ups focusing on the B2B sector

Model variables	Beta coefficient (β)	Standard error	Wald statistic	Degree of freedom	Significance (p-value)	Exp. (β)
Constant	20.138	10270.656	0.000	1	0.998	5.570E8
Prior industry experience of the entrepreneur (fiexp = 1)	0.835	1.408	0.352	1	0.553	2.305
Prior start-up experience of the entrepreneur (fsexp = 1)	1.093	0.591	3.424	1	0.064	2.983
Age of the entrepreneur (fage)	0.026	0.041	0.411	1	0.521	1.027
Education of the entrepreneur – base reference variable (fedn)			0.039	2	0.981	
Education of the entrepreneur – first dummy (fedn1)	–19.032	10270.656	0.000	1	0.999	0.000
Education of the entrepreneur – second dummy (fedn2)	–18.921	10270.656	0.000	1	0.999	0.000
Sales capabilities – base reference variable (csales)			2.557	2	0.278	
Sales capabilities – first dummy (csales1)	0.662	0.646	1.053	1	0.305	1.939
Sales capabilities – second dummy (csales2)	1.073	0.676	2.519	1	0.112	2.925
R&D capabilities – base reference variable (cdev)			6.155	2	0.046	
R&D capabilities – first dummy (cdev1)	1.501	1.444	1.081	1	0.299	4.488
R&D capabilities – second dummy (cdev2)	–1.179	0.903	1.704	1	0.192	0.307
Funding status of the start-up (fin = 1)	–1.244	0.673	3.415	1	0.065	0.288
SDP growth (sdp)	–1.860	5.090	0.134	1	0.715	0.156
Number of deals (deals)	0.006	0.015	0.137	1	0.712	1.006
Number of VCs (vc)	–0.009	0.021	0.173	1	0.677	0.991
Operations in south India (zone = 1)	1.230	0.726	2.867	1	0.090	3.421
Transnational entrepreneur (te=1)	–0.733	0.569	1.661	1	0.198	0.480

Model statistics: Number of Observations = 122

Goodness of fit: Chisq = 33.205 on 15 degrees of freedom, p-value = 0.004

Hosmer and Lemeshow test: Chisq = 3.430 on 8 degree of freedom, p-value = 0.905

Cox and Snell R^2 = 0.238; Nagelkerke R^2 = 0.346

SOURCE: Author.

TABLE 4A.2 Results of logistic regression model of start-ups focusing on the B2C sector

Model variables	Beta coefficient (β)	Standard error	Wald statistic	Degree of freedom	Significance (p-value)	Exp. (β)
Constant	2.648	1.598	2.746	1	0.097	14.121
Prior industry experience of the entrepreneur (fiexp = 1)	-0.223	0.578	0.149	1	0.699	0.800
Prior start-up experience of the entrepreneur (fsexp = 1)	0.287	0.446	0.416	1	0.519	1.333
Age of the entrepreneur (fage)	0.010	0.033	0.090	1	0.764	1.010
Education of the entrepreneur – base reference variable (fedn)			2.503	2	0.286	
Education of the entrepreneur – first dummy (fedn1)	1.194	0.957	1.557	1	0.212	3.301
Education of the entrepreneur – second dummy (fedn2)	0.602	0.899	0.449	1	0.503	1.827
Sales capabilities – base reference variable (csales)			0.926	2	0.629	
Sales capabilities – first dummy (csales1)	-0.199	0.685	0.085	1	0.771	0.820
Sales capabilities – second dummy (csales2)	0.280	0.722	0.150	1	0.698	1.323
R&D capabilities – base reference variable (cdev)			4.986	2	**0.083**	
R&D capabilities – first dummy (cdev1)	0.242	1.364	0.032	1	0.859	1.274
R&D capabilities – second dummy (cdev2)	-1.504	0.765	3.861	1	**0.049**	0.222
Funding status of the start-up (fin=1)	-1.528	0.499	9.362	1	**0.002**	0.217
SDP growth (sdp)	-6.399	4.238	2.280	1	0.131	0.002
Number of deals (deals)	0.000	0.011	0.001	1	0.970	1.000
Number of VCs (vc)	-0.006	0.014	0.167	1	0.683	0.994
Operations in south India (Zone=1)	0.482	0.488	0.979	1	0.323	1.620
Transnational entrepreneur (te=1)	-0.746	0.410	3.309	1	**0.069**	0.474

Model statistics: Number of observations = 153

Goodness of fit: Chisq = 38.594 on 15 degrees of freedom, p-value = 0.001

Hosmer and Lemeshow test: Chisq = 4.941 on 8 degree of freedom, p-value = 0.764

Cox and Snell R^2 = 0.224; Nagelkerke R^2 = 0.300

Source: Author.

TABLE 4A.3 Results of logistic regression model of start-ups operating in North Zone

Model variables	Beta coefficient (β)	Standard error	Wald statistic	Degree of freedom	Significance (p-value)	Exp. (β)
Constant	3.952	3.706	1.137	1	0.286	52.041
Prior industry experience of the entrepreneur (fiexp = 1)	0.629	0.816	0.595	1	0.441	1.876
Prior start-up experience of the entrepreneur (fsexp = 1)	−0.143	0.656	0.047	1	0.828	0.867
Age of the entrepreneur (fage)	0.213	0.069	9.467	1	**0.002**	1.237
Education of the entrepreneur – base reference variable (fedn)			1.299	2	0.522	
Education of the entrepreneur – first dummy (fedn1)	1.053	1.973	0.285	1	0.594	2.866
Education of the entrepreneur – second dummy (fedn2)	0.361	1.931	0.035	1	0.852	1.435
Sales capabilities – base reference variable (csales)			4.153	2	0.125	
Sales capabilities – first dummy (csales1)	1.896	0.985	3.705	1	**0.054**	6.662
Sales capabilities – second dummy (csales2)	1.778	0.967	3.378	1	**0.066**	5.915
R&D capabilities – base reference variable (cdev)			2.420	2	0.298	
R&D capabilities – first dummy (cdev1)	21.096	8111.859	0.000	1	0.998	1.451E9
R&D capabilities – second dummy (cdev2)	−1.625	1.045	2.420	1	0.120	0.197
Funding status of the start-up (fin = 1)	−1.872	0.931	4.040	1	**0.044**	0.154
SDP growth (sdp)	−73.629	29.894	6.066	1	**0.014**	0.000
Number of deals (deals)	−0.060	0.022	7.364	1	**0.007**	0.942
Number of VCs (vc)	−0.008	0.016	0.224	1	0.636	0.993
Target market segment (market_segment = 1)	0.534	0.724	0.543	1	0.461	1.705
Transnational entrepreneur (te = 1)	0.471	0.612	0.594	1	0.441	1.602

Model statistics: Number of observations = 101

Goodness of fit: Chisq = 41.246 on 15 degrees of freedom, p-value = 0.000

Hosmer and Lemeshow Test: Chisq = 4.183 on 8 degree of freedom, p-value = 0.840

Cox and Snell R^2 = 0.335; Nagelkerke R^2 = 0.473

SOURCE: Author.

TABLE 4A.4 Results of logistic regression model of start-ups operating in South Zone

Model variables	Beta coefficient (β)	Standard error	Wald statistic	Degree of freedom	Significance (p-value)	Exp. (β)
Constant	4.483	1.680	7.122	1	0.008	88.460
Prior industry experience of the entrepreneur (fiexp = 1)	0.513	0.743	0.476	1	0.490	1.670
Prior start-up experience of the entrepreneur (fsexp = 1)	0.948	0.436	4.732	1	**0.030**	2.581
Age of the entrepreneur (fage)	-0.031	0.031	1.039	1	0.308	0.969
Education of the entrepreneur – base reference variable (fedn)			0.973	2	0.615	
Education of the entrepreneur – first dummy (fedn1)	-0.192	1.036	0.034	1	0.853	0.825
Education of the entrepreneur – second dummy (fedn2)	-0.564	0.980	0.332	1	0.565	0.569
Sales capabilities – base reference variable (csales)			1.942	2	0.379	
Sales capabilities – first dummy (csales1)	0.276	0.584	0.223	1	0.637	1.317
Sales capabilities – second dummy (csales2)	0.818	0.642	1.623	1	0.203	2.266
R&D capabilities – base reference variable (cdev)			10.367	2	**0.006**	
R&D capabilities – first dummy (cdev1)	0.484	1.128	0.185	1	0.667	1.623
R&D capabilities – second dummy (cdev2)	-1.843	0.767	5.780	1	**0.016**	0.158
Funding status of the start-up (fin = 1)	-1.578	0.482	10.715	1	**0.001**	0.206
SDP growth (sdp)	-3.797	3.871	0.962	1	0.327	0.022
Number of deals (deals)	0.006	0.024	0.055	1	0.814	1.006
Number of VCs (vc)	-0.005	0.040	0.019	1	0.891	0.995
Target market segment (market_segment = 1)	0.726	0.419	2.995	1	0.084	2.066
Transnational entrepreneur (te = 1)	-1.542	0.431	12.792	1	**0.000**	0.214

Model statistics: Number of observations = 174

Goodness of fit: Chisq = 57.715 on 15 degrees of freedom, p-value = 0.000

Hosmer and Lemeshow test: Chisq = 11.623 on 8 degree of freedom, p-value = 0.169

Cox and Snell R² = 0.284; Nagelkerke R² = 0.384

SOURCE: Author.

TABLE 4A.5 Results of logistic regression model of start-ups operated by local entrepreneurs

Model variables	Beta coefficient (β)	Standard error	Wald statistic	Degree of freedom	Significance (p-value)	Exp. (β)
Constant	0.467	2.021	0.053	1	0.817	1.595
Prior industry experience of the entrepreneur (fiexp = 1)	0.142	0.569	0.062	1	0.803	1.153
Prior start-up experience of the entrepreneur (fsexp = 1)	0.433	0.422	1.049	1	0.306	1.541
Age of the entrepreneur (fage)	0.015	0.033	0.199	1	0.656	1.015
Education of the entrepreneur – base reference variable (fedn)			0.760	2	0.684	
Education of the entrepreneur – first dummy (fedn1)	0.564	1.454	0.150	1	0.698	1.757
Education of the entrepreneur – second dummy (fedn2)	0.212	1.410	0.023	1	0.881	1.236
Sales capabilities – base reference variable (csales)			0.408	2	0.815	
Sales capabilities – first dummy (csales1)	-0.141	0.607	0.054	1	0.816	0.869
Sales capabilities – second dummy (csales2)	0.163	0.627	0.068	1	0.794	1.178
R&D capabilities – base reference variable (cdev)			6.240	2	**0.044**	
R&D capabilities – first dummy (cdev1)	0.554	1.055	0.276	1	0.600	1.740
R&D capabilities – second dummy (cdev2)	-1.367	0.722	3.581	1	**0.058**	0.255
Funding status of the start-up (fin = 1)	-1.225	0.476	6.638	1	**0.010**	0.294
SDP growth (sdp)	-0.735	4.432	0.027	1	0.868	0.480
Number of deals (deals)	0.002	0.012	0.033	1	0.855	1.002
Number of VCs (vc)	0.000	0.016	0.001	1	0.981	1.000
Target arket segment (market_segment = 1)	0.658	0.442	2.218	1	0.136	1.932
Operations in south India (zone = 1)	1.173	0.508	5.332	1	**0.021**	3.232

Model statistics: Number of observations = 152

Goodness of fit: Chisq = 35.178 on 15 degrees of freedom, p-value = 0.002

Hosmer and Lemeshow test: Chisq = 8.704 on 8 degree of freedom, p-value = 0.368

Cox and Snell R^2 = 0.208; Nagelkerke R^2 = 0.278

Source: Author.

TABLE 4A.6 Results of regression model of start-ups operated by transnational entrepreneurs

Model variables	Beta coefficient (β)	Standard error	Wald statistic	Degree of freedom	Significance (p-value)	Exp. (β)
Constant	3.095	2.032	2.320	1	0.128	22.095
Prior industry experience of the entrepreneur (fiexp = 1)	0.005	1.043	0.000	1	0.996	1.005
Prior start-up experience of the entrepreneur (fsexp = 1)	0.957	0.613	2.439	1	0.118	2.603
Age of the entrepreneur (fage)	0.024	0.041	0.348	1	0.555	1.024
Education of the entrepreneur – base reference variable (fedn)			0.318	2	0.853	
Education of the entrepreneur – first dummy (fedn1)	0.221	1.090	0.041	1	0.839	1.248
Education of the entrepreneur – second dummy (fedn2)	-0.107	1.028	0.011	1	0.917	0.899
Sales capabilities – base reference variable (csales)			2.837	2	0.242	
Sales capabilities – first dummy (csales1)	0.609	0.715	0.726	1	0.394	1.839
Sales capabilities – second dummy (csales2)	1.337	0.803	2.772	1	**0.096**	3.807
R&D capabilities – base reference variable (cdev)			2.064	2	0.356	
R&D capabilities – first dummy (cdev1)	19.162	8738.701	0.000	1	0.998	2.098E8
R&D capabilities – second dummy (cdev2)	-1.646	1.145	2.064	1	0.151	0.193
Funding status of the start-up (fin = 1)	-1.946	0.754	6.672	1	**0.010**	0.143
SDP growth (sdp)	-6.216	4.935	1.587	1	0.208	0.002
Number of deals (deals)	0.002	0.013	0.015	1	0.901	1.002
Number of VCs (vc)	-.015	0.017	0.750	1	0.386	0.985
Target market segment (market_segment = 1)	0.575	0.576	0.998	1	0.318	1.778
Operations in south India (zone = 1)	-0.038	0.677	0.003	1	0.955	0.963

Model statistics: Number of observations = 123

Goodness of fit: Chisq = 37.752 on 15 degrees of freedom, p-value = 0.001

Hosmer and Lemeshow test: Chisq = 5.136 on 8 degree of freedom, p-value = 0.743

Cox and Snell R^2 = 0.264; Nagelkerke R^2 = 0.384

SOURCE: Author.

TABLE 4A.7 Results of the logistic regression of the overall model

Model variables	Beta coefficient (β)	Standard error	Wald statistic	Degree of freedom	Significance (p-value)	Exp. (β)
Constant	2.145	1.264	2.879	1	0.090	8.538
Prior industry experience of the entrepreneur (fiexp = 1)	0.056	0.498	0.012	1	0.911	1.057
Prior start-up experience of the entrepreneur (fsexp = 1)	0.615	0.332	3.425	1	**0.064**	1.849
Age of the entrepreneur (fage)	0.015	0.024	0.408	1	0.523	1.016
Education of the entrepreneur – base reference variable (fedn)			0.675	2	0.714	
Education of the entrepreneur – first dummy (fedn1)	0.152	0.796	0.036	1	0.849	1.164
Education of the entrepreneur – second dummy (fedn2)	–0.117	0.754	0.024	1	0.876	0.889
Sales capabilities – base reference variable (csales)			2.579	2	0.275	
Sales capabilities – first dummy (csales1)	0.189	0.436	0.189	1	0.664	1.209
Sales capabilities – second dummy (csales2)	0.676	0.469	2.080	1	0.149	1.966
R&D capabilities – base reference variable (cdev)			12.379	2	**0.002**	
R&D capabilities – first dummy (cdev1)	0.984	0.947	1.079	1	0.299	2.674
R&D capabilities – second dummy (cdev2)	–1.367	0.568	5.785	1	**0.016**	0.255
Funding status of the start-up (fin = 1)	–1.352	0.379	12.719	1	**0.000**	0.259
SDP growth (sdp)	–3.224	3.045	1.121	1	0.290	0.040
Number of deals (deals)	0.002	0.008	0.071	1	0.790	1.002
Number of VCs (vc)	–0.006	0.011	0.333	1	0.564	0.994
Target market segment (market_segment = 1)	0.585	0.327	3.191	1	**0.074**	1.795
Operations in South India (zone = 1)	0.718	0.392	3.353	1	**0.067**	2.051
Transnational Entrepreneur (te = 1)	–0.846	0.317	7.117	1	**0.008**	0.429

Model statistics: Number of observations = 275

Goodness of fit: Chisq = 70.950 on 16 degrees of freedom, p-value = 0.000

Hosmer and Lemeshow test: Chisq = 1.453 on 8 degree of freedom, p-value = 0.993

Cox and Snell R² = 0.228; Nagelkerke R² = 0.312

SOURCE: Author.

5

Survival of High-tech Start-ups

Introduction

The phenomenon of high-tech start-up survival has been extensively studied in the entrepreneurship literature from multiple theoretical perspectives, the prominent ones being economic, strategic management and evolutionary and behavioural sciences. The motivation for all these studies are twofold. First, start-ups provide context to examine and interpret the theories of entrepreneurship. This is primarily because start-ups are a vehicle of the acts of entrepreneurship or institutional arrangements for demonstration of entrepreneurship by an entrepreneur (Shane 1995; Sarasvathy 2004). Second, small high-tech start-ups have been recognized as the major drivers of job creation and innovation and thus, economic growth (Birch 1979; Baumol 2002; Kirchhoff and Spencer 2008). Birch (1979) showed that small firms created more jobs than large firms. Scherer (1980) and Scherer and Ross (1990) showed that small firms produced disproportionately more innovations than large firms. Further, Kirchoff and Spencer (2008) hypothesized small firms as the dominant drivers of radical innovations that define new fields.

While high technology start-up firms have been credited with contributing to economic growth by way of job creation and innovation (Kirchhoff 1994; Kirchhoff and Spencer 2008), a review of the characteristics of these start-ups reveal that they have a huge failure rate (Stinchcombe 1965). Given these seemingly contradicting observations, one can infer that the contribution to economic development is through those start-up firms that have successfully managed to overcome the challenges during the initial stages of firm life cycle and emerged successful. It is, therefore, appropriate to understand the process and the characteristics of those few start-ups that braved the uncertainty and ambiguity, and challenged and managed to overcome the liability of newness.

The above-mentioned observations also underlie the shift in the focus of entrepreneurship researchers who earlier focused on explaining the phenomenon of start-up life cycle events, such as survival and success from a static perspective, to the now accepted understanding that entrepreneurship is a complex and dynamic process (Wiklund, Patzelt, and Shepherd 2009). This realization is reflected in Gregoire et al. (2006) who indicate seven major areas of convergence within the entrepreneurship literature. Their work illustrates that an entrepreneur as the central agent who initiates actions, firms as the vehicle of the acts of entrepreneurship, behavioural aspects/characteristics of the entrepreneur, firms, and environmental factors (social capital and financial capital) as the influencers form the common tenets of entrepreneurship field.

The resource-based view (RBV) of the firm contends that firms are a heterogeneous bundle of tangible and intangible resources. As per this theory, the entrepreneur's task is to develop, acquire, and assemble these resources in such a way as to create a competitive advantage (Barney 1991). In the RBV theory, the entrepreneur needs to adapt to a changing competitive environment by reconfiguring existing resource bundles and acquiring new resources and capabilities as required. In this sense, the role of the entrepreneur is dynamic rather than static in nature. This ability of the entrepreneur to adapt to changing circumstances is a resource and it reflects a capability of the firm (Alvarez and Busenitz 2001). Further, it is these capabilities of the entrepreneur and resource bundles of the firm that determine start-up survival (Coleman, Cotei, and Farhat 2013).

From an industrial economics perspective, Geroski (1995) noted that start-ups in high-tech sector are the most exposed to exit or failure, especially in the first few years of their inception. Audretsch (1997) noted that primarily two factors influenced the decision of a firm to exit from the market: one is the gap between firm size and the minimum efficient scale, and the other is the selection mechanism of heterogeneous firms. In proof of Audretsch's first observation, Mahmood (1992) had established that the probability of survival in an industry will be higher in the presence of economies of scale. Further, Geroski (1995) indicated that new firms which enter an industry at a level of production below the minimum efficient scale experience high hazard rates soon after the entry. These observations were further corroborated by Agarwal and Audretsch (2001) who found that survival probability increased with firm size at the time of entry.

As regards to the second factor of Audretsch's observation, we find evidence of the same in Jovanovic's (1982) theory of 'noisy selection'. In Jovanovic's equilibrium model, firm dynamics depend on the learning process that enables firms to discover and adapt to their particular level of efficiency, given the existence of asymmetries in efficiency and imperfect information. Over time, firms discover their levels of efficiency through operating in the industry: those who are more efficient grow and survive while those who discover that they are relatively inefficient, reduce the production and eventually exit the market (Cefis and Marsilli 2006).

Apart from Jovanovic's model, two more models have been significant in explaining the survival of high-tech start-ups. Ericson and Pakes (1995) extended Jovanovic's model to include the investments of individual firms on the R&D. In Ericson and Pakes' model, firms explore the space of technological opportunities by actively investing in research, and by doing so, they improve their efficiency and profitability, and ultimately their chances of survival. This model helped in understanding the role played by uncertainty in influencing start-up survival. Ericson and Pakes (1995) contended that high degrees of uncertainty associated with R&D investments may negatively affect the survival of firms.

Nelson and Winter's (1982) modelling of start-up survival is another significant contribution that has helped shape the understanding of the phenomenon. Nelson and Winter (1982) support Audretsch's (1997) second reason for start-up exit. They interpreted the firms' exit behaviour as the result of out-of-equilibrium processes of learning and market selection. The selection mechanism transforms existing asymmetries in productivity among firms (due to the heterogeneous distribution of knowledge and capabilities) into differential rates of growth and survival. This model also highlighted the influence of innovation impacting start-up survival. In both Ericson and Pakes' model and Nelson and Winter's model, it is the combination of the enhanced opportunities for innovation stemming from the investment in R&D and the uncertainty of the partly random outcomes of this investment that determines survival (Cefis and Marsili 2006).

The contributions from the RBV, entrepreneur learning, and industrial economics theories have shaped the framework of this chapter. Following up from the literature review on survival of high-tech start-ups, this chapter examines the factors grouped under three key dimensions, namely, the entrepreneurial characteristics, the firm (start-up) specific factors, and the external environmental factors that impact the time to survival of high-tech start-ups operating out of India.

Factors Impacting Survival of High-tech Start-ups

The preceding chapter discussed and analysed the key factors that influenced the creation of high-tech start-ups. In the case of high-tech start-ups that are created in the IT sector, the barriers to firm formation are very minimal. Hence, while it may be easier to create a new venture, survival and subsequent growth of the start-up are the most important phases that have the maximum uncertainty to be addressed. These start-ups face many unique constraints during their life cycle that makes them highly amenable to failure. A start-up would be able to survive and sustain only if it can successfully overcome the liability of newness, fighting against the uncertainty of value it promises to its stakeholders, and dealing with undeveloped markets.

Politis (2008) tried to explain entrepreneurship as a continuous learning process (2008). This has resulted in researchers applying the core concepts of learning theory to different entrepreneurial contexts, in particular to high-tech start-up survival. Politis and Gabrielsson (2005) observed that entrepreneurship occurs at the intersection of the individual's perception of an entrepreneurial opportunity and his/her ability to pursue that opportunity (Shane and Venkataraman 2000). Shane (2000) further explained that individuals develop different stocks of information throughout their careers and that these stocks of information influence their ability to recognize, act on, and exploit particular entrepreneurial opportunities.

Research from the past decade has delved deeper into these discussed facets, trying to unravel how entrepreneurs learn from experiences, and how these experiences further help the entrepreneur in enhancing performance of the venture or in reducing time to survival of the start-up. The role of prior start-up experience in entrepreneurial learning (Politis and Gabrielsson 2005), the distinction between entrepreneurial learning and entrepreneurial knowledge (Reuber, Dyke, and Fischer 1990), exploring the intermediate process of entrepreneurial learning where experience is transformed into knowledge (Minniti and Bygrave 2001; Politis and Gabrielsson 2005) are some of the notable contributions that have extended our understanding in this domain.

Aldrich (1999) noted that entrepreneurs need to pursue a lot of activities in the early stages of operation of their new venture. These include establishing the business environment, making legal arrangements, developing new organizational routines, and formulating business plans (Stinchcombe 1965). Research has demonstrated the substantial impacts of initial organizational conditions, including the role of entrepreneurs' social skills (Baron and Markman 2003) and start-ups' resource endowments (Davidsson and Honig 2003; Ruef, Aldrich, and Carter 2003), market opportunities, and environmental constraints (Low and Abrahamson 1997). Because the tasks required for a successful start-up are various and demanding, and must be accomplished within a very short time frame (Brush, Greene, and Hart 2001; Lichtenstein and Brush 2001), the mechanisms for alleviating the liabilities of newness are particularly important from both theoretical and empirical perspectives.

Cefis and Marsili (2006) reviewed the firm level and external environmental factors that influence the survival of high-tech start-ups. At the firm level, size and age of the firm were initially attributed to increasing survival probability (Evans 1987; Hall 1987; Dunne, Robert, and Samuelson 1989; Dunne and Hughes 1994). At the industry level, the characteristics of demand, such as market size and growth rates (Mata and Portugal 1994), the characteristics of technology (Audretsch 1991 and 1995), and the characteristics of life cycle (Suarez and Utterback 1995; Agarwal and Gort 1996), were found to be important determinants of survival.

Cader and Leatherman (2011) stated that the factors that affect survival of a high-tech start-up can be broadly classified into those which are specific to the firm (for example, size, type, and the like), entrepreneur (for example, age, education, and so on), industry (manufacturing, high-tech), region (metro, non-metro), or a combination of these factors. Subsequently, factors such as age, education, previous work experience, and prior start-up experience of the entrepreneur represent the 'entrepreneurial capabilities'. Factors such as financial capitalization of the start-up, R&D, and sales resources of the start-up represent the 'firm-specific resources' in this study.

Based on the preceding discussion and the survey of literature, we aim to validate the following hypotheses regarding the survival of high-tech start-ups.

Hypothesis 1: Prior industry experience of the primary founder positively influences the time to survival of the start-up.

Hypothesis 2: Prior start-up experience of the primary founder positively influences the time to survival of the start-up.

Hypothesis 3: Primary founders of higher ages are more likely to achieve survival of their start-ups earlier than the founders of lesser ages.

Hypothesis 4: Higher educational pedigree positively influences the time to survival of the start-up.

Hypothesis 5: Higher R&D resources with the start-up founders positively influences the time to survival of the start-up.

Hypothesis 6: Higher sales capabilities with the start-up founders positively influences the time to survival of the start-up.

Hypothesis 7: Higher financial resources with the start-up founders positively influences the time to survival of the start-up.

Hypothesis 8: Higher state domestic product (SDP) growth in the region where the start-up is located positively influences the time to survival of the start-up.

Hypothesis 9: The higher the presence of VCs in the region, the faster the start-ups will be able to achieve survival.

These hypotheses will be tested against six survival analysis models, each validating the hypotheses in the context of B2B start-ups, B2C start-ups, start-ups based in North Zone regions in India, start-ups based in South Zone regions in India, start-ups that have local entrepreneurs as founders, and start-ups that have transnational entrepreneurs as founders. Finally, a model will be fitted based on all the data collected across the country which will reveal the key entrepreneurial, firm-specific, and external environment-specific factors that affect start-up survival.

Description of Data and Variables

In this section, we describe the dependent and independent variables that we have used for the study. We also describe the univariate relationships between each of the independent variables with the dependent variable. The method of analysis for this research objective is survival analysis. A description of this method and its relevance for usage to examine this objective have been detailed in Chapter 2. The statistical tool 'SPSS' has been used for the analysis of this research objective.

Dependent Variable

Time to survival of the start-up in months is the dependent variable used in this chapter. The time, in months, of operation of the start-up since its formal incorporation and whether the start-up has achieved survival or not, are taken together to form the dependent variable. The respondents to our questionnaire reported the month and year when they formally created the start-up. The start-up that had achieved product-market fit at the time of conducting the survey is considered to have survived. Start-ups that had not yet achieved this milestone are considered as not survived at the time of observation.

Independent and Control Variables

The relevant industry experience, prior start-up experience, age, and education of the entrepreneur are the entrepreneurial factors that are examined in this study. The sales turnover in Indian currency, R&D capabilities, and the funding status of the start-up form the organizational factors that are examined for impact. The SDP growth of the region, the number of VCs in the region, and the number of VC deals that were signed in the region for a given year form the external environmental variables that are examined for their influence on time to survival of the high-tech start-ups.

Relevant industry experience: A discrete dichotomous variable which indicates whether or not the founder has previous industry experience has been used for analysis. This variable takes the value of 1 for every start-up founder who has industry experience prior to founding the current start-up, considered for the study. A value of 0 for this variable indicates that the founder of the start-up does not possess any previous industry working experience. This variable is labelled in SPSS as *fiexp* for the analysis.

Prior start-up experience: A discrete dichotomous variable which indicates whether or not the founder has prior start-up experience has been used for analysis. This variable takes the value of 1 for every start-up founder who has experience working in a start-up, either as an employee or as a founder prior to founding the current start-up considered for the study. A value of 0 for this variable indicates that the founder of the start-up does not possess any previous start-up experience. This variable is labelled in SPSS as *fsexp* for the analysis.

Age of the entrepreneur: The age of the entrepreneur in years at the time of founding the current start-up has been used for analysis. This variable is labelled in SPSS as *fage* for the analysis.

Education of the entrepreneur: The education of the entrepreneur is categorized using two dummy variables. The base reference variable indicates graduate education without an engineering degree (degree in science, arts, and others), the first dummy variable indicates graduate education with a technical (engineering) degree, and the second dummy variable indicates education with a technical master's degree or above. This variable is labelled in SPSS as *fedn* for the analysis. The base reference variable takes the value of 1 for every founder of the start-up whose educational credentials are a non-engineering degree. A value of 0 for the base reference variable indicates the absence of a non-engineering degree of the founder. The first dummy variable *fedn1* takes the value of 1 for every start-up founder who has a technical (engineering) degree as his/her educational credentials. A value of 0 for this variable indicates the absence of a technical (engineering) degree of the founder. The second dummy variable *fedn2* takes the value of 1 for every start-up founder who has educational credentials of a technical (engineering) master's degree or above. A value of 0 for this variable indicates the absence of a technical master's degree or a higher technical qualification (for example, PhD) of the founder.

Sales capabilities of the start-up: The sales capabilities of the start-up at the time of initiating operations is measured as a categorical value with 3 levels. This variable is labelled as *csales* in SPSS for the analysis. A value of 1 for the base reference variable indicates that the start-up does not possess any sales capabilities. This means either the founders do not have the sales background or they have not yet formalized a co-founder with sales background or the start-up has not yet obtained initial customers and started sales. A value of 0 for the base reference variable indicates the converse. Very few start-ups fall under this category. The first dummy variable *csales1* takes the value of 1 for every start-up that has sales capabilities, but no revenue is yet generated. This value is assigned to all start-ups that either have a co-founder focusing on sales or hired employees who have prior selling experience, but no revenue has been accrued on account of selling the offerings of the start-ups. A value of 0 for this dummy variable indicates the absence of the capabilities as indicated in the preceding sentence. A value of 1 for the second dummy variable *csales2* indicates that the start-up has already clocked up some revenue by selling to initial customers. A value of 0 for this variable indicates the converse.

R&D capabilities of the start-up: The R&D capabilities of the start-up at the time of initiating operations is measured as a categorical variable with 3 levels. This variable is labelled as *cdev* in SPSS for the analysis. A value of 1 for the base reference variable indicates that the start-up does not possess any R&D capabilities. This means either the founders do not have a technological background or they have not yet formalized a co-founder with the technological background. A value of 0 for the base reference variable indicates the converse. A value of 1 for the first dummy variable *cdev1* indicates that the start-up has R&D capabilities, but no viable product prototype has been built yet. This level is assigned to all start-ups that have a founder or co-founder with a technological background or have hired employees with technical capabilities. However, as an entity, the team has not yet produced an initial prototype that could be demonstrated to its prospective customers. A value of 0 for this dummy variable indicates the absence of the capabilities as indicated in the preceding sentence. A value of 1 for the second dummy variable *cdev2* indicates the presence of a working and demonstrable initial product or service offering at the time of beginning the operations. A value of 0 for this variable indicates the converse.

Financial capability of the start-up: Measured by a discrete dichotomous variable which indicates whether or not the start-up obtained funding external to its founder's and his/her family's funds. This variable is labelled as *fin* in SPSS for the analysis. A value of 1 for this variable indicates that the start-up is funded from external sources, and conversely, a value of 0 for this variable indicates that the start-up under consideration is not funded from external sources.

SDP: This variable is used as a proxy for the macroeconomic environment prevalent in the state in which the start-up is located. This variable provides the percentage of change in the SDP in comparison to its previous year (at constant prices). This variable is labelled as *sdp* in SPSS for the analysis.

Number of funded deals: This variable is used to indicate the number of early-stage VC deals that happened for a given year and a given geography. This measure is a proxy to measure the maturity of the start-up ecosystem for the given year and given geography. An increase in the number of funded early-stage deals in a given geography, year on year, indicates a healthy and growing start-up ecosystem. This variable is labelled as *deals* in SPSS for the analysis.

Number of VC funds: This variable indicates the presence of the active VC funds for a given year and a given geography. This variable is a proxy to measure and understand the availability of external funding options for a particular region and year. This variable is labelled as *vc* in SPSS for the analysis.

Control variables

Target market segment: This variable is a dummy variable with two levels. A value of 0 indicates that the target market segment of the start-up is B2B sector, whereas the value of 1 indicates that the target market segment of the start-up is B2C sector. This variable is labelled as *market_segment* in SPSS for the analysis.

Location of operations: This variable is a dummy variable with two levels. A value of 0 indicates that the start-up is located in North Zone region, whereas the value of 1 indicates that the start-up is located in the South Zone region of India. This variable is labelled as *zone* in SPSS for the analysis.

Entrepreneurial background: This variable is a dummy variable with two levels. A value of 0 indicates that the entrepreneur is a local entrepreneur, whereas the value of 1 indicates that the entrepreneur is transnational (which indicates that the entrepreneur has exposure to working or studying in more than one country, other than the country of his/her origin, for a period of at least one year). This variable is labelled as *te* in SPSS for the analysis.

With this background about the variables and measures and the method of analysis, we now proceed to discuss and interpret the univariate analysis of the data.

Discussion of Results

Graphical Examination of Data

The statistical analysis of the data begins with a visual inspection of estimators of survival probability using non-parametric KM plots. To begin with, the survival probability and cumulative probability of survival of entire sample against time are plotted as shown in Figures 5.1 and 5.2. For the purposes of analysis, the event T is defined as the time from formal incorporation till survival. From Figures 5.1 and 5.2, we can observe that on an average, start-ups take anywhere between 6 and 70 months to achieve the survival milestone. Further, from Figure 5.1, we can also infer that after incorporation of a start-up, as time elapses, the probability of not achieving survival begins to decrease. For example, from the data in our sample, a start-up has about 99 per cent probability of not achieving the survival milestone if it is formally incorporated only in the past six months. However, if a start-up has been incorporated for 4 years (48 months), the probability of not surviving of such start-up reduces to about 50 per cent.

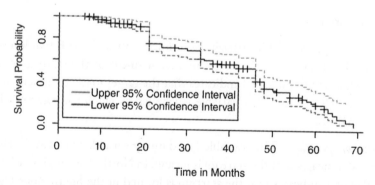

FIGURE 5.1 Survival probability of start-ups in our sample
SOURCE: Author.

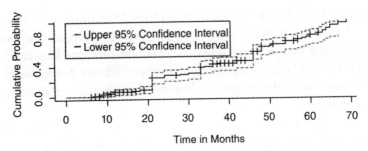

FIGURE 5.2 Cumulative survival probability of start-ups in our sample

SOURCE: Author.

Figure 5.2 indicates the inverse phenomenon, that of the cumulative probability of survival of the start-ups in the sample. From Figure 5.2, we can infer that very few start-ups (about 10 per cent of the sample) are able to achieve the survival milestone within 20 months or roughly 1.5 years' time since their formal incorporation. Further, we can also observe that about 50 per cent of the start-ups in our sample are predicted to have achieved the survival milestone in about 4 years of time. Figure 5.2 also predicts that in about 69 to 70 months' time, about 90 per cent of the start-ups in our sample would have achieved the survival milestone. We need to remember that these predications are estimates based on the data provided in our sample. Later in this chapter, we will verify if these predictions are indeed validated or not.

After the examination of the survival probability and cumulative probability plots, we also visually analyse the continuous variables in our study by examining the box plots for each of these variables against the survival status. To begin with, Figure 5.3 presents the box plot of the founders' ages versus the survival status of their start-ups. From Figure 5.3, we can observe clearly that founders of start-ups in our sample who have not yet achieved the milestone of

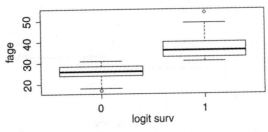

FIGURE 5.3 Box plot of founder's age versus survival status of start-ups

SOURCE: Author.

survival seem to belong to the ages ranging from 25 to 30 years, barring a few outlier observations at both ends. Further, the box plots indicate that founders of start-ups that have achieved milestone of survival are aged between 32 and 40 years. This initial analysis, therefore, seems to indicate that higher the age of the entrepreneur, the greater the likelihood of his start-up achieving the survival milestone.

Figure 5.4 presents the box plot between the percentage of SDP growth in a given region versus the start-up survival status. From the plot, we can infer that start-ups seem to have achieved the survival state in regions where the rate of SDP growth (year-on-year, at constant prices) is higher, in the range of 8 per cent to 14 per cent. Further, we observe that regional SDP growth rates are lower at 5 per cent to 7 per cent in the cases of start-ups that have not yet achieved the product-market fit.

The box plot between the number of VC deals in a given region versus the start-up survival status is presented in Figure 5.5. From the box plot, we can infer that start-ups that are based in regions where more number of VC deals happens per year have a higher likelihood of achieving the survival milestone. From Figure 5.5, we see that start-ups that have achieved the product-market fit are based in regions that have VC deals ranging between 60 and 90 per year. On the other hand, the box plot in Figure 5.5 indicates that all start-ups in our sample that have not achieved the survival milestone are based in the region where the VC deals are between 15 and 40 per year. This indicates that higher the number of VC deals in a given region, higher the likelihood of a start-up survival in that region.

Figure 5.6 presents the box plot between the number of VCs present in a given region versus the start-up survival status. From the box plot, we can infer that wherever there is a larger presence of VCs, the start-ups are more likely

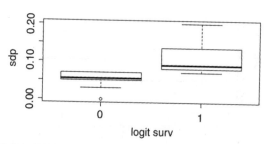

FIGURE 5.4 Box plot of percentage of SDP change versus survival status of start-ups
SOURCE: Author.

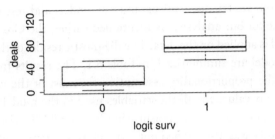

FIGURE 5.5 Box plot of number of VC deals versus survival status of start-ups

SOURCE: Author.

to survive. We observe from the box plot that start-ups that have achieved the survival milestone in our sample are based in those regions where the number of VCs ranges between 50 and 80. The start-ups that have not yet achieved the survival milestone have a lesser number of VC presence in these regions, ranging between 10 and 45.

Aided by the aforementioned initial visual analysis of the data, we now proceed to identify the correct statistical model that is appropriate to be used for analysis of the objectives that are laid out in the chapter.

Model Selection

The initial analysis by visual inspection provides us with some initial hints and directions on which factors may actually affect the time to survival for the high-tech start-ups. However, these are just initial statistical estimates and not proof of influence or absence thereof. Hence, we begin the exercise of fitting the right model to analyse the objectives of our study. As a first step

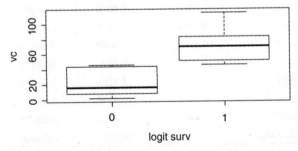

FIGURE 5.6 Box plot of number of VCs versus survival status of start-ups

SOURCE: Author.

in this direction, we try out semi-parametric models and test whether they are appropriate for our analysis. As mentioned earlier, the Cox proportional hazards model is applied on the data. The diagnostic results of the application of the Cox model are summarized in Table 5.1. The results from Table 5.1 indicate that the proportionality assumption for most of the variables does hold. The high p-values for all the variables used in the model indicate that they are suited for usage or analysis using the Cox model. The visual evaluation of proportionality was also carried out – the plots and graphs of the analysis further supported the usage of the Cox model. Therefore, the Cox proportional hazards model will be used for our analysis.

A total of seven survival analysis models are executed to analyse what factors influence the target market segment (B2B versus B2C), location of operations (North Zone versus South Zone), entrepreneurial exposure (local versus transnational), and the final one being the overall model that includes all these dimensions. Table 5.2 provides a summary of which of the hypotheses were

TABLE 5.1 Results from the Cox proportional test diagnostics

Variable	rho	chisq	p-value
fiexp1	0.1254	1.6934	0.19316
fsexp1	−0.0204	0.0477	0.82716
fage	−0.0539	0.3034	0.58176
fedn2	0.0348	0.1085	0.74182
fedn3	−0.1341	1.9563	0.16191
sales2	0.0265	0.0631	0.80162
sales3	0.0837	0.6861	0.40748
dev2	−0.0669	0.6663	0.41436
dev3	−0.0499	0.3488	0.55477
fin1	−0.0665	0.4804	0.48824
sdp	−0.0672	0.5117	0.47442
deals	−0.1113	1.6048	0.20522
vc	0.0987	0.889	0.34575
mkt1	0.1904	4.4269	0.03538
te1	0.0432	0.1948	0.65892
zone1	0.2392	7.2135	0.00724
GLOBAL	NA	18.3811	0.30206

SOURCE: Author.

NOTE: NA = Not applicable.

TABLE 5.2 Summary of Hypotheses Evaluations Related to
Survival of High-tech Start-ups

	B2B	B2C	North Zone	South Zone	Local entrepreneur	T.E.	Overall model
H 1: prior industry experience							
H 2: prior start-up experience			A (–)				
H 3: age of the founder						A (+)	
H 4: education of the founder							
H 5: sales capabilities of the start-up	A (–)			A (–)		A (–)	A (–)
H 6: R&D capabilities of the start-up	A (+)			A (+)	A (+)	A (–)	A (+)
H 7: financial capabilities of the start-up							
H 8: SDP growth				A (+)		A (+)	A (+)
H 9: number of VC funded deals			A (+)	A (–)	A (+)		A (+)
H 10: number of VCs in the region			A (–)	A (+)			

SOURCE: Author.

NOTE: All the empty cells in the table indicate the rejection of the hypotheses.

accepted and rejected across the seven regression models. An entry 'A' in the table indicates acceptance of the hypothesis. The sign in the brackets indicates the direction of the influence of the variable. A '+' sign indicates positive influence, whereas a '–' sign indicates negative influence. The detailed results of each of the regression models are presented in the chapter-end Appendix as Tables 5A.1–5A.7.

Results Based on Target Market Segment

The results of the survival analysis model for start-ups targeting the B2B market segment indicate that *R&D capabilities of the start-up* and *the sales capabilities of the start-up* are the principal influencers on start-ups achieving survival in the B2B sector. Further, apart from these factors, the probability of survival will decrease if these start-ups are located in South Zone. From the results, we can infer that start-ups that have a demonstrable product offering are more likely to survive, whereas start-ups that do not have any revenue generated, although they may possess sales capabilities, have a decreasing likelihood of survival.

In a similar fashion, the results of the survival analysis model that are obtained with the data of start-ups, operating in the B2C market segment, indicate that none of the factors can explain the phenomenon under study. Hence, we do not further analyse the results obtained for this model.

In the B2B sector, we observe that *R&D capabilities of the start-up* contribute to enhancing survival probability of the start-ups. This result can be explained as follows. In the high-tech sector, most entrepreneurs themselves are technically educated, and, therefore, their start-ups will inherently have good R&D capabilities. After formal incorporation when the entrepreneurs start their sales based on the initial prototypes of their products or offerings, they will receive initial feedback from the market about their offerings. This feedback can be broadly classified under two categories.

The first category of the feedback is to deal with feedback coming in the form of rapid acceptance of the product. This will mean that the start-up will now brace itself to scale up by providing the product or service to a larger customer base while maintaining the highest levels of quality. Only if the start-up possesses good R&D capabilities will the firm be able to service such requests. If they do, then these acts will ensure survival of the start-up. The second category of feedback is to deal with cases where the initial features of the offering do not create the expected market demand.

In this case, there will be feedback from the market regarding the product or offering on various aspects, such as the overall value delivered by the offering in solving the customer pain points or requests to enhance the ease of usage of the offering and so on. All the initial customer feedback received by the start-up need to be immediately addressed so that the customers who are not completely convinced can be won over. To be able to quickly respond to such changes, a start-up needs to possess strong R&D capabilities. Without these capabilities, a start-up cannot manage to turn around the feedback from initial prospective into a profitable, recurring revenue stream. Hence, in both cases, the need for a start-up to possess strong R&D capabilities in order to ensure its survival is of paramount importance.

The aspect of lack of revenue from sales activities negatively impacting the likelihood of survival can be explained as follows. Literature, discussing the survival of start-ups, has always noted that any new incumbent start-up needs to deal with the liability of newness across its functional divisions. For example, when it comes to selling a new and unique product offering, the customers would need to be made aware of the value that this new product offering would provide. Further, investments in marketing would need to be made to make sceptic customers aware of the benefits of using the start-up's new offering. All these aspects around sales of the start-up are nothing but dealing with the liability of newness. Further, the outcomes of all these sales activities would be uncertain since there is no precedence of how customers would respond to an awareness building campaign, or how customers would want to try or use the new product offering.

Shepherd and Shanley (1998) explained that when customer knowledge is incomplete on the new product or offering, then market novelty is present and this market novelty can have significant negative impact on the chances of survival of the start-up. They further explained their insight by noting that new product releases from existing companies or even corporate ventures can be viewed as more familiar (less novel) to the market than a new venture, in which the customers are completely ignorant about the organization, launching itself into the market. These aspects explain the influence of sales capabilities on the survival of high-tech start-ups.

Results Based on Location of Operations

The results of the two survival analysis models that analysed the survival impact of factors on start-up samples located in the two Zones of the country are presented in this section. The results of the survival analysis model for start-ups targeting the North Zone indicate that the *prior start-up experience of the founder* and environmental factors, namely, *the number of deals and presence of VCs in the region*, are the principal influencers on start-ups achieving survival in the North Zone. From the results, we can infer that start-ups that have a founder with no start-up experience, a positive year-on-year growth in the number of VC deals, and a decrease in the number of active VCs are factors that increase the likelihood of survival.

The results of the analysis of the model executed on start-up data from the South Zone indicate that *R&D capabilities of the start-up*, *the sales capabilities of the start-up*, and all the three external environmental variables, namely, *SDP growth, number of VC deals*, and *number of VCs present in the region*, are the principal influencers on start-ups' achieving survival in the South Zone. Further, apart from these factors, the probability of survival will increase if these South Zone start-ups focus on the B2C sector. From the results, we can infer that start-ups that have a demonstrable product offering are more likely to survive, whereas start-ups that do not have any revenue generated, although they may possess sales capabilities, have a decreasing likelihood of survival. Further, a positive SDP growth and an increased number of VCs in the region will increase the likelihood of survival of this set of start-ups, whereas an increase in the number of VC deals would affect the chances of start-up survival negatively.

The results of analysis of the two survival analysis models evaluated based on the location of their operations reveal that the external environmental variables included in the study (number of VCs present in the region and the number of funded deals in the region) are the common sets of key influencers of start-up survival.

South Zone region of the country, comprising Karnataka, Tamil Nadu, Andhra Pradesh, Telangana, and Kerala, has three key most vibrant and fastest growing hubs of Bengaluru, Hyderabad, and Chennai. Further, these are relatively well connected with each other (NASSCOM 2014). Given the relatively high start-up activity in the South Zone, and availability of addressable local market, we can interpret that VC firms have set up offices in this Zone to scout for potential investment opportunities. In the North Zone, the situation would be the converse. Given the relative gaps in the ecosystem, fewer start-ups are being funded in the North Zone by these external investors, and the ticket size of these deals have been fairly small till about 2014. Therefore, a steady increase in the funded deals implies better chances of survival of start-ups, based in North Zone.

For the start-ups, operating in South Zone, the R&D capabilities of the start-up is another key factor that can significantly impact the chances of survival of a start-up. This is because, from a technological point of view, during the initial days of operation, only an initial prototype or, at best, the first working version of the offering would be made available by the R&D team of a start-up – to go and seek customer feedback. Based on the feedback, the R&D team would need to be able to quickly respond and make changes to the existing offering or in some cases start afresh since there is no customer interest in the earlier prototype. In all these cases, the R&D team would need to be able to learn and unlearn new technology at a rapid pace and be able to help out the rest of the start-up team by responding to the changes as sought by the product development team. To be able to do so, there is a need to build and possess a strong and skilled R&D team. This capability of the start-up will either enable survival or ensure failure of the start-up, based on how it responds to the market needs.

Shepherd, Douglas, and Shanley (2000) explored the liability of newness contributed by the firm's R&D capabilities and further explained how this can impact start-up survival. They coined a construct named 'novelty to production' that explained *the extent to which the production technology used by the new venture was similar to the technologies in which the production team had experience and knowledge.* They noted that the difficulty of manufacturing the new venture's product, relative to the knowledge and experience of the production team, is a major indicator of the novelty in production. For example, a new venture assembles a new production team – people that have not worked with each other before. There are likely to be some conflicts regarding new organizational roles and the absence of an informal organizational structure. Furthermore, the new venture's production team might be operating with new production technology (or maybe just the newer version of a manufacturing machinery that they had used in the past) which introduces costs associated with learning new tasks. These issues contribute to the liability of newness.

While the R&D capabilities of the start-up helps ensure that there is a good supply of resources to innovate, the SDP growth represents the demand side of the equation – ensuring that there is an addressable market for the start-up to sell to and ensure its sustenance. The macroeconomic environment of any region plays a significant role in affecting the survival rate or failure rate of high-tech start-ups in that region. No start-up can survive if there is no presence of early adopters who are willing to try new and innovative offerings and pay for the same as well. The South Zone region consists of states that have been consistently clocking positive year-on-year SDP growth – signalling an increasing consumer demand in the region. This is the reason why start-ups focusing on the B2C markets in the South Zone will have an increased likelihood of survival.

Results Based on Entrepreneurial Exposure

We now present the results of analysis pertaining to the survival of start-ups based on the two data sets that consist of local and transnational entrepreneurs, respectively. From the results of execution of the most optimal model for local entrepreneurs, we observe that *R&D capabilities of the start-ups* and the *number of funded deals* in the region are significant factors in positively influencing start-ups founded by local entrepreneurs to achieve the survival milestone.

The analyses of the previous set of results have dwelled upon the importance of having a demonstrable product/service offering in order to increase the chances of survival. The increase in funded deals can be viewed as a signal from the external ecosystem for the availability of capital and the willingness of external financiers to invest in practical ideas that would scale. The increasing rate of deals also signals a healthy and vibrant consumer demand.

From the summary of results of execution of the optimal model, examining the factors influencing the survival of start-ups founded by transnational entrepreneurs, we observe that the *age of the entrepreneurs*, the *sales, R&D capabilities of the start-up* that they founded, and the *rate of the SDP growth in the region* come out as the key-influencing factors that determine survival of start-ups founded by transnational entrepreneurs. Further, we can infer that absence of revenue generated by the start-ups (although they may have sales personnel) or absence of a demonstrable product offering (although the start-ups may have technical personnel) decrease the likelihood of survival of the start-ups established by transnational entrepreneurs. Also, we can infer that higher the age of the transnational entrepreneur, the likelihood of survival of start-ups increases. Similarly, a positive year-on-year SDP growth and presence of start-up in North Zone increase the likelihood of survival of the start-ups set up by transnational entrepreneurs.

The entrepreneur-specific factor of age of the entrepreneur being influential in ensuring survival of start-ups can be explained as follows. In emerging markets, the degree of uncertainty that an entrepreneur needs to deal with while navigating the operational and functional aspects of the start-up in the early days is certainly a few notches higher than those in developed economies. Despite the entrepreneur possessing the necessary and sufficient capabilities, skills and knowledge to pursue an entrepreneurial idea, various other factors contribute to increase the inherent uncertainty of outcome in India. Key among them are market- and firm-based challenges. To be able to deal with such unique challenges, the entrepreneur needs to have an increased amount of entrepreneurial judgement, which would accrue on account of spending more number of years in the market that he wishes to sell to. As the age of the entrepreneur increases, he/she will have accumulated more means and resources as well as tacit knowledge of learning to deal with uncertainty by way of pursuing various activities since his/her early days. This capability will help him/her navigate the uncertainty and liability of newness of challenges in the initial days of operation of the start-up.

These results indicate the need for start-ups to acquire key resources in the sales and R&D functions in order to increase the likelihood of survival. As discussed in the previous section of this chapter, the start-ups need to deal with uncertainty and an increased liability of newness. The liability of newness induced by an unknown market and sceptical customers need to be mitigated by hiring an experienced sales force who can deal with these challenges of uncertainty related to the markets. Shepherd, Douglas, and Shanley (2000) noted that potential customers are less likely to purchase from a new and novel organization. They observed that a new venture that is less novel to the market is likely to have fewer advertising expenditures and less variance around those expenditures.

In a similar vein, in the current age of rapid technological change, the R&D team that is in place in any start-up would need to develop the abilities to be able to quickly master new technological developments. This team should have the ability to leverage the new technological developments in the product or service offering developed in the start-up. Shepherd, Douglas, and Shanley (2000) indicated that mortality risk for a start-up increases with novelty in production, because novelty will probably require greater expenditures in terms of dollars and time to overcome the costs associated with overcoming conflicts about new organizational roles, the development of informal organizational structures, and learning new tasks.

Further, from these results, we understand that transnational entrepreneurs scan the regions in their country of origin for suitable anchors to locate their new ventures, use signals such as SDP growth to time the creation of new ventures. A healthy year-to-year growth in the SDP of the region is an indication of market demand which will entice the TEs to leverage their experience, resources, and networks to ensure survival of these new ventures.

Results of the Overall Model

We now present the results of the overall model. Apart from the independent variables that are discussed in the preceding sections, this model includes the three dimensions of market segment, location of operations, and entrepreneurial exposure as control variables. We perform further checks on the data to ensure that the analysis is more robust. A visual inspection of Q-Q plots for continuous covariates of the model is carried out. The Q-Q plot for one of the covariates, the age of the entrepreneur, is presented in Figure 5.7. Based on these checks, we thus arrive at the optimal model to be used for our analysis.

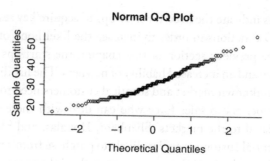

FIGURE 5.7 Q-Q plot for the age of the entrepreneur

SOURCE: Author.

The test results of our analysis using the overall optimized model is presented in Table 5A.7. The test results indicate that this model fits better than the null model which indicates that the results from this model could be used for the analysis.

The results from the overall model indicate that among the entrepreneur related factors, none of the factors has an influence on increasing the likelihood of survival of high-tech start-ups. Among the firm-specific factors, *sales* and *R&D capabilities* of the start-ups have shown to be of paramount importance in influencing the probability of survival of high-tech start-ups. Further, among the external environment-specific attributes, the *SDP growth* in the region is shown to have significant influence on the survival of high-tech start-ups (borderline significant). From Table 5A.7, we can infer that start-ups that have a demonstrable product offering are more likely to survive, whereas start-ups that do not have any revenue generated, although they may possess sales capabilities, have a decreasing likelihood of survival. Further, an increase in the SDP growth rate year on year in the region will increase the likelihood of survival of start-ups.

The other notable aspects coming out of these results are that the entrepreneur-specific factors, such as *prior start-up experience, prior industry experience,* or *education,* do not come out as significant influencers in ensuring survival of high-tech start-ups. Further, among the firm-specific factors, the *funding* or capitalization of the start-up does not come out as significant in ensuring survival of the high-tech start-ups. Finally, among the external environmental variables, the *number of deals* or the *number of VCs in the region* does not seem to matter in influencing survival of high-tech start-ups.

These results have important implications in the context of the life cycle studies of high-tech start-ups, and they need to be explained further. From a firm-specific resources' perspective, we have deliberated in the earlier sections of this chapter, it is of a paramount importance to have a demonstrable product offering very early in the life cycle, using which feedback could be obtained on aspects that need to be addressed before getting to product-market fit. Further, the aspect of lack of revenue early on for the start-up affecting its chances of survival have also been deliberated in the prior sections. The external environmental factors, namely, the SDP growth (borderline significant, from the results indicated in Table 5A.7), indicate the need for a healthy macroeconomic and high-tech start-up-friendly ecosystem in the region, which in turn would result in enabling a higher survival rate of start-ups in the region.

From these results, we also need to understand and interpret the factors which usually are attributed to influence survival – but have not come out as significant in ensuring start-up survival. Notable among them are the entrepreneur-specific factors, such as prior industry experience, prior start-up experience, and the educational credentials of the entrepreneur. Prior industry experience of the entrepreneur did not matter as much as prior start-up experience of the founder when the results related to emergence of the high-tech start-ups are analysed. However, when we analyse the results of start-up survival, we find that both these prior experiences, be it industry experience or start-up experience, do not seem to matter. Interestingly enough, educational pedigree of the entrepreneur did not turn out to be significant in influencing the emergence, not does it seem to influence the survival. Since a direct interpretation of this result would imply inferences contrary to existing literature, there is a need to elaborate on the analysis of these results a bit further.

As regards to education, not appearing significant in any of the models, it has to be noted that all entrepreneurs in this study had the basic level of education or a degree. In the context of our study, all of these individuals would already have had the necessary and sufficient basic skills to pursue an entrepreneurial opportunity. Further, the technological maturity occurred only a couple of decades back, and clearly, the current generation of entrepreneurs can be expected to be more responsive and dynamic in responding to an entrepreneurial opportunity. Hence, these results indicate that given the minimum education, these individuals are more likely to exploit entrepreneurial opportunities.

The prior start-up experience or prior industry experience of the entrepreneur has not come out as a significant influence on the survival of high-tech start-ups. To interpret this result, we need to understand that entrepreneurial activities post start-up emergence are inherently unrepeatable. In fact, it is very difficult to even arrive at a common pattern or common set of task buckets for the activities that entrepreneurs pursue during the initial days of operations. This is fundamentally on account of the pure uncertainty of outcomes that cannot be predicted up front, for the lack of prior evidence of similar product offering being available, or a comparable sales plan being executed in the past. Prior research noted that for tasks that are well defined, repeated often, and for which feedback is provided in a timely and correct manner, entrepreneurial judgement can be improved (Hayward, Shepherd, and Griffin 2006; Wright 2001). In these conditions of pure uncertainty, where the range of activities and the uncertainty in pursuing every new entrepreneurial activity do not lend itself to repeatability, the aspects of prior start-up experience or prior industry experience may be of little help.

From a firm-specific resources' perspective, the aspect of funding or capitalization of the start-up does not come out as a significant factor that influences start-up survival. This result also might be viewed contrary to existing findings if taken at face value. This result can be explained as follows. Viewed in isolation, funding or capital infusion to a firm at any time of its life cycle is considered a necessary factor input. In the case of high-tech start-ups, particularly in the IT sector, the nature of the industry structure is such that the costs of entry for a new venture is very minimal, since there is no need to invest in any physical assets that invite capital expenditure. The only investment comes by way of intellectual and technical capital – which all of the founders of this sample possess – by way of educational pedigree.

Entrepreneurs looking to achieve the survival milestone post formal incorporation usually have to deal with one of the following circumstances. The first one is the initial prototype or offering that they developed does not generate sufficient market traction or demand. This means either the founder does not possess the technical competence or the right R&D skills required to innovate in the area of the offering or does not have the capabilities to articulate the value of the product to the initial sceptic customers. In this case, entrepreneurs usually choose to exit from the current entrepreneurial idea. The second circumstance is the case of rapid acceptance of the initial product offering or good sales in the initial days of the start-up operations. This means that the start-up is close to achieve product-market fit. Usually, start-ups which can demonstrate initial adoption of their product offering can easily avail external funding, particularly when they are located in an ecosystem that is conducive to such activities. Therefore, we can infer that in both of these cases, the ability of the start-up to have good sales and R&D capabilities influence survival, and not just the possession of financial capabilities. In support of this argument, Lloyd-Ellis and Bernhardt (2000) found that entrepreneurs complain frequently about lack of access to finance to often mask their technical and managerial inadequacies. Estrin, Meyer, and Bytchkova (2006) observed that financial constraints are not binding on start-ups and see it to be more important in the expansion of existing businesses rather than in the creation or in ensuring survival of new firms.

Summary

In this chapter, we have provided an insight into the factors that influence and impact the survival of high-tech start-ups in India. Based on prior literature review, we developed hypotheses around the entrepreneurial, firm-specific, and external environment related attributes that impact and influence the survival of high-tech start-ups. We analysed these hypotheses based on the three segments of target market segment (B2B versus B2C), location of operations (North Zone versus South Zone), and entrepreneurial exposure (local versus transnational) culminating with presentation of results of the overall model.

Survival analysis models are built to analyse the entrepreneurial, firm-specific, and external environment-specific factors across all the aforementioned segments. For each of the data set thus created, an initial visual descriptive analysis is performed to obtain the context and nature of relationships between the variables involved in the study.

Appendix: Results of Logistic Regression Models

This section contains the results of the statistical analysis performed on the data for all the seven models. To begin with, Tables 5.3 and 5.4 present the results of the tests carried out for the B2B and B2C sectors. Then, Tables 5.5 and 5.6 provide the results of the tests carried out with the location of operations (north and south India) as the variable differentiator. Last, Tables 5.7 and 5.8 provide the results of tests that were carried out with data groups based on entrepreneurial exposure. Table 5A.7 provides results for the overall model, including the control variables.

TABLE 5A.1 Results of the model of start-ups focusing on the B2B sector

Model variables	Beta coefficient (β)	Standard error	Wald statistic	Degree of freedom	Significance (p-value)	Exp. (β)
Prior industry experience of the entrepreneur (*fiexp* = 1)	1.292	0.856	2.280	1	0.131	3.641
Prior start-up experience of the entrepreneur (*fsexp* = 1)	−0.615	0.390	2.483	1	0.115	0.541
Age of the entrepreneur (*fage*)	0.006	0.027	0.049	1	0.825	1.006
Education of the entrepreneur – base reference variable (*fedn*)			0.230	2	0.891	
Education of the entrepreneur – first dummy (*fedn1*)	0.120	0.614	0.038	1	0.845	1.128
Education of the entrepreneur – second dummy (*fedn2*)	0.230	0.532	0.187	1	0.665	1.259
Sales capabilities – base reference variable (*csales*)			6.004	2	**0.050**	
Sales capabilities – first dummy (*csales1*)	−1.830	0.758	5.828	1	**0.016**	0.160
Sales capabilities – second dummy (*csales2*)	−0.674	0.459	2.163	1	0.141	0.509
R&D capabilities – base reference variable (*cdev*)			13.204	2	**0.001**	
R&D capabilities – first dummy (*cdev1*)	−0.192	0.617	0.097	1	0.756	0.825
R&D capabilities – second dummy (*cdev2*)	1.769	0.622	8.095	1	**0.004**	5.865
Funding status of the start-up (*fin* = 1)	0.078	0.382	0.041	1	0.839	1.081
SDP growth (*sdp*)	5.896	3.642	2.620	1	0.106	363.518
Number of deals (*deals*)	−0.005	0.012	0.162	1	0.688	0.995
Number of VCs (*vc*)	0.012	0.012	1.111	1	0.292	1.013
Operations in south India (*Zone* = 1)	−1.123	0.529	4.508	1	**0.034**	0.325
Transnational entrepreneur (*te* = 1)	−0.134	0.365	0.134	1	0.714	0.875

Model statistics: Number of Observations = 89

Goodness of fit: Chisq = 32.510 on 15 degrees of freedom, p-value = 0.005

Source: Author.

TABLE 5A.2 Results of the model of start-ups focusing on the B2C sector

Model variables	Beta coefficient (β)	Standard error	Wald statistic	Degree of freedom	Significance (p-value)	Exp. (β)
Prior industry experience of the entrepreneur (*fiexp* = 1)	−1.209	0.883	1.875	1	0.171	0.298
Prior start-up experience of the entrepreneur (*fsexp* = 1)	−0.268	0.842	0.101	1	0.751	0.765
Age of the entrepreneur (*fage*)	0.052	0.037	1.968	1	0.161	1.054
Education of the entrepreneur – base reference variable (*fedn*)			1.799	2	0.407	
Education of the entrepreneur – first dummy (*fedn1*)	−0.435	0.926	0.221	1	0.639	0.647
Education of the entrepreneur – second dummy (*fedn2*)	−0.873	0.802	1.186	1	0.276	0.418
Sales capabilities – base reference variable (*csales*)			0.256	2	0.880	
Sales capabilities – first dummy (*csales1*)	−12.237	90.916	0.018	1	0.893	0.000
Sales capabilities – second dummy (*csales2*)	0.229	0.468	0.238	1	0.626	1.257
R&D capabilities – base reference variable (*cdev*)			2.332	2	0.312	
R&D capabilities – first dummy (*cdev1*)	0.871	0.831	1.098	1	0.295	2.388
R&D capabilities – second dummy (*cdev2*)	0.862	0.588	2.149	1	0.143	2.369
Funding status of the start-up (*fin* = 1)	0.136	0.405	0.113	1	0.737	1.146
SDP growth (*sdp*)	5.133	5.029	1.042	1	0.307	169.545
Number of deals (*deals*)	0.022	0.016	1.855	1	0.173	1.022
Number of VCs (*vc*)	−0.009	0.013	0.557	1	0.456	0.991
Operations in south India (*Zone* = 1)	0.291	0.624	0.217	1	0.641	1.338
Transnational entrepreneur (*te* = 1)	0.633	0.528	1.436	1	0.231	1.883

Model statistics: Number of observations = 86

Goodness of fit: Chisq = 47.881 on 15 degrees of freedom, p-value = 0.000

Source: Author.

TABLE 5A.3 Results of the model of start-ups located in the North Zone

Model variables	Beta coefficient (β)	Standard error	Wald statistic	Degree of freedom	Significance (p-value)	Exp. (β)
Prior industry experience of the entrepreneur (fiexp = 1)	-0.616	1.011	0.371	1	0.542	0.540
Prior start-up experience of the entrepreneur (fsexp = 1)	-1.278	0.663	3.724	1	**0.054**	0.278
Age of the entrepreneur (fage)	0.023	0.038	0.381	1	0.537	1.023
Education of the entrepreneur – base reference variable (fedn)			0.384	2	0.825	
Education of the entrepreneur – first dummy (fedn1)	-0.439	0.955	0.211	1	0.646	0.645
Education of the entrepreneur – second dummy (fedn2)	-0.572	0.926	0.382	1	0.537	0.564
Sales capabilities – base reference variable (csales)			2.110	2	0.348	
Sales capabilities – first dummy (csales1)	-12.291	133.540	0.008	1	0.927	0.000
Sales capabilities – second dummy (csales2)	0.773	0.533	2.102	1	0.147	2.165
R&D capabilities – base reference variable (cdev)			2.689	2	0.261	
R&D capabilities – first dummy (cdev1)	-0.278	0.957	0.084	1	0.772	0.758
R&D capabilities – second dummy (cdev2)	0.786	0.706	1.239	1	0.266	2.195
Funding status of the start-up (fin = 1)	0.193	0.515	0.141	1	0.707	1.213
SDP growth (sdp)	7.271	15.789	0.212	1	0.645	1437.287
Number of deals (deals)	0.040	0.024	2.825	1	**0.093**	1.041
Number of VCs (vc)	-0.025	0.015	2.902	1	**0.088**	0.975
Target market segment (Market_Segment = 1)	0.104	0.559	0.035	1	0.852	1.110
Transnational entrepreneur (te = 1)	0.662	0.544	1.480	1	0.224	1.939

Model statistics: Number of observations = 70

Goodness of fit: Chisq = 35.101 on 15 degrees of freedom, p-value = 0.002

SOURCE: Author.

TABLE 5A.4 Results of the model of start-ups located in the South Zone

Model variables	Beta coefficient (β)	Standard error	Wald statistic	Degree of freedom	Significance (p-value)	Exp. (β)
Prior industry experience of the entrepreneur (fiexp = 1)	−0.385	0.687	0.313	1	0.576	0.681
Prior start-up experience of the entrepreneur (fsexp = 1)	−0.088	0.387	0.052	1	0.819	0.915
Age of the entrepreneur (fage)	−0.019	0.026	0.569	1	0.451	0.981
Education of the entrepreneur – base reference variable (fedn)			0.294	2	0.863	
Education of the entrepreneur – first dummy (fedn1)	0.005	0.635	0.000	1	0.994	1.005
Education of the entrepreneur – second dummy (fedn2)	0.173	0.516	0.113	1	0.737	1.189
Sales capabilities – base reference variable (csales)			11.392	2	**0.003**	
Sales capabilities – first dummy (csales1)	−2.150	0.643	11.183	1	**0.001**	0.116
Sales capabilities – second dummy (csales2)	−0.257	0.364	0.499	1	0.480	0.773
R&D capabilities – base reference variable (cdev)			6.522	2	**0.038**	
R&D capabilities – first dummy (cdev1)	0.092	0.567	0.026	1	0.871	1.096
R&D capabilities – second dummy (cdev2)	1.276	0.541	5.570	1	**0.018**	3.581
Funding status of the start-up (fin = 1)	−0.013	0.316	0.002	1	0.967	0.987
SDP growth (sdp)	5.048	2.875	3.084	1	0.079	155.688
Number of deals (deals)	−0.049	0.020	6.106	1	**0.013**	0.952
Number of VCs (vc)	0.087	0.028	9.360	1	**0.002**	1.091
Target market segment (market_segment = 1)	0.931	0.384	5.893	1	**0.015**	2.538
Transnational entrepreneur (te = 1)	−0.149	0.339	0.194	1	0.659	0.861

Model statistics: Number of observations = 105

Goodness of fit: Chisq = 41.065 on 15 degrees of freedom, p-value = 0.000

SOURCE: Author.

TABLE 5A.5 Results of the model of start-ups of local entrepreneurs

Model variables	Beta coefficient (β)	Standard error	Wald statistic	Degree of freedom	Significance (p-value)	Exp. (β)
Prior industry experience of the entrepreneur (fiexp = 1)	−0.071	0.651	0.012	1	0.913	0.931
Prior start-up experience of the entrepreneur (fsexp = 1)	−0.729	0.486	2.249	1	0.134	0.482
Age of the entrepreneur (fage)	−0.006	0.033	0.039	1	0.843	0.994
Education of the entrepreneur – base reference variable (fedn)			1.678	2	0.432	
Education of the entrepreneur – first dummy (fedn1)	0.166	0.983	0.028	1	0.866	1.180
Education of the entrepreneur – second dummy (fedn2)	0.641	0.925	0.480	1	0.489	1.898
Sales capabilities – base reference variable (csales)			0.028	2	0.986	
Sales capabilities – first dummy (csales1)	−12.132	114.185	0.011	1	0.915	0.000
Sales capabilities – second dummy (csales2)	0.055	0.416	0.017	1	0.896	1.056
R&D capabilities – base reference variable (cdev)			4.068	2	0.131	
R&D capabilities – first dummy (cdev1)	1.099	0.697	2.483	1	0.115	3.001
R&D capabilities – second dummy (cdev2)	1.342	0.684	3.852	1	**0.050**	3.828
Funding status of the start-up (fin = 1)	0.222	0.462	0.231	1	0.631	1.249
SDP growth (sdp)	−5.305	4.911	1.167	1	0.280	0.005
Number of deals (deals)	0.037	0.015	6.273	1	**0.012**	1.038
Number of VCs (vc)	−0.002	0.011	0.031	1	0.860	0.998
Target market segment (market_segment = 1)	−0.307	0.488	0.395	1	0.529	0.736
Operations in south India (zone = 1)	0.839	0.619	1.838	1	0.175	2.315

Model statistics: Number of observations = 85

Goodness of fit: Chisq = 45.975 on 15 degrees of freedom, p-value = 0.000

SOURCE: Author.

TABLE 5A.6 Results of the model of start-ups of transnational entrepreneurs

Model variables	Beta coefficient (β)	Standard error	Wald statistic	Degree of freedom	Significance (p-value)	Exp. (β)
Prior industry experience of the entrepreneur (fiexp = 1)	−12.943	567.243	0.001	1	0.982	0.000
Prior start-up experience of the entrepreneur (fsexp = 1)	−0.300	0.405	0.549	1	0.459	0.741
Age of the entrepreneur (fage)	0.062	0.032	3.770	1	**0.052**	1.064
Education of the entrepreneur – base reference variable (fedn)			1.599	2	0.450	
Education of the entrepreneur – first dummy (fedn1)	0.192	0.639	0.091	1	0.763	1.212
Education of the entrepreneur – second dummy (fedn2)	−0.369	0.507	0.531	1	0.466	0.691
Sales capabilities – base reference variable (csales)			12.387	2	**0.002**	0.219
Sales capabilities – first dummy (csales1)	−1.517	0.702	4.676	1	**0.031**	0.219
Sales capabilities – second dummy (csales2)	0.740	0.509	2.112	1	0.146	2.095
R&D capabilities – base reference variable (cdev)			8.195	2	**0.017**	
R&D capabilities – first dummy (cdev1)	−1.502	0.779	3.721	1	**0.054**	0.223
R&D capabilities – second dummy (cdev2)	0.639	0.532	1.444	1	0.230	1.894
Funding status of the start-up (fin = 1)	0.271	0.397	0.468	1	0.494	1.312
SDP growth (sdp)	10.992	3.882	8.017	1	**0.005**	59413.680
Number of deals (deals)	−0.018	0.013	1.837	1	0.175	0.983
Number of VCs (vc)	0.006	0.012	0.230	1	0.631	1.006
Target market segment (market_segment = 1)	0.527	0.413	1.627	1	0.202	1.693
Operations in south India (zone = 1)	−0.981	0.517	3.598	1	**0.058**	0.375

Model statistics: Number of observations = 90

Goodness of fit: Chisq = 39.643 on 15 degrees of freedom, p-value = 0.001

Source: Author.

TABLE 5A.7 Results of analysis of the overall optimized model

Model variables	Beta coefficient (β)	Standard error	Wald statistic	Degree of freedom	Significance (p-value)	Exp. (β)
Prior industry experience of the entrepreneur (fiexp = 1)	−0.320	0.526	0.371	1	0.543	0.726
Prior start-up experience of the entrepreneur (fsexp = 1)	−0.282	0.291	0.942	1	0.332	0.754
Age of the entrepreneur (fage)	0.020	0.018	1.210	1	0.271	1.020
Education of the entrepreneur – base reference variable (fedn)			0.121	2	0.941	
Education of the entrepreneur – first dummy (fedn1)	−0.106	0.481	0.049	1	0.825	0.899
Education of the entrepreneur – second dummy (fedn2)	−0.005	0.401	0.000	1	0.990	0.995
Sales capabilities – base reference variable (csales)			14.271	2	0.001	
Sales capabilities – first dummy (csales1)	−1.985	0.571	12.067	1	0.001	0.137
Sales capabilities – second dummy (csales2)	0.089	0.279	0.102	1	0.749	1.093
R&D capabilities – base reference variable (cdev)			10.631	2	0.005	
R&D capabilities – first dummy (cdev1)	−0.192	0.440	0.190	1	0.663	0.825
R&D capabilities – second dummy (cdev2)	0.951	0.364	6.845	1	0.009	2.589
Funding status of the start-up (fin = 1)	0.010	0.258	0.001	1	0.970	1.010
SDP growth (sdp)	4.227	2.577	2.689	1	0.101	68.484
Number of deals (deals)	0.005	0.009	0.363	1	0.547	1.006
Number of VCs (vc)	0.001	0.008	0.006	1	0.940	1.001
Target market segment (Market_Segment = 1)	0.128	0.275	0.216	1	0.642	1.136
Operations in south India (Zone = 1)	−0.326	0.342	0.909	1	0.340	0.722
Transnational entrepreneur (te = 1)	0.310	0.257	1.455	1	0.228	1.364

Model statistics: Number of observations =175

Goodness of fit: Chisq = 49.609 on 16 degrees of freedom, p-value = 0.000

SOURCE: Author.

6

Growth of High-tech Start-ups

Introduction

In this chapter, we discuss in detail the factors that influence the growth of high-tech start-ups in India. We will be specifically examining the growth of the start-ups based on three vital aspects, namely, the entrepreneur-specific factors that contribute to the growth of high-tech start-ups, the firm-specific factors that impact the growth of high-tech start-ups, and last, the external environment-specific factors that influence the growth of high-tech start-ups. We study the factors impacting growth of start-ups by grouping our sample of start-ups into two distinct categories – *start-ups that have survived but not yet growing* and *start-ups that are growing*. We then perform logistic regression analysis to understand the key factors that are responsible for growth of the high-tech start-ups in the sample.

Growth of firms has been researched extensively in the past, and even as high-tech firms emerged in the 1980s and onwards, there has been analysis of factors that influence and impact growth of these categories of firms as well. The initial key contributions to examination of firm growth can be traced back to Penrose (1959) and Stinchcombe (1965). They provided the perspective that a firm's growth pattern is dependent on its age, size, and industry affiliation. However, these were theoretical contributions only. A few decades later, scholars such as Collins and Porras (1994), Gundry and Welsch (2001), and Kirchhoff (1994) tried to provide empirical evidence to the aforementioned theoretical work but ended with different results and interpretations of growth of firms and the factors influencing the same.

Delmar, Davidsson, and Gartner (2003) observed that this substantial heterogeneity in the results was due to usage of different growth measures in their corresponding studies, and hence these results cumulatively could not help us comprehensively understand the phenomenon of growth in firms' life cycle. After evaluating multiple firm growth measures prior to their work, they concluded that there was no single best way to measure firm growth, and that all high-growth firms do not grow in the same way. Hence, they suggested that researchers use the appropriate measure of growth that suited their approach of study, and also mentioned that the findings of such work to be restricted to enhancing knowledge, related to the theoretical stream of organizational growth.

Some studies measured growth as 'absolute growth of sales' over a period of five years (Dunne and Hughes 1994), whereas other studies used 'relative employment growth over a period of three years to measure the growth (Cooper, Gimeno-Gascon, and Woo 1994; Zahra 1993). The results from these studies could not be compared because the former relied on absolute measures, whereas the latter relied on relative measures.

Further, based on a detailed literature review, Ardishvili et al. (1998) and Davidsson and Delmar (1997) arrived at almost identical lists of possible growth indicators: assets, employment, market share, physical output, profits, and sales. However, Delmar, Davidsson, and Gartner (2003) observed that if only one metric to measure growth was to be chosen then it had to be the sales. Although they recommended usage of sales of the firm as a measure of firm growth, Delmar, Davidsson, and Gartner (2003) indicated that sales is not the perfect indicator of growth for all purposes. They noted that sales are sensitive to inflation and currency exchange rates, while employment is not. For high-tech start-ups and the start-up of new activities in established firms, it is possible that assets and employment will grow before any sales will occur. Based on all these aspects, they stated that it is not always true that sales leads the growth process.

Many other studies have evaluated employment as an alternative metric to measure firm growth and have commented that employment may be a preferable measure if the focus of interest is on the managerial implications of growth (Churchill and Lewis 1983; Greiner 1972). The same line of reasoning about the value of employment-based measures of growth applies for resource- and knowledge-based views of the firm (Penrose 1959; Kogut and Zander 1992). If firms are viewed as bundles of resources, a growth analysis ought to focus on the accumulation of resources such as employees. Furthermore, when a more macro-oriented interest in job creation is the rationale for the study, measuring growth in employment seems the natural choice (Schreyer 2000). Obvious drawbacks of employment as a growth indicator are that the measure is affected by labour productivity increase, machine-for-man substitution, degree of integration, and other make-or-buy decisions. A firm can grow considerably in output and assets without any growth in employment.

From a start-up life-cycle perspective, both of the discussed measures that are dominantly discussed in earlier literature come out as being useful in cross-sectional or point-in-time analysis of the phenomenon. In our case, while we are interested in exploring the factors of growth of high-tech start-ups in India from a cross-sectional study perspective, we also realize that growth of start-ups post the survival stage follows a very heterogeneous path, based on various factors, such as entrepreneurial, firm-specific, and external environment-specific factors. Further, we would also like to examine if the start-up or the entrepreneur having achieved the product-market fit would like to scale up their start-up and transform it into a larger enterprise or would be content to operate as a sustainable and viable business operation. To address and examine these aspects, we have chosen the measure of valuation of the start-up by an entity, external to the firm, in the year of our study as the proxy to indicate the growth.

Using the valuation status of the start-ups in our study, we categorize them into two distinct groups. The first category of start-ups consists of those start-ups that have no reported external valuation, or have valuation less than ₹5 crore if they are services-based, or less than ₹10 crore if they are a manufacturing-based start-up. These start-ups are classified under the category of start-ups that have achieved product-market fit but have not yet found their growth trajectory. The second category of start-ups consists of start-ups that have received external valuation of more than ₹5 crore if they are services-based or more than ₹10 crore if they are a product-manufacturing start-up. The second category start-ups are classified as growth-oriented start-ups. We postulate that higher valuation of the start-up indicates higher growth and vice versa.

A description on why valuation of a start-up is pursued as an indicator of growth is in order. For all the start-ups that had passed the product-market fit milestone in our sample, we had two impediments that prevented us to use the metrics of either 'absolute growth of sales' or 'relative employment growth' to measure the growth of the start-ups in our sample. The first impediment was that a majority of start-up entrepreneurs in this stage were not willing to share data on the previously stated metrics on a year-to-year basis. This meant that we could not arrive at an aggregated metrics across all the start-ups on account of lack of data. Second, even in the data that some of the entrepreneurs provided, we observed different patterns of year-on-year sales or employment growth. This meant that, even if we were to use the metric for our study, we had to normalize it appropriately, so that it would become relevant to compare this metric across the start-ups.

Given these twin challenges, we tried to explore if we could supplement the lack of data in some cases with credible external sources of data – such as Crunchbase, a website of VCs among others – to see if we could obtain the missing data for the years in question. We were not very successful with this effort. The absence of the sources of credible data on the growth metrics of start-ups in India led us to identify other metrics that can be used for our study. We zeroed in on the valuation of the company by external sources as the next best credible metric that we could use for our study. To ensure that we had parity of this metric across all the start-ups, we examined the valuation obtained by the start-ups during the year of our study, 2015.

Second, we found that this metric was shared voluntarily by most entrepreneurs on their websites and in relevant media interviews, probably for marketing and brand-building purposes, including the ones that have not raised external capital (self-funded entrepreneurs). We collated this data and cross-checked the same with the reports of investments and valuations available from the corresponding VCs and other financial intermediaries. We cross-checked the valuation data against the databases that track investments and valuations of start-ups such as Venture Intelligence and VCCircle databases and ensured the accuracy of the data. Hence, this metric, which was evaluated by a credible external entity, was close enough to serve as a measure of overall growth of the start-up for our study.

Factors Influencing Growth of High-tech Start-ups

The growth phase of a high-tech start-up can be viewed as the stage wherein the firms successfully mitigate the risks and uncertainty involving their creation and survival as well as overcome the challenges of scaling the organization. This milestone in the life cycle of a high-tech start-up is also very relevant for the economy, since only at this milestone, the contributions of the high-tech start-up towards innovation, job growth, and technological change become more pronounced.

Three prominent approaches can be found while examining the literature focused on the growth of high-tech start-ups. The phenomenon has been examined from an industrial economics' perspective, from an organizational ecology's perspective, and last, from an examination of individual factors, influencing the growth of high-tech start-ups. From an industrial economics' perspective, Ericson and Pakes (1995) identified the start-up's ability to innovate, the human capital of the founder(s) and employees, and the location and structure of the industry to be key determinants of growth of high-tech start-ups.

The organizational ecology-based approaches primarily analysed the growth of firms by examining factors such as size and age (Bruederl, Preisendoerfer, and Ziegler 1996; Woywode 1998) of the start-up. In the past two decades, these theories were extended to explain the growth of new technology-based firms. Recent literature augments the dynamic capabilities (Teece, Pisano, and Shuen 2007) and organizational change perspectives to the mentioned approach to provide a comprehensive theory of growth of high-tech start-ups.

Storey (1994) noted that growth determinants of young (innovative) firms can be separated into firm-specific, founder-specific, and external characteristics. Lee, Lee, and Pennings (2001) examined the interplay of internal capabilities and external networks in aiding the growth of high-tech firms. Barringer, Jones, and Neubaum (2005) stated that factors influencing high-growth firms can be categorized into four major areas: founder characteristics, firm attributes, business practices, and human resource management (HRM) practices.

Theories and research on firm size and its relationship to growth have been developed in the economic literature in the context of analyses of firm size distribution (Carroll and Hannan 2000). Most well known is Gibrat's law (1931) which holds that growth is proportional to size and the factor of proportionality is random. Gibrat's law has generated a substantial amount of research. Some studies have indicated that growth rates are independent of size, other studies have indicated that Gibrat's law is applicable only to large organizations (but not to small ones), and some studies have found that growth rates diminish with increasing sizes (Dunne and Hughes 1996; Evans 1987; Storey 1995; Sutton 1997). Even if we cannot still determine the direction in which firm size affects growth, we can conclude that size may have an effect on growth. A firm will expand differently, dependent on its size. A more clear relationship is to be found between firm age and growth, where firm growth rates tend to decline with the age of the firm. This result stands out independent of whether the samples of studied firms come from multiple industries or from a single industry (Sutton 1997).

From these contributions, it is evident that the knowledge on high-tech start-up growth incrementally evolved by examination of multiple dimensions and factors over time. Further, the review of literature on the factors impacting start-up growth revealed that the entrepreneurial factors that influence the phenomenon of start-up growth are age and education of the founder, prior industry experience and prior start-up experience of the founder (Storey 1982; Ronstadt 1988).

Similarly, the firm-specific factors that influence the start-up emergence are the functional resources of the start-up, such as human capital, financial capital, and sales and marketing capabilities (Kim, Aldrich, and Keister 2006; Munshi 2007). The start-up's size since inception (measured in terms of number of customers acquired since inception) have also been shown to impact the growth of high-tech start-ups. To represent the macroeconomic environment as well as supporting the external factors of the start-up ecosystem, three variables, namely, the percentage of SDP growth (year-on-year) of the region, the number of VCs present in the region, and the number of VC-funded deals in the region for a given year have been included for the analysis.

Based on these and the survey of literature, we arrive at the following hypotheses regarding growth of high-tech start-ups.

Hypothesis 1: Prior industry experience of the primary founder positively influences the growth of the start-up.

Hypothesis 2: Prior start-up experience of the primary founder positively influences the growth of the start-up.

Hypothesis 3: Primary founders of higher age are more likely to influence the growth of the start-up than the founders of lesser age.

Hypothesis 4: Higher educational pedigree of the founder positively influences the growth of the start-up.

Hypothesis 5: Higher developmental resources with the firm positively influences the growth of the start-up.

Hypothesis 6: Higher number of customers acquired since inception of the firm positively influences the growth of the start-up.

Hypothesis 7: Higher financial resources at the disposal of the firm positively influences the growth of the start-up.

Hypothesis 8: Higher SDP growth in the region positively influences the growth of the start-up.

Hypothesis 9: Higher presence of VCs in the region influences the higher rate of growth of start-ups in that region.

Hypothesis 10: Higher number of funded VC deals in the region influences the higher rate of growth of start-ups in that region.

The discussed hypotheses will be tested by subjecting the data of high-tech start-ups to logistic regression analysis. The data of the high-tech start-ups would be classified under two categories (growth-based and survived-only) based on the valuation of the start-up. We then proceed to perform logistic regression analysis which will help us statistically identify the key factors that affect the growth of high-tech start-ups in the sample. We will execute six logistic regression models to begin with. Each of the two models will be built to analyse the impact on growth for the dimensions of target market segment (B2B and B2C), location of operations (North Zone and South Zone), and entrepreneurial exposure (local and transnational entrepreneurs). Finally, an overall model will be built and analysed to study the impact of factors affecting growth of high-tech start-ups.

Key Semantics of the Data

For the purposes of analysis of this research objective, the start-ups that have a formal registered office in India are considered for the study. The data includes only those start-ups that have already established product-market fit (moved past the survival state). As discussed earlier, the data for the study of growth of high-tech start-ups have been categorized into two groups – survived-only and growth-based. We find that 38 start-ups qualify for the first category (start-ups that have survived, but not grown) from our data. Similarly, 49 start-ups are qualified for the second category (growth-oriented start-ups) from our data.

Most of the data used in our study is collected using our research instrument – the questionnaire. The unit of analysis in our study has been the start-up, represented by the founder. The firm-specific inputs about the start-up were also obtained from the founder of the start-up. The external environmental variables relevant to the study were sourced from secondary data sources, such as *Economic Survey* reports, Venture Intelligence, and VCCircle databases. Logistic regression is used as the method of analysis of this objective. Chapter 2 provides a more detailed overview of the theory and motivation for the usage of this method. The variables and their measures used in the analysis of this research objective is presented next.

Variables and Measures

Dependent variable

The dependent variable for analysis is a dummy (discrete, dichotomous) variable '*growth category of the start–up*'. This variable takes a value of 1 for every start-up in the sample that falls under the second category of growth start-ups. A value of 0 for this variable indicates that the start-up falls under the first category of survived-only start-ups. This variable is labelled in SPSS as *logitgrowth* for the purposes of analysis.

Independent variables

The relevant industry experience, prior start-up experience, age, and education of the entrepreneur are the entrepreneurial factors that are examined in this study. The number of customers that the start-up has served since its inception, the R&D capabilities, and funding status of the start-up form the organizational factors are examined for impact. Further, the SDP growth rate, number of VCs present in the region, and the number of funded deals in the region are considered as the external environmental factors for examination.

Relevant industry experience: A discrete dichotomous variable which indicates whether or not the founder has previous industry experience. This variable takes the value of 1 for every start-up founder who has industry experience prior to founding the current start-up considered for the study. A value of 0 for this variable indicates that the founder of the start-up does not possess any previous industry experience. This variable is labelled in SPSS as *fiexp* for the analysis.

Prior start-up experience: A discrete dichotomous variable which indicates whether or not the founder has prior start-up experience. This variable takes the value of 1 for every start-up founder who has experience working in a start-up either as an employee or as a founder prior to founding the current start-up considered for the study. A value of 0 for this variable indicates that the founder of the start-up does not possess any previous start-up experience. This variable is labelled in SPSS as *fsexp* for the analysis.

Age of the entrepreneur: It is in years at the time of founding the start-up. This variable is labelled in SPSS as *fage* for the analysis.

Education of the entrepreneur: This is categorized using two dummy variables. The base reference variable indicates graduate education without an engineering degree (degree in science, arts, and others), the first dummy variable indicates graduate education with a technical (engineering) degree, and the second dummy variable indicates education with a technical master's degree or above. This variable is labelled in SPSS as *fedn* for the analysis. The base reference variable takes the value of 1 for every founder of the start-up whose educational credentials are a non-engineering degree. A value of 0 for the base reference variable indicates the absence of a non-engineering degree of the founder. The first dummy variable *fedn(1)* takes the value of 1 for every start-up founder who has a technical (engineering) degree as his/her educational credentials. A value of 0 for this variable indicates the absence of a technical (engineering) degree of the founder. The second dummy variable *fedn(2)* takes the value of 1 for every start-up founder who has educational credentials of a technical (engineering) master's degree or above. A value of 0 for this variable indicates the absence of a technical master's degree or a higher technical qualification (for example, PhD) of the founder.

Sales capabilities of the start-up: This variable is measured by the number of customers acquired since inception, standardized for the number of years in operation and for the target market segment. This variable serves as the proxy or indicator for the sales capabilities of the start-up and is measured as a continuous variable. This variable is labelled in SPSS as *sales* for the analysis.

R&D capabilities of the start-up: This variable is measured as the number of people in the R&D team, standardized for their work experience at the time of observation. This variable is measured as a continuous variable. This variable is labelled in SPSS as *dev* for the analysis.

Financial capability of the start-up: Measured by a dichotomous (dummy) variable which indicates whether or not the start-up obtained external funding at the time of data collection. A value of 0 also indicates that the founding team has managed to run the operations and pursue growth opportunities by reinvesting revenue from the operations without any external investor support. A value of 1 for this variable indicates that the start-up was funded from external investors (seed, angel, VCs). This variable is labelled as *fin* in SPSS for the analysis.

SDP: This variable is used as a proxy for the macroeconomic environment prevalent at the state in which the start-up is located. This variable provides the percentage of change in the SDP in comparison to its previous year (at constant prices). This variable is labelled as *sdp* in SPSS for the analysis.

Number of funded deals: This variable is used to indicate the number of early-stage VC deals that happened for a given year and a given geography. This measure is a proxy to measure the maturity of the start-up ecosystem for the given year and geography. An increase in the number of funded early-stage deals in a given geography, year on year, indicates a healthy and growing start-up ecosystem. This variable is labelled as *deals* in SPSS for the analysis.

Number of VC funds: This variable indicates the presence of active VC funds for a given year and a given geography. This variable is a proxy to measure and understand the availability of external funding options for a particular region and year. This variable is labelled as *vc* in SPSS for the analysis.

Control variables

Target market segment: This variable is a dummy variable with two levels. A value of 0 indicates that the target market segment of the start-up is the B2B sector, whereas the value of 1 indicates that the target market segment of the start-up is the B2C sector. This variable is labelled as *market_segment* in SPSS for the analysis.

Location of operations: This variable is a dummy variable with two levels. A value of 0 indicates that the start-up is located in northern part of the country, whereas the value of 1 indicates that the start-up is located in the southern part of the country. This variable is labelled as *zone* in SPSS for the analysis.

Entrepreneurial background: This variable is a dummy variable with two levels. A value of 0 indicates that the entrepreneur is a local entrepreneur, whereas the value of 1 indicates that the entrepreneur is transnational (indicates that the entrepreneur has exposure to working or studying in more than one country, other than the country of his/her origin, for a period of at least one year). This variable is labelled as *te* in SPSS for the analysis. With this background about the semantics of the data, variables and measures, method of analysis, and modes of data collection, we now proceed to discuss and interpret the results of the third research objective.

Discussion of Results

We present the results of analysis of the key factors that impact the growth of high-tech start-ups. We begin with describing the relationships of the independent variables (entrepreneur-specific, firm-specific, and external environment-specific) with the dependent variable (valuation of the start-up). We then proceed to present the bivariate correlations between the variables considered for the analysis. Finally, we present the results of the logistic regression models that were analysed based on the three segments, namely, (a) target market being addressed by the start-ups (B2B versus B2C), (b) location of operation of the start-ups (North Zone versus South Zone), and (c) exposure of the entrepreneurs (local versus transnational). We end with presentation and interpretation of results of the overall model.

As discussed earlier in this chapter, the relevant industry experience, prior start-up experience, and age and education of the entrepreneur are the entrepreneurial input variables. The number of customers that the start-up has served since its inception, the R&D capabilities, and funding status of the start-up form the firm-specific variables are fed as inputs to the analysis. Further, the SDP growth rate and number of VCs present in the region as well as the number of funded deals in the region are fed in as external environmental input variables for the model.

Initial Analysis of Data

To begin with, Figure 6.1 shows the spread of the start-ups in our sample, based on the two categories created, depending on the valuation of the start-up. We observe that the survived-only category represents 44 per cent of the sample, whereas the growth category represents 56 per cent of the sample. In order to obtain a deeper initial insight into the spread and distribution of the start-ups in our sample, we examined the start-ups data against the three segments, namely, (a) target market being addressed by the start-ups (B2B versus B2C), (b) location of operation of the start-ups (North Zone versus South Zone), and (c) exposure of the entrepreneurs (local versus transnational). Figures 6.2–6.4 provide the visual description of the spread of the start-ups for this study under the three dimensions respectively.

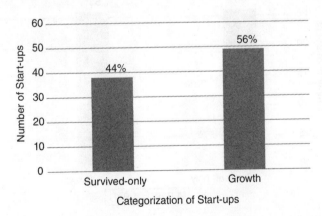

FIGURE 6.1 Distribution of start-ups based on growth categorization

Source: Author.

From Figure 6.2, we observe that visually the distribution of the start-ups across the two market segments appear to be different. We note that there is larger variation in the distribution of the B2C start-ups across these market segments (32 per cent in the survived group versus 47 per cent in the growth group). Further, we see higher variation between B2B- and B2C-focused start-ups in the survived-only category in comparison to the other groups. These visual observations seem to indicate that target market segment of the start-ups may be able to explain the differences between the two groups which are created to study the impact of growth of high-tech start-ups. However, a formal statistical validation will only confirm these initial observations.

The visual analysis of data based on the location of operations as presented in Figure 6.3 clearly brings out that there are more number of start-ups operating in South Zone of the country. Further, the data among the two start-up groups seem to display similar variance between the regions (26 per cent difference in the number of start-ups in the survived-only group versus 30 per cent difference in the number of start-ups in the growth-based group). This observation seems to indicate that the location of operations may not be useful in explaining the difference between these groups. However, as pointed earlier, this result needs to be examined using more rigorous statistical tests.

The visual inspection of Figure 6.4 leads us to make the following observations. We observe that more number of transnational entrepreneurs are

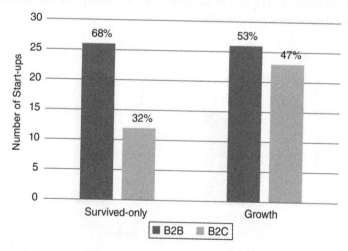

FIGURE 6.2 Distribution of start-ups based on target market segment

SOURCE: Author.

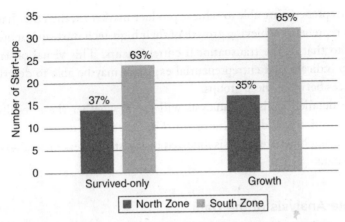

FIGURE 6.3 Distribution of start-ups based on location of operations

SOURCE: Author.

in the survived-only group, whereas local entrepreneurs are more in number in the growth group. This may indicate that transnational entrepreneurs may be able to formally incorporate new ventures as well as survive in their country of origin. But achieving growth may be relatively difficult in comparison to the local entrepreneurs. We can also tentatively note that transnational entrepreneurs may be able to achieve the survival milestone relatively easily to that of the local entrepreneurs on account of higher resources. However, if

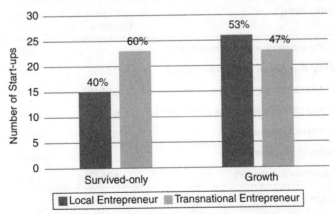

FIGURE 6.4 Distribution of start-ups based on entrepreneur exposure

SOURCE: Author.

local entrepreneurs are able to achieve product-market fit, then the chances of local entrepreneurs achieving growth of their high-tech start-up is more likely relative to that of the transnational entrepreneurs. This visual observation seems to indicate that entrepreneurial exposure may be able to describe the differences between these groups.

More detailed statistical analysis will reveal whether these results from visual inspection would hold true or not. The next section delves into analysing the data using bivariate analysis followed by logistic regression analysis of the start-up data.

Bivariate Analysis of the Data

We present the bivariate analysis of all the independent variables against the dependent variable for the study in Tables 6.1 and 6.2. Table 6.1 presents the bivariate analysis performed against the categorical and dichotomous variables in our study. Chi-square tests are carried out to understand whether the variables of our study are statistically independent when compared against the dependent variable. For all the continuous variables examined in our study, one-way ANOVA were executed to ascertain the statistical relationship between one independent variable with the dependent variable. The results of these one-way ANOVA are presented in Table 6.2.

TABLE 6.1 Chi-square test results of dependent variable against the input variables

Variable name	Chi-square statistic value	p-value
Industry experience of the entrepreneur	—	1.000
Start-up experience of the entrepreneur	0.5339	0.465
Education pedigree of the entrepreneur	0.2548	0.8804
Financial capitalization status of the start-up	5.7866	**0.01615**
Target market segment	1.5097	0.2192
Location of operations	—	1.000
Entrepreneurial exposure	1.0873	0.2971

SOURCE: Author.

NOTE: p-values of significant results are marked in **bold**.

The results from Table 6.1 indicate that barring the variable representing the financial capabilities of the start-up, all other categorical and dichotomous variables reveal a lack of dependence with the category of growth dummy variable. In other words, only the financial capitalization of start-ups variable possesses dependence with the growth dummy variable while all other dichotomous and categorical variables come out as independent with respect to the growth dummy variable. Barring the financial capabilities variable, in each case, the high p-value (greater than 0.1) indicates that the null hypothesis cannot be rejected (null hypothesis states that these two variables are independent of each other), which establishes the independence of these two variables.

Table 6.2 presents the bivariate analysis of the continuous variables that are examined in this study against the growth dummy variable. From Table 6.2, we observe that only the age of the entrepreneur seems to be significant, implying that this variable can explain the differences and potentially influence the growth of high-tech start-ups. All other continuous variables do not seem to differentiate or influence the growth dummy variable.

TABLE 6.2 One-way ANOVA results of dependent variable against continuous input variables

	Computed F-values	p-value	Homogeneity of variance
Age of the founder (years)	4.888	**0.03066**	Yes
Sales capabilities of the start-up	2.3994	0.127	No
R&D capabilities of the start-up	2.775	0.1008	Yes
SDP	0.1321	0.7172	Yes
Number of deals	0.7637	0.3847	Yes
Number of VCs	0.0107	0.918	Yes

SOURCE: Author.

NOTE: The test for equality of means was preceded by the test for equality of variances. In case the variances are equal, the regular F-statistic values have been reported; otherwise Welch-F-statistic values have been reported. p-values of significant results are marked in **bold**.

Table 6.3 summarizes the hypotheses that were supported or rejected based on the analyses. An entry 'Accepted' in the table indicates acceptance of the hypotheses. The sign in the brackets indicates the direction of the influence of the variable. A '+' sign indicates positive influence, whereas a '–' sign indicates negative influence. The detailed results of each of the regression models are presented in the chapter-end Appendix as Tables 6A.1–6A.7.

TABLE 6.3 Summary of hypotheses evaluations related to growth of high-tech start-ups

	B2B	B2C	North Zone	South Zone	Local entrepreneur	T.E.	Overall model
H 1: prior industry experience							
H 2: prior start-up experience				Accepted (–)	Accepted (–)		
H 3: age of the founder	Accepted (–)				Accepted (–)		Accepted (–)
H 4: education of the founder	Accepted (–)		Accepted (–)				Accepted (–)
H 5: sales capabilities of the start-up							
H 6: R&D apabilities of the start-up							
H 7: financial capabilities of the start-up		Accepted (–)					Accepted (–)
H 8: SDP growth	Accepted (+)	Accepted (–)					
H 9: number of VC-funded deals				Accepted (–)			
H 10: number of VCs in the region				Accepted (+)			

SOURCE: Author.

NOTE: All the empty cells in the table indicate the rejection of the hypotheses.

Results of the Analysis Based on Market Segment

The logistic regression model analysis results, based on start-ups, targeting the B2B market sector is presented in the Appendix Table 6A.1. The analysis of model targeting B2C market sector is presented in Table 6A.2. The dependent variable is the dummy growth variable, a discrete dichotomous variable. As discussed earlier, the data for the study of growth of high-tech start-ups has been categorized into two segments – survived-only and growth-based. Start-ups in the first category – survived-only – are those start-ups that have no reported external valuation, have valuation less than ₹5 crore if they are services-based, or have less than ₹10 crore if they are a manufacturing-based start-up. These will be represented by a value of 0 for the dependent variable. Start-ups that have valuation greater than the discussed threshold will have a value of 1 for the dependent variable.

From the results presented in Table 6A.1, the variables that model the *age and education* of the founders emerge as significant factors influencing the start-ups catering to the B2B sector. From the results, we can infer that both age of the entrepreneur and the founders whose educational pedigree is a technical (engineering) degree impact negatively to achieving the growth milestone of the start-ups. Both the factors of age and education of the entrepreneur have been discussed and debated in prior literature with divergent results. These results seem to indicate that entrepreneurs who are aged higher may not be able to rapidly adjust to the new direction of their firm objectives after they surpass the survival milestone. Further, the technical education of the founder may not contribute too much to the growth of the firm, because business and market expansion skills may be more required than technical skills during this phase of the start-up life cycle.

The logistic regression model analysis results based on start-ups targeting the B2C market sector is presented in Table 6A.2. The results indicate that the *financial capitalization of the start-ups* and the *SDP growth in the region* are the key factors influencing the growth of high-tech start-ups focusing on the B2C market segment. From Table 6A.2, we can infer that external capital negatively impacts the likelihood of growth, whereas the positive SDP growth enhances the likelihood of growth of B2C start-ups.

For B2C-focused start-ups, the addressable market is very large and diversified unlike the sector-specific focus of the B2B-focused start-ups. Further, the B2C start-up revenue models are driven by volume of end consumers and massive adoption of the product or service offering by a large customer base. This is because revenue per user or margins per user for the usage of the product or service offering tends to be very marginal in the case of B2C start-ups. Although the B2C start-up would have created a new unique offering and it has been accepted in the market by a few initial enthusiastic customers, its broad-based adoption by larger sets of customers is what transforms this start-up into a larger enterprise.

While the empirical literature indicates that availing external funding would enable a start-up to achieve scale, our results indicate the contrary. One of the possible causes for external funding, hindering the growth prospects of the start-up, is that external funding post the survival milestone achievement may induce complacency and unwanted distraction amongst founders. Founders of these high-tech start-ups may be usually comfortable dealing with uncertainty and may not be very comfortable with the discipline and structure that needs to be in place to transform into a high-growth enterprise. Further, external capital infusion might bring in additional stakeholders (VCs and other investors) whose interests may not be always aligned with that of the entrepreneur's. In most cases, entrepreneurs who have set up the start-up, enabled its survival, would tend to have an emotional connect and their context of how to scale their start-up. When additional external stakeholders like VCs come in at this stage, there are bound to be differences of opinion on a variety of operational aspects. These may keep the entrepreneur busy, distracting him/her from the actual business. These aspects seem to explain why external funding hinders start-up growth.

The result that SDP growth of the region in which the B2C firm operates can also be explained as follows. For B2C start-ups to grow into large enterprises, it is very important that there is a large demand that can be tapped by the start-up. For this market to exist there needs to be a robust external environment that is conducive and favourable to both start-ups and consumers. SDP growth in a given region is a proxy for such an environment. A greater SDP growth implies a larger addressable market and more disposable spending – which augur well for B2C start-ups to grow.

Results of Analysis Based on Location of Operations

The logistic regression model analysis results based on start-ups targeting the North Zone region of the country is presented in Table 6A.3. The model analysing the results based on start-ups targeting South Zone is presented in Table 6A.4.

The results from Table 6A.3 indicate that the *educational pedigree of the founder* and the *SDP growth in the region* are the key factors influencing the growth of high-tech start-ups operating in the North Zone. The results indicate that lack of technical or higher education beyond a technical degree of founders and a negative SDP growth in the region of operations increase the likelihood of growth of high-tech start-ups in the North Zone. The model fit statistics from Tables 6A.3 and 6A.4 indicate that the model is just marginally significant than the baseline.

The educational pedigree of the founders coming out as a significant result for the start-ups operating in the North Zone region of the country is explained as follows. For a start-up that has achieved the survival milestone (product-market fit), the activities of market development would take higher precedence in order to capitalize on the initial acceptance of the offering from the customers. Given the high-tech obsolescence rates, when any start-up achieves initial market traction, most of its focus would then be to sell the offering to invest on marketing to enable rapid penetration of the offering to the market. In such scenarios, the technical qualifications of entrepreneurs may be of less help. Perhaps, the focus to achieve technical perfection and improvisation of the offerings by a highly technically qualified founder may hinder the market development and hence the growth of the high-tech start-up.

The SDP growth of the region as an important contributor to the start-ups operating in the North Zone region can be explained as follows. The SDP growth variable in our study can be treated as the proxy for measuring the demand for new product offerings at the macro level. Our results indicate that negative SDP growth in the region where the start-up is located increases the likelihood of growth of the start-up. Our results seem to indicate that start-ups that target regions other than those of their state may have better growth prospects, since demand to the new offerings in their local market is muted (as indicated by the negative SDP growth). If we study the SDP growth patterns in India, we notice that all states in the South Zone usually record higher SDP growth than the national GDP average. This means that the macroeconomic conditions for consumption of new offerings are usually more favourable in the South Zone. Further, high-tech start-ups can target the global markets for growth, not just to sell within India as a market.

The logistic regression model analysis results based on start-ups targeting the South Zone region of the country is presented in Table 7.6. The results indicate that the *prior start-up experience of the founder* and the *presence of VCs and number of funded deals in the region* are the key factors influencing the growth of high-tech start-ups operating in the South Zone. From Table 7.6, we can infer that lack of start-up experience of entrepreneurs, a negative VC deals growth, and a positive growth on the availability of VC firms increase the likelihood of growth of high-tech start-ups in the South Zone.

The result that the prior start-up experience negatively influencing the growth of high-tech start-ups, operating in the South Zone, can be explained as follows. In the context of emerging economies, it is established that the degree of uncertainty is higher than what an entrepreneur would usually face in the developed countries as one embarks on scaling up the venture (Boyacigiller and Adler 1991). Hence, although the start-up has achieved product-market fit and is earning repeatable revenue, there would be aspects related to scaling up of the start-up from both internal and external perspectives which would still challenge the founder to deal with uncertainty. For example, from an internal organizational perspective, the founder would need to deal with challenges of establishing repeatability of activities across various functions, such as product development, customer relationship management, sales and branding, and so forth, apart from ensuring that he/she is able to hire quality talent to perform all the aforementioned activities for his/her start-up which is rapidly growing. From an activity list external to the organization, there are challenges of ensuring that the customer base of the start-up be increased, fundraising for subsequent rounds to support expansion if required to be done, and so on. These spectra of activities call for a structured and disciplined approach to organize and manage the activities of the start-up. A founder with prior start-up experience would have more expertise in dealing with uncertainty but may find it difficult to lead activities that need structure and discipline. Hence, founders with start-up experience might hinder growth of their start-ups.

The external environmental factors, namely, the presence of VCs in the region and the number of funded VC deals in the region represent the vibrancy and favourable conditions on the demand side of the market. In this case, the results indicate that increasing presence of VCs on a year-to-year basis, but a decreasing trend in deals in the same region, augur well for growth of the start-ups in this Zone. It has been established that VCs tend to invest in start-ups in and around their areas of physical presence for purposes of alleviating the information asymmetry risks (Joshi 2015). An increase in the number of VCs in the region automatically implies that the availability of external capital for the region is increased.

Further, when the number of funded deals in the region have decreased year on year, it is a signal to the start-up entrepreneurs that the immediate past and current situations may not be very conducive for every entrepreneur to raise growth capital. For the VCs, high-tech sector is just one of the sectors they can choose to invest. In India, Joshi (2015) has deduced that VCs most often prefer to invest in less risky but assured-return sectors such as real estate. However, when the number of VCs increases, some of these VCs will examine projects that need capital from the ICT sector, but when they do invest, they will do so after due diligence. From our results, we can suggest that this situation enables the start-ups with strong fundamentals to grow, and also, due diligence for external funding of growth stage start-ups which has a higher-level of maturity in the South Zone.

Results of Analysis Based on Entrepreneurial Exposure

The logistic regression model analysis results based on start-ups that are founded by local entrepreneurs are presented in Table 6A.5. The results from Table 6A.5 indicate that *prior start-up experience* and *age of the founder* are the key factors influencing the growth of high-tech start-ups operated by the local entrepreneurs. The results indicate that lack of prior start-up experience and lesser age of the founders increase the likelihood of growth of start-ups founded by local entrepreneurs.

The result of prior start-up experience as being one of the contributors to growth of high-tech start-ups is a result which has mixed reviews from prior literature. Most of the earlier findings is contrary to our current result (Storey 1982; Ronstadt 1988), although there is some support from the results discussed out of the work pursued by Clement et al. (2007). Proponents of entrepreneurial learning theory and organizational behaviour stated that prior start-up experience will be an invaluable asset in influencing the growth of high-tech start-ups (Politis 2008). This is because they argue that by indulging in start-up-related activities either as a founder or as an initial team member, the prospective entrepreneur would obtain tacit knowledge (which cannot be codified and easily transferable) and expertise in dealing with situations of uncertainty and ambiguity (Ensley 2006). While this tacit knowledge may come in handy during the inception and survival stages of the start-up, our results indicate that lack of start-up experience of the local founders actually increases the likelihood of growth of the start-ups. The possible reasons for this result could be that growth stage of the firm demands skills of repeatable operations, creation of structure in the organization, which calls for mean optimizing behaviour. However, if founders who are comfortable dealing with uncertainty and chaos on account of their prior start-up experience, they tend to be trying out different experiments as response to the growth challenges of their start-up – which may prove ineffective and hinder growth.

The age of the entrepreneur as the other significant factor, influencing the growth of the start-ups founded by local entrepreneurs, is in line with the earlier results of the univariate and bivariate analyses that was carried out prior to execution of these models. As mentioned earlier, prior literature has discussed in detail about age of the entrepreneur acting as a proxy to knowledge accumulation by the entrepreneur (Wennberg and Lindqvist 2010; Coleman, Cotei, and Farhat 2013). However, our results point out that this accumulated knowledge might come in as a barrier to start-ups manned by local entrepreneurs – indicating that their overconfidence or enhanced assessment of capabilities gained on account of higher age would hinder the growth prospects of their start-ups.

The logistic regression model analysis results for start-ups that are founded by transnational entrepreneurs are presented in Table 6A.6. The results indicate that the model is not a good fit for the data present for our study and do not provide any factor as being significant influencer in the growth of start-ups owned by transnational entrepreneurs. Hence, we do not further interpret or analyse the results emanating out of the execution of this model.

Results of the Overall Model

The visual inspection of the raw data by graphical methods have provided us initial insights on what factors might influence and differentiate the growth of high-tech start-ups present in our sample. Further, the results based on the three segments – target market, location of operations, and entrepreneur exposure – have provided insights in to the key factors that enable growth in the corresponding segments. In this section, we present the results of the logistic regression analysis carried out to statistically validate and understand the key factors that drive the growth of high-tech start-ups.

Prior to execution of the logistic regression analysis, we need to ensure that the assumptions of this statistical technique are met by the data of start-ups that we have in our study. We validate these assumptions by graphical examination of the statistical plots of the independent variables to begin with and later, based on the logistic regression analysis, we build the optimal model that fits the data in our study. Then, we analyse the results obtained by the execution of this optimal logistic regression model and discuss the outcomes and implications.

Graphical validation of assumptions

The first step involved in execution of any regression analysis technique is to visually or graphically analyse the independent continuous variables in the study and understand its distribution. To begin with, Figure 6.5 presents the box plot of the founders' ages versus the two categories of the start-ups.

From Figure 6.5, we can observe clearly that as the age of the entrepreneur increases, the probability of them operating growth start-ups increases. For example, we see that the ages of the entrepreneurs in the survived-only start-ups group (indicated by the group number 0 under the x-axis) lie between 24 and 29 years. The growth group of start-ups in our sample has entrepreneurs aged between 30 and 45 years. Therefore, from Figure 6.5, we can find some initial support for our hypothesis on founder's age influencing the start-up growth.

The box plot presented in Figure 6.6 provides us insight about how the SDP influences the different groups of start-ups that are classified based on their growth potential. We can clearly observe that each of the group of start-ups has a different range of SDP growth. From Figure 6.6, we see that survived-only start-up group is based in regions where there is relatively lower SDP growth (in the range of 5 per cent to 6 per cent year-on-year growth) along with a few outliers in the lower band of SDP growth, whereas the growth start-ups are based in the regions where the SDP growth (year-on-year) is between 9 per cent and 13 per cent, along with a few outliers. This seems to indicate that start-ups based in regions that are witnessing higher SDP growth are likely to scale up.

The box plots, indicating the relationship between the number of VC deals in a given region versus the categories of start-ups, is grouped based on their growth potential is presented in Figure 6.7. From Figure 6.7, we can observe that number of VC deals positively seems to influence the growth of start-ups. In other words, as the number of VC deals in a region grows, we can infer that the start-ups in that region are likely to register a higher growth.

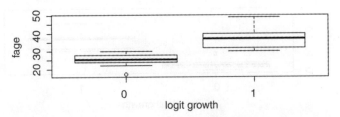

FIGURE 6.5 Box plot of founder's age versus valuation of start-ups

SOURCE: Author.

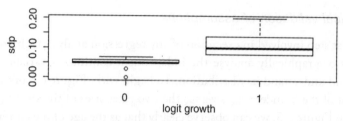

FIGURE 6.6 Box plot of SDP growth in the region versus valuation of start-ups

Source: Author.

From the data of start-ups in our study, we can observe that the survived-only group of start-ups is based in regions where lesser number of VC deals in a year happens – in the range of 15 to 22 deals per year – along with the presence of a few outlier observations at the top of the range. The growth-related start-up group seems to be based in region where the number of VC deals ranges between 45 and 75 deals per year with the average closer to the higher bound of about 65 to 70 deals per year. These observations imply that the number of VC deals in the region might positively influence the growth of start-ups.

Figure 6.8 presents the box plot obtained by comparison of number of VCs present in a given region versus the categories of growth potential of the start-ups. From Figure 6.8, we can infer that the larger the presence of VCs in a given region, more the number of growth start-ups. An analysis of the correlations between the two groups and the number of VCs in the corresponding regions indicates that survived-only group of start-ups has lesser number of VCs, physically located in their region of operation, ranging from about 10 to 24 VC firms with the average value of about 20 VCs in the region. However, we observe from Figure 6.8 that about 50 to 70 VCs are present in the regions of the start-ups that are experiencing growth, with the average being biased towards the lower limit of about 55 VCs in that region.

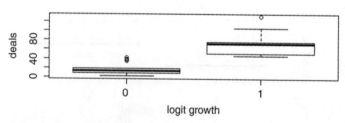

FIGURE 6.7 Box plot of number of VC deals in the region versus valuation of start-ups

Source: Author.

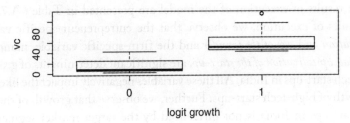

FIGURE 6.8 Box plot of number of VCs in the region versus valuation of start-ups

SOURCE: Author.

After the graphical analysis of the continuous variables, we now proceed to build and obtain the optimal model that could be used for analysis of factors impacting the growth of high-tech start-ups in India.

Results of the optimal model

The initial analysis by visual and graphical inspection provides us with some initial hints and directions on which factors might actually affect and differentiate the growth of high-tech start-ups in India. However, these are just initial statistical estimates and not evidence of influence or absence thereof. Hence, we begin the exercise of fitting the right model to analyse the objectives of our study. As a first step in this direction, we build a full model consisting of all the variables that are hypothesized to have an influence on the growth of the high-tech start-ups in India. These variables include the entrepreneur-specific variables, such as prior start-up experience, prior industry experience, and the age and education of the founder of the start-up.

Further, the firm-specific variables that are included in the model are sales capabilities, R&D capabilities, and financial capitalization status of the start-up at this juncture. The SDP growth (year-on-year) of the region, the number of VCs that is present in the region as well as the number of funded VC deals that occurs in the region for a given year form the external environment variables in the model. Further, to control specific dimensions, we have used three dummy variables to account for the target market segment that is being addressed by the start-ups, the location of operations of the start-up, and whether the founder is a local or a transnational entrepreneur. The status of growth of the firm categorized into two groups – survived-only and growth – based on the range of valuation is the dichotomous dependent variable in this case.

The results of execution of the model are presented in Table 6A.7. From the results of execution, we observe that the entrepreneur-specific variables of *education* and *age of the founder* and the firm-specific variable, namely, the *financial capitalization of the start-up*, are significant determinants of growth of high-tech start-ups in India. All these variables negatively impact the likelihood of growth of high-tech start-ups. Further, we observe that growth of the high-tech start-ups in India is not influenced by the target market segment, the location of operations in which the start-up operates, or the entrepreneurial exposure.

We also notice that there are a few other variables that do not come out significant in explaining the growth of the high-tech start-ups. From the entrepreneur-specific variables, neither the prior industry experience of the founders nor the prior start-up experience seems to statistically influence the growth of high-tech start-ups in India. Among the firm-specific variables, our results indicate that the R&D capabilities and the sales capabilities of the start-up do not influence the growth of the high-tech start-ups. Further, none of the external environment-specific variables comes out as significant in explaining or influencing growth of the start-ups, present in our study. Therefore, the hypotheses related to the aforementioned variables as proposed in the earlier sections of this chapter stand rejected.

The result from Table 6A.7 shows that education of the entrepreneur impacts growth of high-tech start-ups is a finding which is in line with previous such examinations. From the early years of research on entrepreneurial traits to recent examinations of entrepreneurial behaviour, education of the entrepreneur has always been considered an important factor influencing the growth of high-tech start-ups. Jo and Lee (1996) found that the lead entrepreneur's educational level are positively correlated with his/her firm's profitability. However, our results indicate that higher level of education of the founder actually hinder the growth prospects of the start-up. It is useful to note that most of the founders considered for this study are technically qualified. This indicates that while basic technology skills and domain knowledge of entrepreneurs could be a prerequisite for starting up a new venture, high technical qualification would hinder growth prospects.

The age of the entrepreneur, emerging significant in influencing the growth of high-tech start-ups, revalidates the prior findings in this regard that have argued on the lines of age of the entrepreneur becoming a barrier to start-ups' growth. As noted before, with age, the entrepreneur may develop overconfidence and accumulation of individual experiences might hinder the him/her to objectively assess the current demands to scale the organization.

Financing or capitalizing a start-up that has already achieved product-market fit sets up the firm on a positive trajectory to scale up its operations and transform itself into a full-fledged enterprise. Adequate financial capital is the basis on which the start-up which has validated the product or offering can now increase the market penetration externally and establish repeatable routines to execute the internal operations of the start-up. From a perspective, external to the firm, increasing the market penetration requires more spending on advertising, brand building, and awareness creation among the market segments that have hitherto not embraced the product offering.

From a perspective, internal to the start-up, when demand generation activities create new customers looking to use the offering, the quality of deliverables, customer support functions, and allied activities need to be in pace with the increase in customer demand, so that all users get the same quick and high-quality experience as they use the services or product offered by the start-up. To enable both these external and internal activities, financing of the start-up is the key. Existing literature seems to indicate that external funding of a start-up is crucial to ensure its growth and transformation. Estrin, Meyer, and Bytchkova (2006) indicated that financial capitalization of the start-up is more important in the expansion of existing businesses rather than in the creation of new firms. However, our results indicate that firms that are able to manage this financial capitalization through internal accruals – revenue from sales and promoter-capital infusion – have higher chances of achieving growth.

The result that neither the R&D capabilities nor the sales capabilities of the start-up are influential in impacting the growth of the high-tech start-ups needs further explanation. Prior literature has emphasized on sales growth of a firm as a proxy to growth, as it is discussed in the earlier in this chapter (Dunne and Hughes 1994; Davidsson and Delmar 2003). In similar lines, the R&D capabilities of the start-up has usually been held important in the growth of high-tech start-ups (Zahra and George 2002b). We need to understand that during the scale-up or transformation of a start-up to a full-fledged enterprise, it is certainly important to ensure that sales and development activities of the start-up support this transition. However, for a start-up that has achieved product-market fit, attracting key sales or development resources will not be a constraint because the rapid acceptance of the product in the market signals potential sales personnel that this start-up is a good bet to further the career aspirations of that function. In similar lines, the novelty, present in the offering that has got initial customer acceptance, will attract the R&D personnel to work on such product offerings without hesitation. Hence, all that is required at this juncture is adequate financial capitalization to attract and incentivize talented and skilled workforce to support the scale-up activities of the start-up.

On the same line, when the start-up is on an expansion and growth path beyond that of a small firm, it cannot confine its sales or R&D activities to a particular region. Hence, irrespective of how external environment conditions are, the start-up will need to gain new markets and expand its presence beyond just one region. These aspects explain as to why the external environment variables, such as SDP growth, may not be significant. Further, as regards to the number of funded deals and the presence of VCs in the region not being significant in our final result, we need to understand and interpret this result in the context of growth of start-ups.

The absence of significance of these funding ecosystem variables does not imply that they are not required. For a start-up that has proven its business model in terms of customer acquisition, robustness of the product or offering, it will be easy to access the VCs and sign up for equity-based funding arrangements with them. Availability of credit or access to finance will not be an impediment to any firm that has validated its basic entrepreneurial idea. However, to ensure that the firm is capitalized at the right time to leverage the opportunities for growth is the key for the founders of that start-up to work with these external funding entities. These aspects explain why the funding related external environmental variables have not appeared significant in our final results.

Summary

In this chapter, we have attempted to understand the factors that influence and impact growth of the high-tech start-ups in India. Drawing from our literature review, we have analysed the factors that contribute to the growth of the start-ups from three specific dimensions: entrepreneur-specific, firm-specific, and external environment specific aspects.

The valuation of the firm was chosen as the proxy to measure growth of the high-tech start-ups in India. The data for the study of growth of high-tech start-ups was categorized into two segments: survived-only and growth-based. Once these groups were identified, we examined these groups using three segments, namely, the target market segment, location of operations of the start-up, and the entrepreneur exposure. The examination across these two groups, using the variables from these three segments (B2B versus B2C, North Zone versus South Zone, and local versus transnational entrepreneurs) provided us with a deeper understanding of factors that may influence the growth of the high-tech start-ups. We performed univariate and bivariate tests to understand how the relationship of these variables worked at the univariate and bivariate levels. Chi-square tests were performed for categorical and dichotomous variables used for the study, and one-way ANOVA were performed to examine the relationship between the continuous independent variables with the dummy growth-dependent variable.

We then executed tests to understand the factors that impact growth of high-tech start-ups. In all, we executed seven logistic regression models. Our results indicate that the age and education of the entrepreneur, financial capitalization, and SDP growth in the region influence the growth of B2C and B2B focused high-tech start-ups. The logistic regression models targeting the location of operations revealed to us that education of the entrepreneur and the SDP growth in the North Zone was important to spur growth of high-tech start-ups in that region. Similarly, prior start-up experience and a favourable external funding ecosystem by way of presence of VCs and number of funded deals in the region influence the growth of start-ups in the South Zone. Factors of prior start-up experience and age of the entrepreneurs came out as significant in the analysis of growth of start-ups founded by local entrepreneurs. Our model for transnational entrepreneurs' growth did not yield any significant results, hence we do not further analyse the results for the same.

Finally, we built the overall model to analyse the growth of high-tech start-ups. The results from the overall model indicate that age and education of the founders and financial capitalization of the start-ups are the key factors in driving growth of high-tech start-ups in India.

Appendix: Results of Logistic Regression Models

This section contains the results of the statistical analysis performed on the data for all the seven models. To begin with, Tables 6A.1 and 6A.2 present the results of the tests carried out for the B2B and B2C sectors. Then, Tables 6A.3 and 6A.4 provide the results of the tests carried out with the location of operations (north and south India) as the variable differentiator. Last, Tables 6A.5 and 6A.6 provide the results of tests that were carried out with data, grouped and based on entrepreneurial exposure. Table 6A.7 provides the results for the overall model, including the control variables.

TABLE 6A.1 Results of model execution based on B2B sector focused start-ups

Model variables	Beta coefficient (β)	Standard error	Wald statistic	Degree of freedom	Significance (p-value)	Exp (β)
Constant	5.405	2.985	3.279	1	0.070	222.589
Prior industry experience of the entrepreneur (fiexp = 1)	-1.529	1.463	1.093	1	0.296	0.217
Prior start-up experience of the entrepreneur (fsexp = 1)	-1.264	0.792	2.545	1	0.111	0.283
Age of the entrepreneur (fage)	-0.119	0.069	3.009	1	0.083	0.888
Education of the entrepreneur – base reference variable (fedn)			3.577	2	0.167	
Education of the entrepreneur – first dummy (fedn1)	-2.480	1.355	3.350	1	0.067	0.084
Education of the entrepreneur – second dummy (fedn2)	-0.828	1.007	0.677	1	0.411	0.437
Sales capabilities – base reference variable (csales)	0.000	0.002	0.055	1	0.814	1.000
R&D capabilities – base reference variable (cdev)	0.100	0.113	0.792	1	0.374	1.105
Funding status of the start-up (fin = 1)	0.160	0.907	0.031	1	0.860	1.174
SDP growth (sdp)	-12.067	7.796	2.396	1	0.122	0.000
Number of deals (deals)	0.005	0.029	0.033	1	0.857	1.005
Number of VCs (vc)	0.015	0.028	0.272	1	0.602	1.015
Operations in south India (Zone = 1)	-0.590	1.106	0.285	1	0.594	0.554
Transnational entrepreneur (te = 1)	0.475	1.012	0.220	1	0.639	1.608

Model statistics: Number of observations = 52

Goodness of fit: Chisq = 19.217 on 13 degrees of freedom, p-value = 0.117

SOURCE: Author.

TABLE 6A.2 Results of model execution based on B2C sector focused start-ups

Model variables	Beta coefficient (β)	Standard error	Wald statistic	Degree of freedom	Significance (p-value)	Exp (β)
Constant	1.066	3.606	0.087	1	0.768	2.903
Prior industry experience of the entrepreneur (fiexp = 1)	16.541	25849.363	0.000	1	0.999	15270220.874
Prior start-up experience of the entrepreneur (fsexp = 1)	-1.138	1.646	0.479	1	0.489	0.320
Age of the entrepreneur (fage)	-0.009	0.087	0.011	1	0.916	0.991
Education of the entrepreneur – base reference variable (fedn)			1.448	2	0.485	
Education of the entrepreneur – first dummy (fedn1)	-1.902	2.382	0.638	1	0.425	0.149
Education of the entrepreneur – second dummy (fedn2)	-0.828	1.007	0.677	1	0.411	0.437
Sales capabilities – base reference variable (csales)	0.004	0.005	0.613	1	0.434	1.004
R&D capabilities – base reference variable (cdev)	-0.049	0.067	0.530	1	0.467	0.952
Funding status of the start-up (fin = 1)	-2.968	1.307	5.158	1	**0.023**	0.051
SDP growth (sdp)	41.168	23.126	3.169	1	**0.075**	7.56e[17]
Number of deals (deals)	0.001	0.039	0.001	1	0.977	1.001
Number of VCs (vc)	-0.011	0.041	0.069	1	0.793	0.989
Operations in south India (Zone = 1)	0.374	1.501	0.062	1	0.803	1.454
Transnational entrepreneur (te = 1)	0.514	1.495	0.118	1	0.731	1.673

Model statistics: Number of observations = 35

Goodness of fit: Chisq = 18.122 on 13 degrees of freedom, p-value = 0.153

Hosmer and Lemeshow test: Chisq = 7.532 on 7 degrees of freedom, p-value = 0.376

Cox and Snell R^2 = 0.404; Nagelkerke R^2 = 0.559

SOURCE: Author.

TABLE 6A.3 Results of model execution based on start-ups operating in the North Zone

Model variables	Beta coefficient (β)	Standard error	Wald statistic	Degree of freedom	Significance (p-value)	Exp (β)
Constant	19.569	9.520	4.226	1	0.040	315305713.054
Prior industry experience of the entrepreneur (fiexp = 1)	0.056	1.952	0.001	1	0.977	1.057
Prior start-up experience of the entrepreneur (fsexp = 1)	-2.835	2.019	1.970	1	0.160	0.059
Age of the entrepreneur (fage)	-0.160	0.130	1.520	1	0.218	0.852
Education of the entrepreneur – base reference variable (fedn)			4.110	2	0.128	
Education of the entrepreneur – first dummy (fedn1)	-7.129	3.634	3.849	1	**0.050**	0.001
Education of the entrepreneur – second dummy (fedn2)	-5.875	3.049	3.712	1	**0.054**	0.003
Sales capabilities – base reference variable (csales)	0.003	0.006	0.276	1	0.599	1.003
R&D capabilities – base reference variable (cdev)	-0.021	0.093	0.053	1	0.817	0.979
Funding status of the start-up (fin = 1)	-1.438	1.624	0.784	1	0.376	0.237
SDP growth (sdp)	-91.271	54.292	2.826	1	**0.093**	0.000
Number of deals (deals)	-0.032	0.072	0.196	1	0.658	0.969
Number of VCs (vc)	0.023	0.049	0.215	1	0.643	1.023
Target market segment (market_segment = 1)	-0.051	1.860	0.001	1	0.978	0.950
Transnational entrepreneur (te = 1)	0.725	2.375	0.093	1	0.760	2.066

Model statistics: Number of observations = 31

Goodness of fit: Chisq = 18.775 on 13 degrees of freedom, p-value = 0.130

Hosmer and Lemeshow test: Chisq = 7.687 on 8 degrees of freedom, p-value = 0.465

Cox and Snell R^2 = 0.454; Nagelkerke R^2 = 0.608

SOURCE: Author.

TABLE 6A.4 Results of model execution based on start-ups operating in the South Zone

Model variables	Beta coefficient (β)	Standard error	Wald statistic	Degree of freedom	Significance (p-value)	Exp (β)
Constant	1.323	2.296	0.332	1	0.564	3.756
Prior industry experience of the entrepreneur (fiexp = 1)	−0.479	1.540	0.097	1	0.756	0.619
Prior start-up experience of the entrepreneur (fsexp = 1)	−1.426	0.804	3.148	1	**0.076**	0.240
Age of the entrepreneur (fage)	−0.063	0.058	1.174	1	0.279	0.939
Education of the entrepreneur – base reference variable (fedn)			1.286	2	0.526	
Education of the entrepreneur – first dummy (fedn1)	−1.571	1.386	1.285	1	0.257	0.208
Education of the entrepreneur – second dummy (fedn2)	−0.831	1.052	0.624	1	0.429	0.435
Sales capabilities – base reference variable (csales)	0.002	0.002	0.893	1	0.345	1.002
R&D capabilities – base reference variable (cdev)	0.068	0.059	1.328	1	0.249	1.071
Funding status of the start-up (fin = 1)	−0.426	0.716	0.354	1	0.552	0.653
SDP growth (sdp)	−4.409	6.382	0.477	1	0.490	0.012
Number of deals (deals)	−0.090	0.045	3.961	1	**0.047**	0.914
Number of VCs (vc)	0.163	0.068	5.833	1	**0.016**	1.177
Target market segment (market_segment = 1)	0.633	0.867	0.534	1	0.465	1.884
Transnational entrepreneur (te = 1)	1.015	0.917	1.226	1	0.268	2.759

Model statistics: Number of observations = 56

Goodness of fit: Chisq = 20.405 on 13 degrees of freedom, p-value = 0.086

Hosmer and Lemeshow test: Chisq = 25.056 on 7 degrees of freedom, p-value = 0.001

Cox and Snell R² = 0.305; Nagelkerke R² = 0.410

Source: Author.

TABLE 6A.5 Results of model execution based on start-ups founded by local entrepreneurs

Model variables	Beta coefficient (β)	Standard error	Wald statistic	Degree of freedom	Significance (p-value)	Exp (β)
Constant	10.544	5.415	3.791	1	0.052	37954.774
Prior industry experience of the entrepreneur (fiexp = 1)	-2.242	1.789	1.571	1	0.210	0.106
Prior start-up experience of the entrepreneur (fsexp = 1)	-4.128	1.817	5.163	1	**0.023**	0.016
Age of the entrepreneur (fage)	-0.222	0.103	4.675	1	**0.031**	0.801
Education of the entrepreneur – base reference variable (fedn)			2.908	2	0.234	
Education of the entrepreneur – first dummy (fedn1)	-4.620	3.235	2.039	1	0.153	0.010
Education of the entrepreneur – second dummy (fedn2)	-2.857	3.028	0.890	1	0.345	0.057
Sales capabilities – base reference variable (csales)	0.002	0.003	0.320	1	0.572	1.002
R&D capabilities – base reference variable (cdev)	0.045	0.038	1.378	1	0.240	1.046
Funding status of the start-up (fin = 1)	-1.890	1.494	1.602	1	0.206	0.151
SDP growth (sdp)	2.316	16.760	0.019	1	0.890	10.133
Number of deals (deals)	0.053	0.036	2.213	1	0.137	1.055
Number of VCs (vc)	0.002	0.026	0.008	1	0.928	1.002
Target market segment (market_segment = 1)	0.105	1.322	0.006	1	0.936	1.111

Model statistics: Number of observations = 41

Goodness of fit: Chisq = 24.735 on 12 degrees of freedom, p-value = 0.016

Hosmer and Lemeshow test: Chisq = 11.697 on 8 degrees of freedom, p-value = 0.165

Cox and Snell R^2 = 0.453; Nagelkerke R^2 = 0.620

SOURCE: Author.

TABLE 6A.6 Results of model execution based on start-ups founded by transnational entrepreneurs

Model variables	Beta coefficient (β)	Standard error	Wald statistic	Degree of freedom	Significance (p-value)	Exp (β)
Constant	−0.138	2.683	0.003	1	0.959	0.871
Prior start-up experience of the entrepreneur (fsexp = 1)	−0.169	0.701	0.058	1	0.810	0.845
Age of the entrepreneur (fage)	−0.037	0.061	0.370	1	0.543	0.964
Education of the entrepreneur – base reference variable (fedn)	0.561	0.592	0.896	1	0.344	1.752
Sales Capabilities – base reference variable (csales)	0.001	0.002	0.257	1	0.612	1.001
R&D Capabilities – base reference variable (cdev)	0.039	0.043	0.816	1	0.366	1.040
Funding Status of the start-up (fin = 1)	0.544	0.717	0.575	1	0.448	1.723
SDP growth (sdp)	−0.768	6.556	0.014	1	0.907	0.464
Number of deals (deals)	0.013	0.027	0.224	1	0.636	1.013
Number of VCs (vc)	−0.018	0.030	0.335	1	0.563	0.983
Target market segment (market_segment = 1)	0.301	0.795	0.143	1	0.705	1.351
Operations in south India (zone = 1)	−0.361	0.901	0.161	1	0.688	0.697

Model statistics: Number of observations = 46

Goodness of fit: Chisq = 7.227 on 11 degrees of freedom, p-value = 0.780

Cox and Snell R^2 = 0.145; Nagelkerke R^2 = 0.194

SOURCE: Author.

TABLE 6A.7 Results of logistic regression execution of the full model

Model variables	Beta coefficient (β)	Standard error	Wald statistic	Degree of freedom	Significance (p-value)	Exp (β)
Constant	3.864	1.855	4.338	1	0.037	47.649
Prior industry experience of the entrepreneur (fiexp = 1)	-0.446	1.125	0.157	1	0.692	0.640
Prior Start-up Experience of the entrepreneur (fsexp = 1)	-0.894	00.587	2.316	1	0.128	0.409
Age of the entrepreneur (fage)	-0.076	0.042	3.279	1	**0.070**	0.927
Education of the entrepreneur – base reference variable (fedn)			4.900	2	**0.086**	
Education of the entrepreneur – first dummy (fedn1)	-2.091	0.968	4.664	1	**0.031**	0.124
Education of the entrepreneur – second dummy (fedn2)	-1.493	0.775	3.712	1	**0.054**	0.225
Sales capabilities – base reference variable (csales)	0.001	0.001	0.656	1	0.418	1.001
R&D capabilities – base reference variable (cdev)	0.032	0.028	1.277	1	0.258	1.032
Funding status of the start-up (fin = 1)	-0.914	0.542	2.843	1	**0.092**	0.401
SDP growth (sdp)	-0.571	5.329	0.011	1	0.915	0.565
Number of deals (deals)	0.015	0.018	0.651	1	0.420	1.015
Number of VCs (vc)	-0.001	0.019	0.006	1	0.937	0.999
Target market segment (market_segment = 1)	-0.182	0.537	0.115	1	0.735	0.834
Operations in south India (zone = 1)	0.027	0.671	0.002	1	0.968	1.028
Transnational entrepreneur (te = 1)	0.738	0.611	1.461	1	0.227	2.092

Model statistics: Number of observations = 87

Goodness of fit: Chisq = 21.210 on 14 degrees of freedom, p-value = 0.096

Hosmer and Lemeshow test: Chisq = 9.635 on 8 degrees of freedom, p-value = 0.292

Cox and Snell R^2 = 0.216; Nagelkerke R^2 = 0.290

SOURCE: Author.

7

Factors Influencing Life Cycle of High-tech Start-ups

Introduction

In this chapter, we discuss in detail, the factors that influence the life cycle of high-tech start-ups with respect to our total sample as a whole. Further, we ascertain the factors that are responsible for variance across the different life cycle phases of the start-ups involved in our study. To begin with, we will be specifically examining the factors that differentiate the start-ups among the three milestones of emergence, survival, and growth by way of MANOVA. We then study and identify the factors impacting the entire life cycle of start-ups by subjecting the entire data of start-ups to a multinomial regression. Further, we assess how high-tech start-ups differ between the three milestones in terms of their orientation towards the market segment that they target, the location in which they operate as well as based on the exposure of the founders.

The preceding chapters analysed the impact of entrepreneurial, firm-specific, and external environment-related factors that are influential in impacting the individual milestones of emergence, survival, and growth respectively. The focus of evaluation in those chapters was to understand what factors would help contribute towards attainment of the particular milestone under study. We grouped the data of our sample accordingly to examine each of the earlier objectives. However, in this chapter, we aim to supplement the insights obtained from the preceding chapters by enquiring if there are factors that influence the entire life cycle of high-tech start-ups. In other words, we wish to evaluate and understand whether there are factors in the entrepreneurial, firm-specific, and external environment-specific categories that pervade influence across all the key milestones of a start-up's journey. We consider the entire data of our sample to analyse this research objective. This insight would be useful for the entrepreneurs, ecosystem partners, and policymakers as well, who will then understand the key ingredients that are required to create, sustain, and grow successful high-tech start-ups.

In order to study the impact of factors affecting the life cycle of start-ups, we organize the data of start-ups that are collected during our study into three distinct categories based on their current status of the life cycle milestone achieved. The first category of start-ups would be those start-ups that have formally been incorporated, but who have not yet achieved the product-market fit. This category of start-ups constitutes the 'emerged only' start-ups group. The second category of start-ups that we created for this study are those who are formally incorporated as well as achieved the product-market fit but have not yet crossed beyond the SME valuations of ₹5 crore if their offerings are services-based or ₹10 crore if their operations are based on capital investment. This category of start-ups constitutes the 'survived-only' start-ups group. The third category of start-ups are those who have been formally incorporated, have achieved the product-market fit as well as have obtained the valuations that are beyond the current Indian SME definitions. These start-ups are classified as 'grown' start-ups – indicating that they are on the path of transformation from a start-up to a large enterprise.

By conducting MANOVA across these three categories of start-ups, we identify the key factors among the entrepreneurial, firm-specific, and external environment-specific domains that can help explain the differences prevailing in these three categories. Further, the multinomial logistic regression would be conducted to understand and statistically validate which of the factors have an influence on the entire start-up life cycle.

Factors Influencing the Life Cycle of High-tech Start-ups

Researchers have examined the life cycle of firms from the 1970s. The earliest examination of the life cycle of firms and their benefits can be traced back to Greiner (1972) who proposed a phase-based model to study the firm life cycle. This model was subsequently adopted to study small business firm life cycle during the 1980s by Churchill and Lewis (1983). The same model was enhanced to study the life cycle of high-tech start-ups by Masurel and Montfort (2006). As regards to the high-tech start-up life cycle, Masurel and Montfort (2006) observed that while the growth model that they proposed was stage-based (existence, survival, success, take-off, and resource maturity), each stage was characterized by size, diversity, complexity, and combinations of management factors.

Hite and Hesterly (2001) reviewed the stage-based life cycle models and commented that while a stage approach has clear limitations, this perspective was useful in framing the general processes of firm evolution and continuous change over time, particularly during the dynamic early stages of the firm. They described that the key point about firm stages was that each stage represented more than mere changes over time, rather they functioned as proxies for many strategic issues (Quinn and Cameron 1983; Reese and Aldrich 1995), such as goals, asset stocks, resource needs, and resource acquisition challenges. The presumption in life cycle approaches was that each stage represented a unique, strategic context that influenced the nature and extent of a firm's external resource needs and acquisition challenges. Thus, they explained that firms must overcome the resource acquisition challenges of each stage in order to successfully survive and grow (Bhide 2000; Churchill and Lewis 1983).

Aldrich (1999) and Pavia (1990) developed stage-based process model to study high-tech start-ups based on the genetic evolution theory of humans. Bhide (2000) explained the life cycle of firms in terms of the varying degrees of investment–uncertainty–profit trilogy. As can be observed, the literature till 1995 studied the activities along the life cycle of high-tech start-ups as being homogeneous between the phases of transition, and any heterogeneity signalled their transition from one phase to another. However, researchers, post 1995, questioned this almost static treatment of firms' activities when deciding about which phase they operated in. Chan, Bhargava, and Street (2006) acknowledged that a firm's journey towards attaining high growth and sustainable development is heterogeneous, but differences in the challenges that firms face decrease, once sustainable high growth is attained.

Blank (2010) tried to provide a set of new definitions to the life cycle of high-tech start-ups by explaining the differences that existed between start-ups and large businesses. He explained that start-ups were not smaller versions of large businesses. Blank (2012) used three primary aspects of strategy, process, and structure to explain the differences between start-ups and large established firms and thereby justified the need to arrive at a new life cycle model to explain start up life cycle. Ries (2011; 2014) further extended Blank's work and proposed the 'lean start-up' method for developing business and products in the high-tech sector. The objective of this methodology was to reduce product development cycles by execution of hypotheses-driven experiments, iterative product releases, and incremental learning of what worked and did not work from these experiments. Ries (2014) claimed that high-tech start-ups could limit failure and expensive spending if they invested their time in the initial days of operation in building products and services iteratively that met the needs of their early customers. The lean start-up method now encompasses Blank's customer development methodology, and also, leverages Osterwalder and Pigneur's (2010) business model canvas, combined with agile programming to complete the loop.

These recent contributions to high-tech start-up life cycle have meant that researchers have started the exploration of the micro aspects of activities of each phase of the start-up life cycle, in order to better explain the different phenomena related to high-tech start-ups. They have also helped to understand that small firms can switch between two types – entrepreneurial and life-style based – depending on the customer traction and founders' intention.

Summarizing this, we can conclude that high-tech start-ups can be viewed as operating in three key milestones of their life cycle: creation/emergence, survival, and growth. A rapid growth of the start-up transforms the firm to a midsize business or to a large business as the case may be, marking the end of it being termed or viewed as a start-up. Similarly, the start-up can end its operations or cease to exist at any of the aforementioned stages in the life cycle, either due to lack of customers or viable business model or due to entrepreneurial actions or intents.

From these contributions, it is evident that the knowledge on high-tech start-up life cycle incrementally evolved by an examination of multiple dimensions and factors over time. Further, the review of literature on factors impacting start-up life cycle revealed that the entrepreneurial factors that influence the phenomenon of start-up life cycle are age and education of the founder, prior industry experience, and prior start-up experience of the founder (Storey 1982; Ronstadt 1988).

Similarly, the firm-specific factors that influence the start-up life cycle are the functional resources of the start-up, such as human capital, financial capital, and sales and marketing capabilities (Kim, Aldrich, and Keister 2006; Munshi 2007). Last, to represent the macroeconomic environment as well as supporting external factors of the start-up ecosystem, three variables, namely, the percentage of SDP growth (year-on-year) of the region, the number of VCs present in the region, and the number of VC-funded deals in the region for a given year have been included in our study.

Based on these, we arrive at the following hypotheses regarding life cycle of high-tech start-ups.

Hypothesis 1: Prior industry experience of the primary founder positively influences all the three key life cycle milestones of emergence, survival, and growth of the start-up.

Hypothesis 2: Prior start-up experience of the primary founder positively influences all the three key life cycle milestones of emergence, survival, and growth of the start-up.

Hypothesis 3: Age of the founder positively influences all the three key life cycle milestones of emergence, survival, and growth of the start-up.

Hypothesis 4: Higher educational pedigree of the founder positively influences all the three key life cycle milestones of emergence, survival, and growth of the start-up.

Hypothesis 5: Higher development resources with the firm positively influences all the three key life cycle milestones of emergence, survival, and growth of the start-up.

Hypothesis 6: Higher number of customers acquired since inception of the firm positively influences all the three key life cycle milestones of emergence, survival, and growth of the start-up.

Hypothesis 7: Higher financial resources at the disposal of the firm positively influences all the three key life cycle milestones of emergence, survival, and growth of the start-up.

Hypothesis 8: Higher SDP growth in the region positively influences all the three key life cycle milestones of emergence, survival, and growth of the start-up.

Hypothesis 9: A higher presence of VCs in the region influences all the three key life cycle milestones of emergence, survival, and growth of the start-ups in that region.

Hypothesis 10: A higher number of funded VC deals in the region, influences all the three key life cycle milestones of emergence, survival, and growth of the start-ups in that region.

These hypotheses will be tested by subjecting the data of high-tech start-ups to multinomial logistic regression analysis. Prior to the regression analysis, the data of the high-tech start-ups would be classified under three categories (the start-ups that have been formally incorporated but not survived, start-ups that have survived but not grown, and start-ups that have experienced growth) based on the response the start-up founders provided to us. A statistical comparison of these three groups using MANOVA and two-way ANOVA is carried out using the grouping variables – life cycle status of the start-up, the target market segment, location of operations, and entrepreneurial exposure as baseline of comparison. These comparisons will reveal to us the key entrepreneur-specific, firm-specific, and external environment-specific factors that differentiate the three phases of start-up life cycle. With this initial insight, we then proceed to perform the multinomial regression analysis to ascertain the key factors that influence the entire life cycle of the high-tech start-ups.

Key Semantics of the Data

For the purposes of this analysis, the start-ups that have a formal registered office in India are considered for the study. The data of start-ups are divided into three groups as per the following description. The first group of the data consists of those start-ups that have formally incorporated their start-up in India but have not yet achieved the product-market fit (survival milestone). The second group of data consists of those start-ups that have already established product-market fit (formally incorporated and moved past the survival state), but have not yet achieved valuation beyond US$800,000 (equivalent to appropriately ₹5 crore) if their offerings are primarily services or valuation greater than US$1.6 million (equivalent to approximately ₹10 crore) if their offerings are based on manufacturing, are considered for this study. The third group of data consists of those start-ups that have been formally incorporated and those who have already established product-market fit, and ones that have their valuation above ₹5 crore (in case of services-based start-ups) or above ₹10 crore (in case of manufacturing-based start-ups).

This grouping is done to identify and classify start-ups into three distinct groups – start-ups that are emerged-only, start-ups that are survived-only, and start-ups that have grown. The emerged-only group consists of data of 88 start-ups. The survived-only group comprises of 38 start-ups, and the grown start-ups group has data from 49 start-ups. Most of the data used in our study are collected using our research instrument – the questionnaire. The secondary data are collected primarily to obtain the entrepreneur profile. The unit of analysis in our study has been the start-up represented by the founder. The firm-specific inputs about the start-up are also obtained from the founder of the start-up. The external environment variables relevant to the study are sourced from secondary data sources, such as *Economic Survey* reports, Venture Intelligence, and VCCircle.

We use the statistical techniques of multinomial regression analysis and MANOVA to analyse the life cycle of high-tech start-ups in this chapter. A brief overview of these methods has been provided in Chapter 2. Our initial step towards analysis is to identify, categorize, and quantify the factors that impact the entire life cycle of high-tech start-ups. We use the current life cycle status of the start-up as a measure to help classify the start-ups in our data. We then examine the three groups obtained by conducting MANOVA and two-way ANOVA, using the dimensions of target market segment (B2B or B2C), location of operations of the start-up (North Zone or South Zone), and entrepreneurial exposure (local or transnational). This profiling will help us in identifying the factors that differentiate for the different phases of the life cycle of start-ups across these groups.

Based on the insights obtained from this analysis, we then proceed to conduct multinomial regression with the life cycle status of the start-up as the dependent variable and the entrepreneur-specific, firm-specific, and external environment-specific factors as the independent variables. We also add three control variables to the model to moderate for the effects related to target market segment, location of operations, and entrepreneurial exposure.

Variables and Measures

We use the following independent and dependent variables as inputs for carrying out the various statistical tests in this chapter.

Dependent variable

The dependent variable for analysis is *life cycle status of the start-up*, a categorical variable. This variable has three levels, with the base level of 0, indicating that the start-up belongs to the emerged start-ups group. The second level of 1 represents that the particular start-up belongs to the survived start-ups group, and the third level of 2 represents that the start-up belongs to the growth category in the data. As discussed earlier, this categorization is done based on the status of the start-up as indicated by the founders during the data collection exercise. This variable is labelled in SPSS as *stage* for the purposes of analysis.

Independent variables

The relevant industry experience, prior start-up experience, and age and education of the entrepreneur are the entrepreneurial factors that are examined in this study. The number of customers that the start-up has served since its inception, the R&D capabilities, and funding status of the start-up form the organizational factors are examined for impact. Further, the SDP growth rate, number of VCs present in the region as well as the number of funded deals in the region are considered for examination in this study.

Relevant industry experience: It is a discrete dichotomous variable which indicates whether or not the founder has previous industry experience. This variable takes the value of 1 for every start-up founder who has industry experience prior to founding the current start-up considered for the study. A value of 0 for this variable indicates that the founder of the start-up does not possess any previous industry-working experience. This variable is labelled in SPSS as *fiexp* for the analysis.

Prior start-up experience: This is a discrete dichotomous variable which indicates whether or not the founder has prior start-up experience. This variable takes the value of 1 for every start-up founder who has experience in working in a start-up, either as an employee or as a founder prior to founding the current start-up considered for the study. A value of 0 for this variable indicates that the founder of the start-up does not possess any previous start-up experience. This variable is labelled in SPSS as *fsexp* for the analysis.

Age of the entrepreneur: This is in years at the time of founding the start-up. This variable is labelled in SPSS as *fage* for the analysis.

Education of the entrepreneur: It is categorized by using two dummy variables. The base reference variable indicates graduate education without an engineering degree (degree in science, arts, and others), the first dummy variable indicates graduate education with a technical (engineering) degree, and the second dummy variable indicating education with a technical master's degree or above. This variable is labelled in SPSS as *fedn* for the analysis. The base reference variable takes the value of 1 for every founder of the start-up whose education credentials are a non-engineering degree. A value of 0 for the base reference variable indicates the absence of a non-engineering degree of the founder. The first dummy variable *fedn(1)* takes the value of 1 for every start-up founder who has a technical (engineering) degree as his/her educational credentials. A value of 0 for this variable indicates the absence of a technical (engineering) degree of the founder. The second dummy variable *fedn(2)* takes the value of 1 for every start-up founder who has education credentials of a technical (engineering) master's degree or above. A value of 0 for this variable indicates the absence of a technical master's degree or a higher technical qualification (for example, PhD) of the founder.

Sales capabilities of the start-up: This variable is measured by the number of customers acquired since inception, standardized for the number of years in operation and for the target market segment. This variable serves as the proxy or indicator for the sales capabilities of the start-up and is measured as a continuous variable. This variable is labelled in SPSS as *sales* for the analysis.

R&D capabilities of the start-up: The R&D capabilities of the start-up is measured as the number of people in the R&D team, standardized for their work experience. This variable is measured as a continuous variable. This variable is labelled in SPSS as *dev* for the analysis.

Financial capabilities of the start-up: It is measured by a dichotomous (dummy) variable which indicates whether or not the start-up obtained funding, external to its founder's and his family's funds. A value of 0 also indicates that the founding team has managed to run the operations and pursue growth opportunities by reinvesting revenue from the operations without any external investor's support. A value of 1 for this variable indicates that the start-up is funded from external investors (seed, angel, VCs). This variable is labelled as *fin* in SPSS for the analysis.

SDP: This variable is used as a proxy for the macroeconomic environment prevalent at the state in which the start-up is located. This variable provides the percentage of change in the SDP in comparison to its previous year (at constant prices). This variable is labelled as *sdp* in SPSS for the analysis.

Number of funded deals: This variable is used to indicate the number of early-stage VC deals that happened for a given year and a given geography. This measure is a proxy to measure the maturity of the start-up ecosystem for the given year and geography. An increase in the number of funded early-stage deals in a given geography, year-on-year, indicates a healthy and growing start-up ecosystem. This variable is labelled as *deals* in SPSS for the analysis.

Number of VC funds: This variable indicates the presence of active VC funds for a given year and a given geography. This variable is a proxy to measure and understand the availability of external funding options for a particular region and year. This variable is labelled as *vc* in SPSS for the analysis.

Control variables

Target market segment: This variable is a dummy variable with two levels. A value of 0 indicates that the target market segment of the start-up is B2B sector, whereas the value of 1 indicates that the target market segment of the start-up is B2C sector. This variable is labelled as *market_segment* in SPSS for the analysis.

Location of operations: This variable is a dummy variable with two levels. A value of 0 indicates that the start-up is located in northern part of the country, whereas the value of 1 indicates that the start-up is located in the southern part of India. This variable is labelled as *Zone* in SPSS for the analysis.

Entrepreneurial background: This variable is a dummy variable with two levels. A value of 0 indicates that the entrepreneur is a local entrepreneur, whereas the value of 1 indicates that the entrepreneur is transnational (which indicates that the entrepreneur has exposure to working or studying in more than one country, other than the country of his/her origin, for a period of at least one year). This variable is labelled as *te* in SPSS for the analysis. The control variables are used for profiling the categories obtained by dividing the start-ups data, based on the life cycle stage of start-ups. As part of the MANOVA, we compare the groups across these control variables to arrive at additional insights about the factors that help differentiating the life cycle of high-tech start-ups. With the aforementioned background, we now move on to discuss the results obtained by executing the statistical methods on the variables outlined.

Discussion of Results

We present the results of the analysis of the key factors that impact the overall life cycle of high-tech start-ups. We begin with describing the relationships of the independent variables (entrepreneur-specific, firm-specific, and external environment-specific) with the dependent variable (life cycle status of the start-up). We then proceed to present the bivariate correlations between the variables considered for the analysis. Next, we present the results of the MANOVA performed to understand which factors differentiate amongst the three groups of start-ups that portray different stages in the overall life cycle. The MANOVA is conducted by using the life cycle status of the start-up, market segment targeted by the start-up, location of operations of the start-up, and entrepreneurial exposure as the baseline for comparison. Finally, we present the multinomial logistic regression model that is built to understand the factors affecting overall life cycle of high-tech start-ups in the sample.

As discussed in the earlier section of this chapter, the relevant industry experience, prior start-up experience, and age and education of the entrepreneur are the entrepreneurial input variables. The number of customers that the start-up has served since its inception, the R&D capabilities, and funding status of the start-up form the firm-specific variables that are fed as inputs to the analysis. Further, the SDP growth rate, number of VCs present in the region as well as the number of funded deals in the region are fed in as external environmental input variables for the model.

Univariate Analysis of Data

To begin with, the relationship of the dependent variable with the three segments, namely, (a) target market being addressed by the start-ups (B2B versus B2C), (b) location of operation of the start-ups (North Zone versus South Zone), and (c) exposure of the entrepreneurs (local versus transnational) are presented. As discussed earlier, the life cycle status of the start-up has been used as a baseline to categorize the start-ups in our sample into three groups. The distribution of high-tech start-ups based on their current phase in the start-up life cycle is presented in Figure 7.1.

We observe that about 50 per cent of the start-ups in our sample fall under the emerged-only category and about 22 per cent under the survived-only category while the remaining 28 per cent of the start-ups getting categorized under the grown category. The high percentage of the start-ups in the emerged-only category is reflective of the general trend in start-up life cycle across the geographies. Further, in the case of India, this higher percentage of presence of the emerged-only category of start-ups is indicative of the fact that many start-ups have started their operations in the recent years.

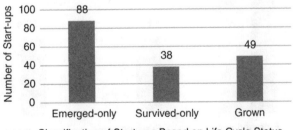

FIGURE 7.1 Distribution of start-ups based on their current start-up life cycle phase

SOURCE: Author.

In order to obtain a deeper initial insight into the spread and distribution of the start-ups in our sample, we examined the start-ups data against three segments, namely, (a) target market being addressed by the start-ups (B2B versus B2C), (a) location of operation of the start-ups (North Zone versus South Zone), and (c) exposure of the entrepreneurs (local versus transnational). Figures 7.2–7.4 provide the visual description of the spread of start-ups under the three dimensions respectively.

From Figure 7.2, we can make the following observations. First, the visual examination of the graph indicates that a large number of start-ups are in the emergence stage, reflecting that many start-ups are recently incorporated. We observe that B2C start-ups account for a majority (58 per cent of the group) in comparison to the B2B start-ups (42 per cent of the group). Second, in the survived group, we observe that B2B start-ups account for the majority (68 per cent of the group) relative to B2C start-ups (32 per cent of the group). Finally, in the growth group, we observe that B2C start-ups account for about 47 per cent of the group relative to B2B start-ups which comprise of 53 per cent of the group.

The visual analysis of data based on the location of operations as presented in Figure 7.3 clearly brings out that there are more number of start-ups operating in the South Zone of the country. The aforementioned observation can also be interpreted as South Zone region being the preferred location for start-up operations irrespective of milestone of operation of the start-up.

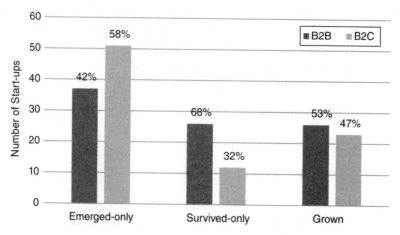

Figure 7.2 Distribution of start-ups based on target market segment

Source: Author.

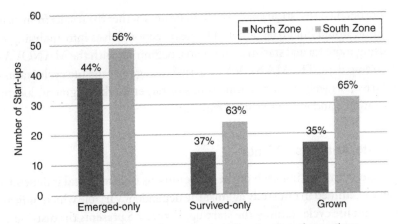

FIGURE 7.3 Distribution of start-ups based on location of operations

Source: Author.

The visual inspection of Figure 7.4 based on entrepreneurial exposure indicates a similar spread of start-ups that we observed with the target market segment. We see that the emerged-only and the grown categories of start-ups are having minimal variance (between 0 and 6 per cent) between the local and transnational entrepreneurs, whereas in the second category of the survived-only start-ups, we see that transnational entrepreneur led start-ups being in the majority with about 61 per cent of the sample represented by them. These observations indicate that transnational entrepreneurship effects may be prominent in ensuring survival but may not be influential in impacting the emergence or growth of high-tech start-ups in India.

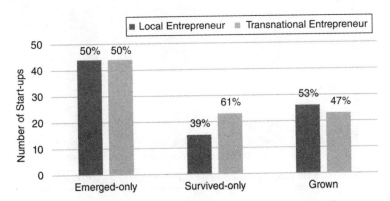

FIGURE 7.4 Distribution of start-ups based on entrepreneurial exposure

Source: Author.

More detailed statistical analysis will indicate whether the results from visual inspection would hold true or not. The next section delves into analysing the data using more formal statistical methods, beginning with the MANOVA of the start-up data. The MANOVA is carried out against the life cycle status of the start-up as well as on the dimensions of target market segment, location of operations, and entrepreneurial exposure.

Bivariate Analysis of Data

We begin with plotting each of the dichotomous or categorical independent variable examined in our study against the dependent variable which indicates the current life cycle status of the start-up. Figure 7.5 presents the distribution of start-ups based on the prior industry experience of the founders. We observe that across all the groups, the founders of the start-ups have prior industry experience. Among the two groups – survived-only and grown – about 95 per cent of the sample has founders with prior start-up experience, with the first group having about 85 per cent representation. This similarity of presence of founders with prior industry experience across all the groups indicates that this variable may not help in differentiating across the three groups. However, a statistical test like MANOVA can formally validate these initial observations.

Figure 7.6 presents the distribution of start-ups across the three categories when distributed against the values of prior start-up experience of the founders

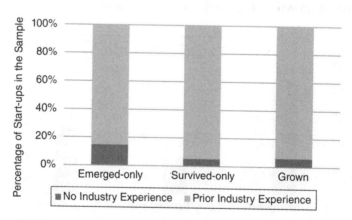

FIGURE 7.5 Distribution of start-ups based on founders' prior industry experiences
SOURCE: Author.

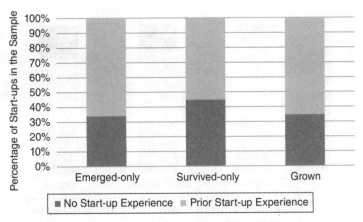

FIGURE 7.6 Distribution of start-ups based on founders' prior start-up experiences

SOURCE: Author.

in our sample. We observe that in this case as well, there seems to be lesser variance (about 10 per cent) among the three categories of start-ups when the data are divided based on the prior start-up experience of the founders. While the first group of emerged-only and the third group of grown start-ups have about 35 per cent of founders with no prior start-up experience, about 45 per cent of start-up founders in the second group of survived-only start-ups represent this segment. This minimal variance across the three categories seems to indicate that prior start-up experience may not be able to explain better the differences between the three categories of start-ups.

The distribution of start-ups across the three life cycle categories when compared against the educational credentials of the start-up founders is presented in Figure 7.7. We can observe that education seems to influence the transition of start-ups from one life cycle milestone to the next. In particular, educational credentials of masters' degree and above seem to distinctly influence the survival and growth of start-ups in the respective groups. The variance in the contribution of each type of educational degree across the three life cycle categories of start-ups seems to indicate that the education of the founders would have an influence across the entire life cycle of high-tech start-ups, and in particular, it would be helpful in explaining the differences among the three categories of the start-ups.

Figure 7.8 presents the distribution of start-ups across the three life cycle stages when compared against the funding or financial capitalization status of the start-ups. From these visuals, we can infer that external funding seems

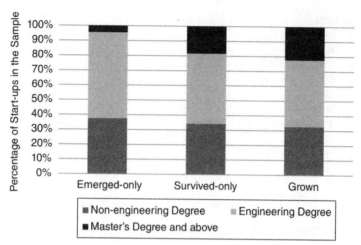

Figure 7.7 Distribution of start-ups based on founders' educational backgrounds

Source: Author.

to influence the growth of high-tech start-ups, whereas it may have limited influence in impacting the emergence or survival of the start-ups. However, a formal statistical validation will let us know if these initial observations are indeed valid.

As a first step towards formal statistical validation of these initial visual observations, we present the bivariate analysis of all variables performed against

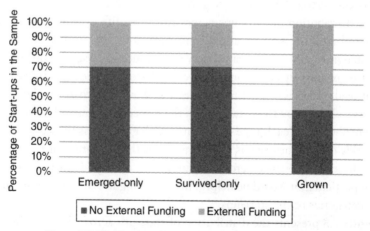

Figure 7.8 Distribution of start-ups based on funding status

Source: Author.

TABLE 7.1 Chi-square test results of life cycle status of start-up against the input variables

Variable name	Chi-square statistic value	p-value
Industry experience of the entrepreneur	3.8792	0.1438
Start-up experience of the entrepreneur	1.4001	0.4966
Education pedigree of the entrepreneur	10.757	**0.02944**
Financial capitalization status of the start-up	11.6639	**0.002932**
Target market segment	7.5196	**0.02329**
Location of operations	1.4164	0.4925
Entrepreneurial exposure	1.7264	0.4218

SOURCE: Author.

NOTE: P-values of significant results are in **bold**.

the dependent variable (current life cycle status of the start-up) for the study in Tables 7.1 and 7.2. Table 7.1 presents the bivariate analysis performed against the categorical and dichotomous variables in our study. Chi-square tests are carried out to understand whether the variables of our study are statistically independent when compared against the dependent variable. For all the continuous variables examined in our study, one-way ANOVA are executed to test the statistical relationship between an independent variable with the dependent variable. The results of these one-way ANOVA are documented in Table 7.2.

TABLE 7.2 One-way ANOVA results of life cycle status of start-up against continuous input variables

	Computed F-values	p-value	Homogeneity of variance
Age of the founder (years)	3.580	**0.030**	Yes
Sales capabilities of the start-up	5.631	**0.004**	Yes
R&D capabilities of the start-up	1.384	0.253	Yes
SDP	2.046	0.132	Yes
Number of deals	4.847	**0.009**	Yes
Number of VCs	3.948	**0.021**	No

SOURCE: Author.

NOTE: The test for equality of means was preceded by the test for equality of variances. In case the variances are equal, the regular F-statistic values have been reported; otherwise Welsch-F-statistic values have been reported. p-values of significant results are in **bold**.

The chi-square tests of the dichotomous and categorical variables indicate that educational qualification of the founder, the financial capitalization of the start-up, and the target market segment which the start-up is focusing on are significant. In other words, these three factors are shown to be individually demonstrating dependence on the life cycle status of the start-up. The low p-values against these variables indicate the rejection of the null hypothesis (null hypothesis states that these two variables are independent of each other) which establishes the dependence of these two variables on each other. These results also imply that factors such as prior industry and prior start-up experience of the founders, the location of operations of the start-up, and the entrepreneurial exposure turn out to be statistically independent with respect to the life cycle status of the start-up at the univariate level.

The one-way ANOVA results indicate that age of the entrepreneur, sales capabilities of the start-up, presence of VCs in the region, and number of funded VC deals in the region can help in explaining the differences among the three start-up groups. In the case of one-way ANOVA, the null hypothesis would be that the means of all the continuous variables that are examined against the dependent variable are the same. Therefore, a very low p-value in this case implies that the null hypothesis is rejected – indicating that there are significant differences in the distributions of values of the continuous variable across the three categories. This implies that all variables that have a low p-value (lesser than 0.05) would actually be able to explain the differences across the three stages of emergence, survival, and growth of the high-tech start-ups in the sample. In contrast, the variables capturing the R&D capabilities and the percentage of SDP growth in the region do not come out as significant, which indicates that these variables may not be able to explain the differences across the three start-up groups at a univariate level.

MANOVA Results

The classification of start-ups into three distinct categories based on their current milestone and their visual analysis have provided an initial insight on what factors can affect the entire life cycle of high-tech start-ups. However, we need to further obtain formal validity by pursuing MANOVA on the data we have for the study and revalidate the initial observations. In this section, we report the MANOVA results that we obtained by subjecting the three different sets of input variables, namely, the entrepreneur-specific variables, the firm-specific variables, and the external environment-specific variables against the life cycle status of the start-up. We then pursue the same method

TABLE 7.3 MANOVA, based on life cycle status of the start-ups

	Approximate value of the test statistic	Approximate F-statistic value	p-value
Pillai's race	0.19648	3.0503	**0.0004264**
Wilks' lambda	0.81192	3.0559	**0.0004181**
Hotelling's trace	0.22129	3.0612	**0.0004105**
Roy's largest root	0.15416	4.3166	**0.0004466**

SOURCE: Author.

NOTE: p-values of significant results are in **bold**.

and perform the MANOVA of these input variables on the three segments, namely, (a) target market being addressed by the start-ups (B2B versus B2C), (b) location of operation of the start-ups (North Zone versus South Zone), and (c) exposure of the entrepreneurs (local versus transnational).

MANOVA, based on life cycle status of the start-ups

The MANOVAs are carried out in two steps. In the first step, the MANOVA is carried out with the entrepreneur-specific, firm-specific, and external environment-specific input variables as the dependent variables and the grouping variable as the independent variable. The results of this step will let us know if the input variables differ at a multivariate level. In the second step, we perform F-tests against each individual dependent variable of the group, against the independent variable. The results of these F-tests will help us determine as to what factors from this input group will actually help differentiate across the groups of the start-ups at a micro level.

TABLE 7.4 F-test results of individual variables against life cycle status of start-ups

Variable name	Mean square value	F-statistic value	p-value
Founder's age	175.166	3.5795	**0.02999**
Sales capabilities of the start-up	255077	5.6308	**0.004279**
R&D capabilities of the start-up	184.28	1.3843	0.2533
Percentage of SDP change in the region	0.004233	2.0461	0.1324
Number of funded deals in the region	6175.5	4.8468	**0.008959**
Number of VCs in the region	3251.1	3.9479	**0.02107**

SOURCE: Author.

NOTE: p-values of significant results are in **bold**.

The results from MANOVA of the input variables are presented in Table 7.3. We observe that all the p-values corresponding to the four different variants of MANOVA are significant. This implies that at the outset, there are significant differences between the two groups at the multivariate level. However, in order to ascertain that the insignificant individual input variables do not potentially mask the significance of the other significant ones at the *multivariate* level, we performed separate F-tests for all the individual variables. The individual F-tests of each variable will also help us to ascertain which of the input variables actually are responsible for the influence on the life cycle of high-tech start-ups. Accordingly, the results obtained from the individual F-tests have been presented in Table 7.4. From the individual F-test results presented in Table 7.4, we can infer that the age of the founder, sales capabilities of the start-up, presence of VCs in the region, and the number of funded VC deals in the region are the key factors that help differentiate across the three life cycle groups of high-tech start-ups.

MANOVA, based on target market segment

The results of the MANOVA, performed on the input variables against the target market segment in which the start-ups operate (B2B or B2C) are presented in Table 7.5. In this case, the entrepreneur-specific, firm-specific, and environment-specific continuous variables are the dependent variables for the MANOVA and the grouping dummy variable capturing the target market segment is the independent variable. We perform a two-step execution here as well, similar to the test execution and analysis carried out in the previous section. In the first step, the MANOVA results are obtained and are presented in Table 7.5. From the results presented in Table 7.5, we observe that for all the four variant tests of MANOVA, the input variables display significant variance, implying that the target market segment variable may be useful in explaining the difference across the groups at the multivariate level.

However, in order to ensure that individual input variables do not mask the presence or influence of significant input variables, we conduct F-tests against each firm-specific input variable. The results of these individual F-tests are summarized in Table 7.6. From the results, we can infer that only one factor, namely, the age of the founder is the key influencing factor among the input attributes that differentiate across the life cycle of high-tech start-ups.

TABLE 7.5 MANOVA, based on target market segment

	Approximate value of the test statistic	Approximate F-statistic value	p-value
Pillai's trace	0.092451	2.8523	**0.01136**
Wilks' lambda	0.90755	2.8523	**0.01136**
Hotelling's trace	0.10187	2.8523	**0.01136**
Roy's largest root	0.10187	2.8523	**0.01136**

Source: Author.

Note: p-values of significant results are in **bold**.

MANOVA, based on location of operations

The results of MANOVA of the input variables against the location of operations (North Zone or South Zone) of the start-ups is presented in Table 7.7. The results indicate that the input variables influence variance across the groups. In other words, the location of operations may be able to explain the differences between the groups of start-ups.

To understand precisely the contributions of the individual environment-specific variables to the life cycle of the start-ups in these groups, F-tests are conducted for each of the dependent–independent variable pairs. The results from the individual F-tests are presented in Table 7.8. The results statistically confirm that the number of VC-funded deals in the region help in differentiating the life cycle of high-tech start-ups.

TABLE 7.6 F-test results of individual variables against target market segment

Variable name	Mean square value	F-statistic value	p-value
Founder's age	561.2	11.831	**0.00073**
Sales capabilities of the start-up	92855	1.9569	0.1636
R&D capabilities of the start-up	12.8	0.0951	0.7581
Percentage of SDP change in the region	0.00008	0.037	0.8476
Number of funded deals in the region	197	0.1476	0.7013
Number of VCs in the region	1126	1.3249	0.2513

Source: Author.

Note: p-values of significant results are in **bold**.

TABLE 7.7 MANOVA, based on location of operations

	Approximate value of the test statistic	Approximate F-statistic value	p-value
Pillai's trace	0.33455	14.077	**5.942e⁻¹³**
Wilks' lambda	0.66545	14.077	**5.942e⁻¹³**
Hotelling's trace	0.50274	14.077	**5.942e⁻¹³**
Roy's largest root	0.50274	14.077	**5.942e⁻¹³**

Source: Author.

Note: p-values of significant results are in **bold**.

MANOVA, based on entrepreneurial exposure

The results of MANOVA of the input variables against entrepreneurial exposure (local or transnational) of the start-ups is presented in Table 7.9. The results indicate that for all the four variants of the MANOVA, the input variables influence variance across the groups. In other words, entrepreneurial exposure may be able to explain for a significant portion of the differences across the groups of start-ups considered for this study.

We also notice that the p-values across all the four variants of the test are the same, indicating that there is good convergence of the model results despite examining with multiple available techniques. Further, to understand precisely the contributions of the individual variables to the life cycle of the start-ups in both these groups, F-tests are conducted for each of the dependent–independent variable pairs. The results from the individual F-tests are presented in Table 7.10. The results statistically confirm that age of the entrepreneur is the only factor that helps to differentiate the life cycle of high-tech start-ups.

TABLE 7.8 F-test results of individual variables against location of operations

Variable name	Mean square value	F-statistic value	p-value
Founder's age	34	0.6739	0.4128
Sales capabilities of the start-up	32156	0.6727	0.4132
R&D capabilities of the start-up	229.8	1.7257	0.1907
Percentage of SDP change in the region	0.00093	0.4444	0.5059
Number of funded deals in the region	31587	27.334	**4.892e⁻⁰⁷**
Number of VCs in the region	409	0.4785	0.49

Source: Author.

Note: p-values of significant results are in **bold**.

TABLE 7.9 MANOVA, based on entrepreneurial exposure

	Approximate value of the test statistic	Approximate F-statistic value	p-value
Pillai's trace	0.10697	3.354	**0.003792**
Wilks' lambda	0.89303	3.354	**0.003792**
Hotelling's trace	0.11978	3.354	**0.003792**
Roy's largest root	0.11978	3.354	**0.003792**

SOURCE: Author.

NOTE: p-values of significant results are in **bold**.

Summary of the MANOVA

Based on the results obtained from four sets of MANOVA, we can draw the following conclusions. When we review the start-ups with the lens of their current life cycle status, we find that age of the entrepreneur, the sales capabilities of the start-up, and the number of VCs and funded VC deals in the region are able to differentiate the start-up categories. However, with just the MANOVA, we cannot quantify the degree of influence of these factors for each of the groups in our data. Further, if we were to analyse which factors differentiate the start-ups life cycle from the lens of market segment being targeted or by the entrepreneurial exposure of the founders of these start-ups, it appears that the age of the entrepreneur is able to differentiate the groups of start-ups statistically.

TABLE 7.10 F-test results of individual variables against entrepreneurial exposure

Variable name	Mean square value	Fstatistic value	p-value
Founder's age	897.9	19.738	**1.58e^{-05}**
Sales capabilities of the start-up	420	0.0088	0.9255
R&D capabilities of the start-up	52.2	0.3892	0.5335
Percentage of SDP change in the region	0.00001	0.0028	0.958
Number of funded deals in the region	495	0.3711	0.5432
Number of VCs in the region	233	0.2722	0.6026

SOURCE: Author.

NOTE: p-values of significant results are in **bold**.

Results of the Multinomial Regression Analysis

The previous tests of MANOVA and the initial visual inspection of the raw data by graphical methods have provided us initial insights on what factors might influence and differentiate the entire life cycle of high-tech start-ups present in our sample. In this section, we present the results of the multinomial regression analysis carried out to statistically validate and understand the key factors that impact the entire life cycle of high-tech start-ups in India.

Prior to execution of the multinomial regression analysis, we need to ensure that the assumptions of this statistical method are met by the data. We validate these assumptions by graphical examination of the statistical plots of the independent variables to begin with and later, based on the multinomial regression analysis, we build the optimal model that fits the data in our study. Then, we analyse the results obtained by the execution of this optimal multinomial regression model and discuss the outcomes and implications.

Graphical validation of assumptions

We need to first validate the assumptions that are required to be satisfied for the application of the multinomial regression analysis. The first step involved in execution of any regression analysis technique is to visually or graphically analyse the independent continuous variables in the study and understand its distribution.

To begin with, Figure 7.9 presents the box plot of the founders' age versus the valuation categories of the start-ups. From Figure 7.9, we can observe clearly that as the age of the entrepreneur increases, the probability of them operating growth start-ups increases. For example, we see that the age of the entrepreneurs in the emerged-only group of start-ups (indicated by the group number 0 under the x-axis) lies between 25 and 30 years. Further, we see that the survived-only start-up group has founders aged between 32 and 37 years. The growth group of start-ups in our sample has entrepreneurs aged 40 years and above along with a few outliers. From Figure 7.9, we, therefore, can find some initial support for our hypothesis on founder-age influencing the start-up life cycle.

The box plot indicating the relationship between the number of VC deals in a given region versus the categories of life cycle of start-ups is presented in Figure 7.10. We can observe that deals positively seem to influence the life cycle of the start-ups. In other words, as the number of deals in a region grows, we

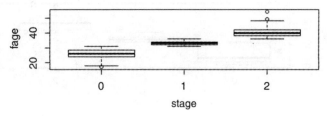

FIGURE 7.9 Box plot of founders' age versus life cycle status of start-ups

SOURCE: Author.

can infer that the start-ups in that region are likely to register higher growth. From the data of start-ups in our study, we can observe that the emerged-only group of start-ups is based in regions where lesser number of deals happens in a year – in the range of 18 to 42 deals per year. The survived-only related start-up group seems to be based in regions where the number of deals ranges between 65 and 75 per year with the average closer to the lower bound of about 65 to 70 deals per year. Further, we observe that growth group of start-ups are based in the region where about 85 to 120 deals per year take place. These observations imply that the number of deals in the region might positively influence the life cycle of the start-ups.

Figure 7.11 presents the box plot obtained by a comparison of number of VCs present in a given region versus the categories of life cycle status of the start-ups. We can infer that the larger the presence of VCs in a given region, the more number of growth start-ups we can expect operating in that region. An analysis of the correlations between the three groups and the number of VCs in the corresponding regions indicate that emerged-only group of start-ups has a lesser number of VCs, physically located in their region of operation, ranging between 10 and 45 with the average value of about 20 VCs in the

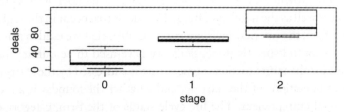

FIGURE 7.10 Box plot of number of VC deals in the region versus life cycle status of start-ups

SOURCE: Author.

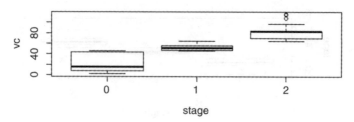

FIGURE 7.11 Box plot of number of VCs in the region versus life cycle status of start-ups

SOURCE: Author.

region. However, we observe from Figure 7.11 that about 50 to 60 VCs are present in the regions of start-ups that are in the survived-only group, with the average being biased towards the lower limit of about 50 VCs in that region. Similarly, we see that in the regions where growth-based start-up groups are operating, we have a higher presence of VCs in the range of 70 to 90 VCs, with an average of 80 VCs operating in these regions.

Armed with these initial observations, we now proceed to build and obtain the optimal model that could be used for analysis of factors impacting the life cycle of high-tech start-ups.

Model selection

To begin with, we build a full model consisting of all the variables that are hypothesized to have an influence on the life cycle of high-tech start-ups. These variables include the entrepreneur-specific variables, such as prior start-up experience, prior industry experience, and age and education of the founder of the start-up.

Further, the firm-specific variables that are included in the model are sales capabilities, R&D capabilities, and the financial capitalization status of the start-up. The SDP growth (year-on-year) of the region, the number of VCs present in the region as well as the number of funded VC deals that occur in the region for a given year form the external environmental variables that are used in this model. Further, to control specific dimensions, we have used three dummy variables to account for the target market segment that is addressed by the start-ups, the location of operations of the start-up, and whether the founder is a local or a transnational entrepreneur. The life cycle status of the firm, categorized into three groups – emerged, survived, and growth – based on the current status of their start-up, is the multinomial dependent variable in this case.

To validate whether the full model will be able to adequately and accurately provide a statistically significant result, we executed the chi-square results between the base model, containing only the intercept, and the full model that has all the variables loaded on to it, using the SPSS statistical package. The results of these tests are presented in Table 7.11. We found that our full model is able to explain a lot more variance in the model (on account of presence of independent variables in the model) as compared to the base model with only the intercept. The very low p-value of 0.000 in the 'model fitting information' column indicates that the two models that are compared with each other are statistically very different, implying that the full model that has been constructed is apt for usage and analysis.

Results of the optimal model

The results from the execution of the optimal model for multinomial regression analysis are presented in Table 7.12. From the results of execution, we observe that the entrepreneur-specific variables of *education of the founder*; the firm-specific variables, namely, the *financial capabilities of the start-up*; and among the external environment variables, namely, *SDP growth and the number of VC-funded deals in the region,* are significant influencers across the entire life cycle of high-tech start-ups. Further, the life cycle of high-tech start-ups operating in the South Zone region tend to accomplish key milestones across the entire life cycle faster, based on the results obtained from this study.

From the parameter estimates obtained out of the execution of this model (presented in the chapter-end Appendix as Tables 7A.1 and 7A.2), we can observe the following aspects. An increase in year-on-year SDP growth would benefit the survived group of start-ups relative to the emerged-only start-ups, whereas an increase in VC deals in the region would likely benefit the emerged-only start-ups group. Similarly, in the North Zone, we could likely see more number of start-ups in the emerged phase than the ones in the survived phase.

Further, founders with no prior start-up experience are more likely to be expected in the emerged-only start-ups group, rather than in the grown start-ups group. Similarly, founders with technical (engineering) degrees or degrees higher than technical degrees are more likely to be found in the emerged-only start-ups group rather than in the grown start-ups group. Also, a start-up with no external funding is more likely to belong to the emerged-only group of start-ups, rather than in the grown start-ups group. In the North Zone, we could likely see more number of start-ups in the emerged phase than the ones in the growth phase.

TABLE 7.11 Optimal model selection test results

Model fitting information: Final model – Chisq = 65.141 with 28 degrees of freedom, p-value = 0.000	Cox and Snell R^2 = 0.311, Nagelkerke R^2 = 0.356
Goodness of fit-Pearson: Chisq = 365.511 on 318 degrees of freedom, p-value = 0.034	Goodness of fit-Pearson–Deviance: Chisq = 296.667 on 318 degrees of freedom, p-value = 0.799

SOURCE: Author.

The other notable aspects coming out of these results are that prior industry experience of the entrepreneur does not seem to contribute across the entire life cycle of high-tech start-ups. In similar fashion, we observe that the sales and R&D capabilities of the high-tech start-ups do not seem to have an influence across the entire life cycle of start-ups, whereas they have been found to be important in influencing emergence and survival of

TABLE 7.12 Results of multinomial regression execution of the optimal model

Effect	-2 log likelihood of reduced model	Chi-square	Degree of freedom	Sig.
Intercept	296.667(a)	0.000	0	
fage	299.942	3.274	2	0.195
sales	300.765	4.097	2	0.129
dev	298.481	1.814	2	0.404
sdp	301.489	4.822	2	0.090
deals	303.911	7.243	2	0.027
vc	297.533	0.865	2	0.649
fiexp	298.641	1.974	2	0.373
fsexp	300.865	4.197	2	0.123
fedn	307.177	10.509	4	0.033
fin	302.738	6.070	2	0.048
market_segment	299.462	2.794	2	0.247
te	298.653	1.985	2	0.371
zone	301.738	5.070	2	0.079

SOURCE: Author.

the start-ups in some contexts. Further, among the three segments that are controlled to develop further insights on the life cycle of high-tech start-ups, our results indicate that the target market segment and entrepreneurial exposure of the founders are not significant enough to impact across the entire life cycle of high-tech start-ups. We also note that prior start-up experience comes out significant in comparison between the emerged-only and growth-only start-ups.

These results have important implications in the context of the life cycle studies of high-tech start-ups, and they need to be explained further. First, we will explain the relevance of the factors, which have been a significant influence on the entire life cycle of high-tech start-ups. The result that education of the entrepreneur impacts the entire life cycle of high-tech start-ups is a finding that is in line with previous such examinations. Davidsson and Honig (2003) argued that educational pedigree of the entrepreneur is often a proxy for the social capital and access to additional resources. During the development stages of the start-up, these additional resources are most needed in order to fulfil the myriad requirements of scaling up of the start-up. It is important to note that in our sample of study of high-tech start-ups, all the founders are technically qualified. This implies that basic technology skills and domain knowledge is a prerequisite for starting up and growing new ventures in the high-tech sector.

Financial capitalization as one of the key factors, influential across the life cycle of high-tech start-ups, is a finding that validates similar observations done in different geographies. Audretsch (1991) had detailed the importance of a firm being financially capitalized, particularly if the firm were to operate in the emerging technology sector. The reasons for the relevance of adequate capitalization is explainable as follows. Financial capital is one of the key factor inputs across any stage in the life cycle of a high-tech start-up. Without this factor input, acquisition of any other resource across all phases gets into a jeopardy. Our results indicate that financial capitalization through internal sources augur well for start-ups in India.

The external ecosystem parameters of percentage of SDP growth in the region as well as the number of VC-funded deals in the region, coming out as significant influencers across the overall life cycle of high-tech start-ups, can be explained as follows. The SDP variable in particular is taken as a proxy to represent the total market demand that exists in the economy or the region in which the start-up is operating. Apart from the market demand, the SDP growth also points out to the stability of the macroeconomy that includes the policy postures of the local and central governments, the governance, and grievance redressal mechanisms that are in place at any given region. A healthy year-to-year growth in SDP indicates the vibrancy of the economy and its ability to accommodate new economic ideas. On the same lines, the variable indicating the number of VC-funded deals in the given region acts as a proxy for us to understand the financial mechanisms that are in place to support growth in emerging and new technologies. Both of these factors, therefore, contribute to creation and sustenance of a vibrant start-up ecosystem in their respective regions.

We now examine the results to understand the absence of a few hypothesized variables in the final results. Among the entrepreneur-specific factors, prior start-up experience and prior industry experience of the entrepreneur were thought of to be significant influencers across the life cycle of the high-tech start-ups. From our results, it is evident that these factors play a key role in the initial phases of the start-up life cycle but may not be too useful in the growth stage of the start-up. Clement et al. 2007 did not find evidence of either prior start-up experience or prior industry experience as being influential across the entire life cycle. Earlier work by Storey (1982) and Ronstadt (1988) also indicated that these aspects would be important in reaching specific milestones such as survival, and not across the entire life cycle.

We obtain the results that age of the entrepreneur may not statistically influence the life cycle of the start-ups as a whole. Prior literature, studying the influence of age on start-up life cycle, indicated age as a proxy for accumulation of knowledge, insight, and experience (Wennberg and Lindqvist 2010). This knowledge and insight were hypothesized to aid the entrepreneurs in dealing with all the operational challenges during the growth phase in a much better manner in comparison to the younger counterparts. However, the formal results point out that age of the entrepreneur may not aid across the entire life cycle. These findings provide support to the prior findings of Gimeno et al. (1997) who argued that higher age hinders the entrepreneurs in contributing effectively across the life cycle of high-tech start-ups on account of higher switching costs in comparison to their younger counterparts.

The result that neither the R&D capabilities nor the sales capabilities of the start-up are influential in impacting across the life cycle of the high-tech start-ups is explained as follows. If one reviews the literature landscape across the phases of the high-tech start-up life cycle, we find evidence of

R&D capabilities being key factor during the early stages of start-up life cycle (emergence and survival), and in similar vein, the sales capabilities have found to be crucial in influencing survival and growth of high-tech start-ups (Davidsson and Delmar 2003). However, in this case, we have evaluated these variables for impact across the life cycle. The absence of statistical significance for these two variables does not indicate that they are not important. Instead, we need to understand that through the financial capitalization of the start-up at various stages of the life cycle, these capabilities can be acquired by the start-up, as and when needed. This is the reason we have the financial capabilities of the start-up being significant across the entire life cycle. Adequate financial capitalization will pave way to attract and incentivize talented and skilled workforce to support the scale-up of the R&D as well as the sales activities of the start-up.

Summary

In this chapter, we have attempted to understand the factors that influence and impact the entire life cycle of the high-tech start-ups in India. Drawing from our literature review, we have analysed the factors that contribute to the life cycle of the start-ups from three specific dimensions: entrepreneur-specific, firm-specific, and external environment-specific aspects.

In order to study the impact of factors affecting the life cycle of start-ups, we grouped the data of start-ups that are collected during our study into three distinct categories based on their current status of the life cycle milestone achieved. The first category of start-ups included those start-ups that have formally been incorporated – but who have not yet achieved the product-market fit. This category of start-ups constituted the 'emerged-only' start-ups group. The second category of start-ups included are those who are formally incorporated as well as have achieved the product-market fit – but have not yet crossed beyond the SME valuations of ₹5 crore if their offerings are services-based or ₹10 crore if their operations are based on manufacturing. This category of start-ups constituted the 'survived-only' start-ups group. The third category of start-ups comprised of those who have been formally incorporated, have achieved the product-market fit as well as have obtained valuations that are beyond the current Indian SME definitions. These start-ups are classified as 'grown' start-ups – indicating that they are on the path of transformation from a start-up to a large enterprise.

Once these groups are identified, we examined these groups using three segments, namely, the target market segment, location of operations of the start-up, and the entrepreneurial exposure. The examination across these groups using the variables from these three segments provided us with a deeper understanding of factors that may influence the entire life cycle of high-tech start-ups. By conducting MANOVA across these three categories of start-ups, we identified the key factors among the entrepreneurial, firm-specific, and external environment-specific domains that explain the differences prevailing in these three categories.

Based on the results obtained from the four sets of MANOVA, we can draw the following conclusions. When we review the start-ups with the lens of their current life cycle status, we find that age of the entrepreneur, the sales capabilities of the start-up, and the number of VCs and funded-VC deals in the region are able to differentiate the start-up categories. However, with just MANOVA, we cannot quantify the degree of influence of these factors for each of the groups in our data. Second, the age of the entrepreneur is able to differentiate the groups of start-ups statistically if we group the start-ups from the lens of market segment (B2B versus B2C) or by the entrepreneurial exposure (local versus transnational).

The MANOVA of the start-ups based on location of operations indicate that largely, the presence of a favourable ecosystem for start-ups, by the way of a healthy number of VC-funded deals, seems to differentiate the life cycles of start-ups. These results imply that entrepreneurs need to accumulate knowledge, skills, and experience in order to set up and grow a new venture. Further, the results also indicate the need of an enabling financial support system that helps in growth of start-ups.

Armed with the statistical results of comparison across multiple groups based on different dimensions of analysis, we then conducted tests to understand the factors that impact the entire life cycle of high-tech start-ups. The multinomial regression analysis revealed that the start-ups operating in South Zone are more likely to prosper well in comparison to the North Zone counterparts. Table 7.13 summarizes the hypotheses that were supported or unsupported based on the analyses. An entry 'Accepted' in the table indicates acceptance of the hypotheses. The sign in the brackets indicates the direction of the influence of the variable. A '+' sign indicates positive influence, whereas a '–' sign indicates negative influence.

TABLE 7.13 Summary of hypotheses evaluations related to the life cycle of high-tech start-ups

	Survived-only group against emerged-only group (baseline)	Grown-only group against emerged-only group (baseline)
H 1: Prior industry experience		
H 2: Prior start-up experience		Accepted (−)
H 3: Age of the founder		
H 4: Education of the founder		Accepted (−)
H 5: Sales capabilities of the start-up		
H 6: R&D capabilities of the start-up		
H 7: Financial capabilities of the start-up		Accepted (−)
H 8: SDP Growth	Accepted (+)	
H 9: Number of VC-funded deals	Accepted (−)	
H 10: Number of VCs in the region		

SOURCE: Author.

NOTE: All the empty cells in the table indicate the rejection of the hypotheses.

Appendix: Parameter Estimates of Both Stages of Multinomial Regression

TABLE 7A.1 Parameter estimates of the multinomial regression – emerged versus survived

Model variables (stage = 1; results between emerged-only and survived-nly groups)	Beta coefficient (β)	Standard error	Wald statistic	Degree of freedom	Significance (p-value)	Exp. (β)
Intercept	−1.385	1.699	0.664	1	0.415	
Age of the entrepreneur (fage)	0.055	0.037	2.224	1	0.136	1.056
Sales capabilities of the start-up (sales)	0.001	0.002	0.637	1	0.425	1.001
R&D capabilities of the start-up (dev)	−0.034	0.031	1.204	1	0.273	0.966
SDP growth (sdp)	9.582	4.730	4.103	1	0.043	14494.609
Number of deals in the region (deals)	−0.033	0.013	6.236	1	0.013	0.967
Number of VCs in the region (vc)	0.013	0.014	0.852	1	0.356	1.013
No industry experience (fiexp = 0)	−0.598	0.892	0.449	1	0.503	0.550
Prior industry experience (fiexp = 1)	0(b)			0		
No start-up experience (fsexp = 0)	0.114	0.475	0.057	1	0.811	1.120
Prior start-up experience (fsexp = 1)	0(b)			0		
Education of the entrepreneur – base reference variable (fedn = 1)	−0.112	0.895	0.016	1	0.900	0.894
Education of the entrepreneur – first dummy (fedn = 2)	−0.990	0.791	1.568	1	0.210	0.372
Education of the entrepreneur – second dummy (fedn = 3)	0(b)			0		
No external funding for the start-up (fin = 0)	−0.235	0.496	0.224	1	0.636	0.790
External funding of the start-up (fin = 1)	0(b)			0		
B2B market focus (market_segment = 0)	0.728	0.481	2.289	1	0.130	2.070
B2C market focus (market_segment = 1)	0(b)			0		
North Zone (zone = 0)	−1.045	0.558	3.501	1	0.061	0.352
South Zone (zone = 1)	0(b)			0		
Local entrepreneur (te = 0)	0.039	0.515	0.006	1	0.939	1.040
Transnational entrepreneur (te = 1)	0(b)			0		

SOURCE: Author.

TABLE 7A.2 Parameter estimates of the multinomial regression – emerged versus grown

Model variables (stage = 2; results between emerged-only and growth-only groups)	Beta coefficient (β)	Standard error	Wald statistic	Degree of freedom	Significance (p-value)	Exp. (β)
Intercept	2.311	1.563	2.187	1	0.139	
Age of the entrepreneur (fage)	-0.013	0.035	0.133	1	0.715	0.987
Sales capabilities of the start-up (sales)	0.002	0.001	2.437	1	0.119	1.002
R&D capabilities of the start-up (dev)	0.000	0.016	0.000	1	0.991	1.000
SDP growth (sdp)	6.702	4.385	2.336	1	0.126	813.973
Number of deals in the region (deals)	-0.019	0.012	2.361	1	0.124	0.981
Number of VCs in the region (vc)	0.007	0.014	0.224	1	0.636	1.007
No industry experience (fiexp = 0)	-1.030	0.788	1.708	1	0.191	0.357
Prior industry experience (fiexp = 1)	0(b)			0		
No start-up experience (fsexp = 0)	-0.823	0.474	3.013	1	0.083	0.439
Prior start-up experience (fsexp = 1)	0(b)			0		
Education of the entrepreneur – base reference variable (fedn = 1)	-1.809	0.841	4.622	1	0.032	0.164
Education of the entrepreneur – first dummy (fedn = 2)	-1.989	0.747	7.089	1	0.008	0.137
Education of the entrepreneur – second dummy (fedn = 3)	0(b)			0		
No external funding for the start-up (fin = 0)	-1.032	0.430	5.762	1	0.016	0.356
External funding of the start-up (fin = 1)	0(b)			0		
B2B market focus (market_segment = 0)	0.507	0.437	1.350	1	0.245	1.661
B2C market focus (market_segment = 1)	0(b)			0		
North Zone (zone = 0)	-0.987	0.541	3.327	1	0.068	0.373
South Zone (zone = 1)	0(b)			0		
Local entrepreneur (te = 0)	0.619	0.466	1.765	1	0.184	1.857
Transnational entrepreneur (te = 1)	0(b)			0		

Source: Author.

8

Conclusions

Introduction

High-tech start-ups are now being recognized as the engines of economic growth in the knowledge-driven society. Their ability to generate new products, services, and business models has helped nations to leapfrog its output in comparison to others (Saxenian 2002). Developed economies in particular have benefited the most by supporting and nurturing high-tech start-ups. Several studies examining economic progress of developed economies have noted small high-tech start-ups as being the major drivers of job creation and innovation and thus, the economic growth (Birch 1979; Baumol 2002; Kirchhoff and Spencer 2008).

As an example of this, in the USA, these entrepreneurial companies contributed 20 per cent of the US employment in the 1980s. Even though in recession, from March 2009 and March 2010, 394,000 new businesses were formed in the USA, creating 2.3 million jobs (Mutikani 2012). Some of the leading companies in the technology industry today, such as Apple, Cisco, eBay, Qualcomm, Intel, were incubated as tiny start-ups during their formative years (Barringer, Jones, and Neubaum 2005; Paulraj 2012).

Over the last decade, the emerging economies across the world also have witnessed a surge in the creation of high-tech start-ups. The rapid proliferation and use of the Internet across the world has accelerated the process of globalization, aided by disruptive technological changes in just a matter of a decade and half (Startup Genome 2012). India has emerged as the third-largest base for high-tech start-ups in the world, with approximately 3100 start-ups operating in the country. The start-up ecosystem in India attracted 300 VC/private equity and 225 angel investment deals worth over US$2.3 billion since 2010 and over 20 mergers and acquisitions worth US$1 billion in the last 3 years. Over the last 12 months alone, 805 technology product/digital start-ups were set up across the country, which is projected to grow fourfold to hit 2,000 by 2020 (NASSCOM 2014).

While the aforementioned data paint an impressive picture, it must be noted that across the world, these contributions are made from a very small percentage of high-tech start-ups which have successfully managed to overcome the challenges during initial stages of the firm life cycle. It has been well established that high-tech start-ups suffer a very heavy failure rate (Stinchcombe 1965; Certo 2003). These start-ups face many unique constraints during their initial stages of operation that makes them highly amenable to failure. Therefore, a start-up would be able to survive and sustain only if it can successfully overcome the liability of newness, fights against the uncertainty of value it promises to its stakeholders, and deals with underdeveloped markets (Bala Subrahmanya 2015). India too has not been different in experiencing a high failure rate of start-ups (Microsoft Accelerator India 2012).

Further, in the area of high-tech start-ups, all the prior knowledge that is currently available is in the context of developed economies. Many scholars have observed that there is limited investigation of the various phenomena concerning the high-tech start-ups in the emerging countries (Bruton and Rubanik 2002; Song et al. 2008). Added to this, from a policy angle, Gilbert, Audretsch, and McDougall (2004) observed that policymakers in the emerging markets had limited inputs or knowledge related to the high-tech start-up life cycle, and, therefore, were finding it difficult to respond appropriately to the structural changes in the economy that are happening on account of technological innovations.

These observations drive the need for a better understanding of the Indian high-tech start-up life cycle. There is very little knowledge and know-how about what factors contribute to the key milestones of start-up life cycle, particularly in the context of an emerging economy, like India. The primary aim of this study was to fill that gap.

Background and Details of the Current Study

This study attempted to provide an exploratory and empirical evaluation of the Indian high-tech start-up life cycle. To be able to do this, we first identified the three critical milestones in the high-tech start-up life cycle. We then critically evaluated the key factors that impacted each of these milestones. To draw deeper and actionable insights, at every such identified milestone, we examined the contribution of key factors from a variety of theoretical lenses.

At the outset, we surveyed the theoretical and empirical literature in this domain, in order to familiarize ourselves with the findings from the previous studies. We first started by understanding the formal definitions that are prevalent in the developed economies related to high-tech start-ups. We observed that there was no formal definition of high-tech start-ups in the case of India. Therefore, we arrived at a definition of high-tech start-up for India, based on NIC 2008 classification as well as in compliance with the formal definitions that are in practice in the USA and EU. Further, since the distinction between small businesses and high-tech start-ups only became clearer after the 2000s, we found it appropriate to examine and understand the key differences between these two forms of organizations and clarify the definition and usage of high-tech start-ups in the context of the study. For the purposes of this study, we adopt the definition put forth by Blank and Dorf (2012) that high-tech start-ups are a temporary organization formed to search for a repeatable and scalable business model. By this definition, we also clarified that the high-tech start-ups considered for our study were both entrepreneurial in nature and were focused on creating new products, services, or business models.

With the definitions of high-tech start-ups clarified, we focused our attention to review the existing literature that examined the life cycle of high-tech start-ups. We traced the roots of these studies to Greiner's (1972) phase-based model of firm life cycle. We understood that subsequent studies leveraged the phase-based model for firms to explain the life cycle of small businesses (Churchill and Lewis 1983; Scott and Bruce 1987). The distinction between the life cycle models of small businesses and that of high-tech start-ups emerged in the early 1990s, with contributions from Pavia (1990) and Hanks et al. (1993) who proposed life cycle models explicitly for high-tech start-ups. Subsequent to their contributions, Bhide (2000) explained the life cycle of high-tech start-ups using a three-factor trilogy. Recent contributions by Blank (2010; 2012), Ostwalder (2013), and Ries (2014) provided more clarity in identifying and delineating the key milestones in the life cycle of high-tech start-ups. Based on these studies, the current study used 'emergence', 'survival', and 'growth' as the three key milestones that are relevant for examination in the life cycle of high-tech start-ups.

With the key milestones for the study of high-tech start-ups identified, we then shifted our focus to arrive at the appropriate framework that we could leverage to examine the key milestones of the high-tech start-up life cycle. To arrive at this framework, we examined the prevailing literature about frameworks that had been used in the past studies (North 1990; Gartner 1985). The literature survey covered both – macro ecosystem-related aspects and the aspects pertinent to the micro firm and entrepreneur-level attributes (Wiklund, Patzelt, and Shepherd 2009). Based on the insights obtained from the review of literature, for the present study, the literature review was carried out in the context of these three dimensions: (a) entrepreneur-based characteristics, (b) start-up (organization/firm) related characteristics, and (c) ecosystem-related characteristics. Among these, the entrepreneur and the firm constitute the micro factors while the ecosystem constitutes the macro factors influencing the phenomenon under study. For each milestone of the high-tech start-up life cycle, literature was reviewed in the context of the three identified dimensions. This approach helped us frame a conceptual model for our study.

The literature review related to study of 'emergence' of high-tech start-ups revealed that predominantly, most of the contributions in this context were derived from the theories of the firm (Coase 1937; Penrose 1959). The concepts of pre-organization (Van de Ven, Hudson, and Schroeder 1984) and resource-based theories of firm emergence (Vesper 1980; Gartner 1985) seem to dominate the explanation of emergence. However, it is to be noted that these studies were carried out during the time when the distinction between small businesses and high-tech start-ups was not made very clear. Recent studies attempted to provide a complementary perspective in explaining the emergence of high-tech start-ups. Prominent among these were legitimacy-based theory (Tornikoski and Newbert 2007), complexity science theory (McKelvey 2004; Liechenstein et al. 2007), and entrepreneurial behavioural theory (Sarasvathy 2001; Dimov 2010).

From an entrepreneurial context, factors such as the prior industry and prior start-up experience of the founders (Ronstadt 1988) and the age and education of the founders (Storey 1982) were found to be key in influencing the emergence of high-tech start-ups. Literature pertaining to evaluation of firm-specific factors contributing to emergence of high-tech start-ups revealed that the human capital of the firm, comprising R&D personnel and sales personnel at the time of formal incorporation (Kim, Aldrich, and Keister 2006), and the financial capitalization of the firm at the time of inception (Gries and Naude 2008) are being the key factors, influencing the emergence of high-tech start-ups.

For the study of prior literature, related to 'survival' of high-tech start-ups in India, the organizational behaviour theory (Schoonhoven and Eisenhardt 1990), legitimacy theory (Williamson 2000), and risk-based theory (Shepherd,

McMullen, and Jennings 2007) stood out in prominence along with the most used resource-based theories of firm (Cader and Leatherman 2011). Entrepreneur-specific factors such as entrepreneurial alertness (Kaish and Gilad 1991), learning ability (Politis 2008), and entrepreneurial orientation and motivation (Furdas and Kohn 2011) came out as being the key factors that have been studied in prior literature as influencing the survival of high-tech start-ups. Apart from these personal characteristics of the entrepreneur, the background of the entrepreneur such as entrepreneur's previous employment experience (Ronstadt 1988), age (Storey 1982), and gender (Kolvereid, Shane, and Westhead 1993) were also identified as being influencing the survival of high-tech start-ups in prior studies.

From a firm-specific perspective, factors such as learning ability of the firm (Geroski 1995), the dynamic capabilities of the firm (Teece, Pisano, and Shuen 1997), integrative capabilities of the firm (Eisenhardt and Martin 2000), and the resources of the firm such as the firm size (Evans 1987) were found to be prominent in explaining survival. It has to be noted again that most of these explanations were provided when the distinctions between small business and high-tech start-ups were not very clearly laid out. However, studies examining the role of external environmental parameters, influencing survival, have been found to take note of this distinction – and a recent set of scholarly works deals with examination of tax regulations impacting high-tech start-ups (Fertala 2008), the concept of clusters as applied to high-tech start-ups (Wennberg and Lindquist 2010), and the effect and role of government policies in promoting high-tech start-ups (Millán, Congregado, and Román 2012).

The growth of high-tech start-ups has been mostly discussed under the organization-based theory (Lee, Lee, and Pennings 2001), resource-based theory (Barringer, Jones, and Neubaum 2005), and ecology- and evolution-based theories (Nelson and Winter 2009). The initial literature, examining the entrepreneurial characteristics responsible for growth of high-tech start-ups, revolved around analysing the impact of factors such as relevant industry experience of the entrepreneur (MacMillan and Day 1987), prior entrepreneurial experience (Singer 1995), and education of the entrepreneur (Sapienza and Grimm 1997). Recently, the entrepreneurial motivation and orientation influencing the growth has been a subset of growing contributions (Furdas and Kohn 2011).

The prior studies that examine firm-specific factors, affecting the growth of high-tech start-ups, have predominantly not distinguished between small businesses and high-tech start-ups. However, the review of past literature in the context of small businesses is important, because, it is the same set of factors that also have an influence on high-tech start-ups. Factors such as firm's age and size (Jovanovic 1982), its strategy (Sandberg 1986), technological capabilities (Zahra 1996), and innovation (Deeds, DeCarolis, and Coombs 1999) stand out as important contributions that helped us understand the current knowledge available in this area of study. In similar fashion, prior literature reviewing the impact of external environmental factors has studied the contribution of market demand (North and Smallbone 1993) and industry structure (Porter 1998) without any distinction towards high-tech start-ups. However, since 2000, the role of government policies (Rose, Kumar, and Yen 2006) and the contributions of the VC industry towards the growth of new ventures (Colombo and Grilli 2010) have clearly focused on high-tech start-ups.

One of the key gaps emanating out of the aforesaid literature review was that most studies limited themselves in examining a set of factors on one or more phases of the life cycle of the start-ups. This partial treatment did not provide a complete perspective of the entire range of factors that come to play at a given time in the life cycle of a start-up. Reviewing the literature from a horizontal (broad-based, using key dimensions) approach as well as with a vertical (narrow, phase/milestone-based) approach, it was important to study the aspects of high-tech start-ups by integrating both these approaches. The integration of both these approaches allowed us to critically examine the changes in the core dimensions that describe the start-ups at a particular milestone event in the life cycle of the start-up. It is in this context that a deeper review of the key factors that influence the high-tech start-up at various phases of its life cycle in relation to the core dimensions of analysis (entrepreneurial, firm-specific, and external environment-related dimensions) becomes important.

Second, after the clear distinction between small businesses and high-tech start-ups, since 2000, there has not been any significant contribution in enhancing the knowledge of the high-tech start-up life cycle and its related phenomena, particularly in the context of emerging countries such as India. This limited investigation of the high-tech start-up life cycle in emerging economies (Song et al. 2008) and the observation that there were limited knowledge and support available to policymakers in the emerging markets to deal with the surge of high-tech start-ups (Gilbert, Audretsch, and McDougall 2004) motivated our study to plug these gaps.

The overarching research objective of this study is to investigate the dynamics involved in the life cycle of high-tech start-ups in the context of

India. To be able to realize the aforementioned, the following macro level objectives were outlined:

1. To determine the entrepreneurial, firm-specific, and external environmental factors that influences the *emergence* of high-tech start-ups in India;
2. To understand the entrepreneurial, firm-specific, and external environmental factors that contribute to early *survival* of high-tech start-ups in India;
3. To understand and determine the entrepreneurial, firm-specific, and external environmental factors that ensures the *growth* of high-tech start-ups in India;
4. To examine whether any of the entrepreneurial, firm-specific, and external environmental factors are relevant and impactful across the entire *life cycle* of high-tech start-ups in India; and
5. To derive implications to the entrepreneurs, start-up ecosystem partners, and policymakers, based on the analysis of our study, with a view to enable them to overcome the key impediments across the high-tech start-up life cycle.

Further, to obtain deeper insights into the interplay of factors at each of the milestones in its life cycle, the high-tech start-ups in our sample have been analysed based on three distinct segments of comparison, namely, (a) B2B versus B2C start-ups, (b) start-ups based in the North Zone versus those based in the South Zone, and (c) start-ups created by transnational entrepreneurs versus those created by local entrepreneurs. The analyses of these segments have yielded useful interpretations and have paved way to recommend appropriate policy interventions.

The B2B versus B2C start-up segmentation is considered primarily to understand the nuances of start-ups catering to different market segments. For example, the sales cycle in a B2B start-up is expected to be much longer in comparison to the sales cycle for a B2C start-up. However, the revenue generated per customer will be higher in B2B start-ups in comparison with the B2C start-ups. Segmenting the start-ups along the lines of targeted customer market will help us identify specific factors that impact the time to survival and growth in an effective manner.

In our study, we have also analysed the start-ups by differentiating them based on location of their operations. Prior literature suggests that high-tech economic activity is usually influenced by the location of operations. The analysis of start-ups operating in cities based in north India versus those operating in south India helped us to understand the extent of proliferation of high-tech economic activity across the country. Second, it helped us analyse different factors that may come to play in impacting start-ups, purely based on the location of operations. Last, we have analysed the start-ups based on the entrepreneurial background and experience, in particular, whether they are local or transnational. Prior research has suggested that transnational entrepreneurs and their communities enable diffusion of knowledge and creation or upgrading of local capabilities. Saxenian and Li (2003) noted that transnational entrepreneurs built specialization and innovation by simultaneously maintaining connections with their host country and the country of origin. They observed that this mechanism helped them to monitor and respond to changes in markets and technology. Given these backgrounds, this study investigated whether the transnational entrepreneurs who create and operate high-tech start-ups in India are more likely to survive, sustain, and grow relative to local entrepreneurs.

To enable the analysis of the research objectives, this study was confined to ICT start-ups operating in India. To ensure homogeneity of data, only the high-tech start-ups that are offering products and cloud-based solutions in the ICT sector were considered for the study. This implied that start-ups that have an established headquarters in India and have majority of investments or R&D personnel in India (in cases where the start-up has multiple global offices) are also qualified.

Further, we restricted our study to cover start-ups that started operations after 2005. This restriction allowed us to get a good spread of start-ups that initiated operations from 2005 to 2015. It also provided sufficient room to analyse the end to end life cycle of high-tech start-ups across the key milestones of start-up creation, survival, and growth. The data were collected using multiple methods that comprised of in-person meetings, telephonic interviews, and by soliciting responses via online survey websites. The analysis of responses yielded a final set of about 275 start-ups for the purposes of our study. The unit of analysis in our study was the start-up represented by the founder. We understand that most start-ups in the high-tech fields start up with multiple co-founders. However, in most cases, there would be one founder who would have the most of the context about the start-up and its operations. We were fairly successful in targeting such founders for our study.

A questionnaire was developed to collect primary data and validate the objectives of this study. To be able to accurately develop the questionnaire, selective case analysis of about six high-tech start-ups was carried out in the first stage. We have used multiple statistical techniques for the analysis of our data set. The same were chosen based on the characteristics of the data fields (type of variables) and the purpose of the analysis.

To analyse the emergence of high-tech start-ups, we used the binary logistic regression analysis for building and analysing the model. These analyses were carried out under three segments to get further insights related to target market segment, location of operations, and the background of founders. In all, a total of seven logistic regression models were executed and results and conclusions were drawn from these analyses. Statistical techniques such as one-way ANOVA and chi-square tests of independence were used as part of the preliminary analysis on each of the variables involved in this study.

Next, we analysed the factors that influence the survival of high-tech start-ups. To analyse this objective, we used the statistical techniques of survival analysis or time to event analysis. We performed the survival analysis on the data set, wherein the time in months of operation of the start-up, and whether the start-up has achieved survival or not, taken together formed the dependent variable. The entrepreneurial and firm-specific factors that are captured as part of the questionnaire formed the independent variables for this analysis. We also examined the data using survival analysis against our three segments of target market segment, location of operations, and the background of founders to obtain a deeper understanding of the factors that influence survival of high-tech start-ups. Statistical techniques such as one-way ANOVA and chi-square tests of independence were used as part of the preliminary analysis on each of the variables involved in this study.

To understand what factors contribute to the growth of the start-ups, we categorized the start-ups that had already achieved survival into two groups – *start-ups that have survived but not yet growing*, and *start-ups that are growing*. We then performed logistic regression analysis to understand the key factors that are responsible for the growth of high-tech start-ups in each of the three categories. Further, we assessed how high-tech start-ups differed between these three categories in terms of their orientation towards the market segment that they target, the location in which they operate as well as based on the exposure of the founders. We executed seven regression models, two each to understand respectively the aspects of variance in market segment, location, and the background of the entrepreneurs; and one for the overall model. Statistical techniques such as one-way ANOVA and chi-square tests of independence were used as part of the preliminary analysis on each of the variables involved in this study.

For the analysis of the objective to find out which factors are relevant and contributed to the entire life cycle of the high-tech start-up, we first grouped the data of all the start-ups in our sample into three distinct categories, based on their current status of the life cycle milestones achieved. The first category of start-ups were those start-ups that were formally been incorporated – but who did not yet achieved the product-market fit. This category of start-ups constitute the 'emerged-only' start-ups group. The second category of start-ups that we created for this study comprised of those who were formally incorporated as well as had achieved the product-market fit but had not yet crossed beyond the SME valuations of ₹5 crore if their offerings were services-based or ₹10 crore if their operations were based on capital investment. These category of start-ups constituted the 'survived-only' start-ups group. The third category of start-ups were those who were formally incorporated, had achieved the product-market fit as well as had obtained valuations that are beyond the current Indian SME definitions. These start-ups were classified as 'grown' start-ups – indicating that they were on the path of transformation from a start-up to a large enterprise.

By conducting MANOVA across these three categories of start-ups, we identified the key factors among the entrepreneurial, firm-specific, and external environment-specific domains that can help explain the differences prevailing among these three categories. Further, the multinomial logistic regression was adopted to ascertain the factors that had an influence on the entire start-up life cycle.

Prior to discussing the results and inferences of the study, a brief profile of the start-ups that constituted our data are presented in these paragraphs. We find that majority of the high-tech start-ups in our sample are relatively young in terms of their years of operations in India – about 95 per cent of them have been established in the post-2008 period. In particular, there has been a systematic increase in the number of start-ups incorporated since 2013, reflecting the trend in the Indian economy. Further, we observe that the gender-wise distribution of founders is heavily skewed towards the male founders. The male founders constituted about 96 per cent of the population in our sample, in line with the trends observed across the country from other industry reports.

In our sample, about 88 per cent of the start-ups had been reported to be operating in metro cities and the remainder from non-metro cities. In terms of cities where start-ups are located, Bengaluru had a major share with about 49 per cent of the overall sample followed by start-ups in the NCR. From a target market segment perspective, our sample was fairly equally spread across the B2B and B2C sectors. The B2B start-ups constituted about 44 per cent of the sample while the remaining 56 per cent being B2C start-ups. A similar spread was observed from our sample if we would look over it from the lens of entrepreneur's exposure. In our sample, about 56 per cent of the founders were local entrepreneurs, and about 44 per cent of the samples were transnational entrepreneurs.

With this background and context about the objectives of the study and the composition of the data related to the study, we now move forward to discuss the results and inferences we obtained by executing the statistical tests and their analyses.

Summary of Findings and Inferences

The findings and inferences from this research study have been discussed under four broad heads: (a) those pertaining to the emergence of high-tech start-ups, (b) those related to the survival of high-tech start-ups, (c) results, related to the growth of high-tech start-ups, and (d) factors that are found to influence the start-ups across their life cycle. These have been discussed in details in few successive pages, respectively.

Emergence of High-tech Start-ups: Findings and Inferences

We modelled the status of *formal incorporation* of every high-tech start-up in our data set as the dependent variable for evaluating this objective. Since this variable was dichotomous in nature, we utilized logistic regression to execute the tests. In total, we built seven logistic regression models to analyse the emergence of high-tech start-ups under different contexts. Each one of the models helped us in validating the formulated hypotheses in the context of the B2B start-ups, B2C start-ups, start-ups based in north Indian cities, start-ups based in south Indian cities, start-ups with local entrepreneurs as founders, and start-ups that have transnational entrepreneurs as founders. Finally, a model fitted based on all the data, collected across the country, revealed the key entrepreneurial and firm-specific factors that affect start-up emergence.

The results of the statistical analyses carried out across the seven models have been summarized in the Summary section of Chapter 4. The negative sign in the block indicates that the factor under the study negatively influences on the emergence of high-tech start-up in the given context. A positive sign in the block indicates that the factor under the study positively influences the emergence of high-tech start-up in the given context. While the results of each model has been discussed in detail in Chapter 4, here we provide a summary and interpretation of results of the overall model, since the overall model more accurately captured the objective that needed to be examined for the purposes of the study. The results from the execution of this model indicate that prior start-up experience of the entrepreneur, absence of R&D, and financial capabilities increase the likelihood of high-tech start-up emergence. In addition to these, the logistic regression model results also indicate that high-tech start-up emergence is likely from *local* entrepreneurs, focusing on the *B2C* markets and who have operations in *South Zone* of the country.

The results from our analysis of factors impacting the emergence of high-tech start-ups indicated that entrepreneurs who do not have prior start-up experience take more time to incorporate their new venture formally. Second, hiring too many technical people prior to formal incorporation will further delay the founding of the firm. On similar lines, possession of external funding delays the chances of incorporation of the start-up. None of the external environmental factors seemed to impact the emergence of the high-tech start-ups.

These results on factors influencing the emergence of high-tech start-ups provide insights that will be helpful to entrepreneurs, policymakers, and external start-up ecosystem partners. From the results, we understand that entrepreneurs with prior start-up experience will be the ones who would more likely incorporate their start-up, irrespective of whether they have the right resources to further sustain their start-up. In contrast, those entrepreneurs who do not have prior start-up experience would take time to formally set up their new venture. The results indicate that knowledge, learning, and entrepreneurial judgement gained from the past stints would alert the entrepreneur to make a start with larger/bigger scope of the entrepreneurial idea, whereas the uncertainty of outcomes in the pre-entrepreneurial phase might constrain the founders with no prior start-up experience and make them go slowly on formal incorporation.

We also have been able to gain useful insights on which firm-specific factors impact the emergence of high-tech start-ups in India, and how do these influence play out? The results from our analysis indicated that obtaining initial financial capitalization prior to starting up delayed the emergence of a high-tech start-up. In the early stages of start-up life cycle, it is usually the self-funding routes, or funds lent by family and friends towards commercializing an entrepreneurial idea, that contribute to capitalizing the firm to be incorporated.

The outcome of having sufficient funds to initiate the initial activities of the start-up operations would lead the entrepreneur to focus on key activities of building the product/service. Since, the entrepreneur no longer needs to raise funds immediately, this may cause delay in the emergence of a start-up. Further, as an alert to what sort of firm-specific resources might be harmful in the pre-emergence phase, our results indicated that having too much of R&D personnel at the pre-emergence stage would actually hinder the process of emergence of high-tech start-ups in India. This result indicates that hiring high-skilled R&D team members at a stage when even initial market acceptance is not proven will create unnecessary distractions and drain on pre-start-up finances.

Our results on start-up emergence also provided new insights, such as in what type of markets might we expect the start-ups to emerge faster and in which location in the country, and whether it is led by a transnational entrepreneur or might make any difference on the emergence of high-tech start-ups. From our results, we observe that any start-up idea concentrating on the B2C market will emerge quickly. This is explainable from the fact that any entrepreneurial idea in the B2C market segment would perhaps provide rapid feedback on product development, initial customer segments to be targeted, and other strategies, since the target audience is not any particular subset of customers, and that they can easily be tapped for initial feedback collection.

In a similar manner, our results indicated that start-ups having ideas would take relatively less time to emerge in south India. The external ecosystem knowledge present in south Indian region will ensure that entrepreneurs in this region are well prepared prior to formal incorporation of their start-up. Further, our results indicated that local entrepreneurs show a bias to quickly set up their new venture in their country of origin. This result is also understandable, since most often, local entrepreneurs have better insight on the market requirements of the entrepreneurial idea that they wish to pursue. This aspect would spur them to begin the operations.

Survival of High-tech Start-ups: Findings and Inferences

We utilized the techniques of survival analysis to understand the key factors that determine the survival of high-tech start-ups in India. A combination of two factors, namely, the time to survival of the start-up in months (if the milestone was achieved) and the status of survival (dichotomous variable) formed the dependent variable used in this study. In total, we built seven survival analysis models to analyse the time to survival of high-tech start-ups under different contexts. Each one of the models helped us in validating the formulated hypotheses in the context of the B2B start-ups, B2C start-ups, start-ups based in North Zone, start-ups based in South Zone, start-ups that have local entrepreneurs as founders, and start-ups that have transnational entrepreneurs as founders. Finally, a model fitted based on all the data, collected across the country, revealed the key entrepreneurial, firm-specific, and external environment-specific factors that affected start-up survival.

The summary of results obtained across these seven models is presented in the Summary section of Chapter 5. An entry in the table indicates that the factor influences the survival of high-tech start-ups. The negative sign accompanying the entry indicates that the factor under study reduces the time to survival (helps the start-up to achieve the survival milestone faster), and a positive sign indicates the opposite. While the results of all the seven models were discussed in detail in the chapter dealing with survival of high-tech start-ups, here we recollect the results for the overall model and discuss the implications of the same.

The results of analyses on the factors that influence the time to survival of high-tech start-ups indicate that none of the entrepreneur-specific characteristics seem to influence the survival of the overall sample. From the results, we can infer that the firm-specific and external environment-specific attributes have a better role in guiding the survival of the start-ups. This is an important result and an insight that has implications to entrepreneurs, policymakers, and external start-up ecosystem partners.

The most important insight about the survival analysis results were the R&D and sales capabilities of the start-up, playing a key role in determining the survival of high-tech start-ups. During the pre-emergence stages, we observed that the R&D capabilities of a start-up may be an overhead and an unnecessary distraction. However, for getting the start-up to achieve the survival milestone, the presence of deep R&D skills is of paramount importance, since it is only on account of these resources that a start-up will be able to respond very quickly to positive and negative feedback from the initial customers.

Similarly, the sales capabilities of the start-up are another key factor that enables the firm to achieve the survival milestone faster. In most high-tech start-ups and in our particular case as well, the founders are mostly from a technical background. These founders do not always possess the market and business development skills that are required to obtain initial customers by selling a completely new product or service offering to the market. Also, most importantly, the ability to gauge whether the new offering is resonating at the marketplace and the gaps in the current version of the solution being offered are the important skill that will enable the start-up to achieve the survival milestone faster in comparison to the others. Combined with R&D skills, the selling capabilities of the start-up will be a key factor influencing the survival of high-tech start-ups in India.

From an external environmental factors perspective, the SDP growth of the region is shown to enable the survival of start-ups operating in that region. This result provides us with the insight that start-ups can look to achieve the product-market fit more quickly in a region where there is an addressable market demand that willfully consumes new products and services. The SDP growth rate in this case should be viewed as a proxy for the macroeconomic environment, prevalent in that region. This factor acts as a signal to entrepreneurs who are confident of their entrepreneurial idea to reach out to the external capital providers.

It is also observed that none of the control variables considered for the study, namely, the preference to selection of target market, preference of location of operations, or the exposure of entrepreneurs, seem to have an influence on the survival of high-tech start-ups. The specific data sets derived to draw insights on these control variables, however, have helped in understanding, in more depth, the actual aspects that help to enable the survival of start-ups in the corresponding markets/locations and entrepreneurial exposure.

Growth of High-tech Start-ups: Findings and Inferences

To analyse the factors that impact the growth of high-tech start-ups, we categorized the start-ups that had already achieved survival into two groups – *start-ups that have survived but not yet growing* and *start-ups that are growing*. We then performed logistic regression analysis to understand the key factors that are responsible for the growth of high-tech start-ups. In all, we executed seven logistic regression models. Two models each were built to analyse the impact on growth for the dimensions of target market segment (B2B and B2C), location of operations (North Zone and South Zone), and entrepreneurial exposure (local and transnational entrepreneurs). Finally, an overall model was built and analysed to study the impact of factors affecting the growth of high-tech start-ups.

The summary of results obtained across these seven models is presented in the Summary section of Chapter 6. An entry in the table indicates that the factor influences the growth of high-tech start-ups. The negative sign accompanying the entry indicates that the factor under study impedes the growth of the high-tech start-up, and a positive sign indicates the opposite. While the results of all the seven models were discussed in detail in the chapter dealing with the growth of high-tech start-ups, here we discuss the results for the overall model and outline the implications of the same.

The results, examining the growth of high-tech start-ups, indicated that age of the entrepreneur was one of the significant factors affecting the growth of high-tech start-ups. It has to be noted that entrepreneur's age has a negative effect on the growth of high-tech start-ups, indicating that higher the age, the difficult it may be for the entrepreneur to drive growth, when the requirement is to scale up the operations of the start-up and transform itself into a large enterprise.

The reasons for why higher age might be a hindrance in influencing growth of high-tech start-ups can be explained as follows. While higher age of the entrepreneur is generally considered a good proxy for experience and capabilities, higher age may also result in deteriorating learning ability of the entrepreneur. Further, some of the past experiences and capabilities acquired by the entrepreneur might actually hinder the growth prospects on account of over-optimism or overconfidence, developed by the entrepreneur on account of his/her past experiences. Hence, our results indicate that entrepreneurs who are not too young (less than 30 years) nor too old (age greater than 45 years) are the best fit to drive the growth of high-tech start-ups.

Our results also indicate that higher educational pedigree of the entrepreneur has a negative influence on the growth of high-tech start-ups. This is understandable, because most entrepreneurs in the high-tech start-up sector possess technical degrees, and a very few portions of them possess management or business development related educational pedigree. This observation was made from the sample that we used for our study as well as the same was corroborated from other data sources that we initially contacted for the purposes of data collection towards this study. Since the majority of the founders were technically qualified, and during growth phase, the business development aspects were the ones that need primary attention, a very technically-oriented entrepreneur may, in fact, act as a bottleneck in driving the scale-up activities of the high-tech start-up. Hence, the results indicate that a balance between the technical and business development capabilities in the founding team or the leadership team of the start-up is an essential ingredient to drive the growth.

The most significant finding from our results is that financial capitalization would act as a deterrent to the growth of high-tech start-ups. Taken in verbatim, this result may appear contradictory to the prevalent knowledge. However, this result needs to be analysed and interpreted in the correct context. We interpret that financial capitalization of the start-up would certainly enable the start-up to grow. However, capitalization beyond the immediate requirements of scaling up of operations would lead to unnecessary distractions and investments, leading the capital to be considered a hindrance to growth. At the growth stage, usually, the start-up go for funding from established VC companies and would be looking to raise Series A and above class of funding which typically runs into millions of dollars of funding. If this capital was not appropriately deployed for the right reasons, there are chances that this capital may become the cause of distraction by way of unsuccessful experiments to drive growth, leads to draining of the start-up's resources and capital as well.

The specific data sets derived to draw insights on these control variables, however, have helped in understanding in more depth, the actual aspects that help enable growth of start-ups in the corresponding markets/locations and entrepreneurial exposure.

Factors Impacting the Entire Life Cycle of High-tech Start-ups: Findings and Inferences

The previous objectives of this study were focused on analysing the key factors that contribute to achieve the corresponding milestones as identified in the life cycle of high-tech start-ups. In this section, we discuss and interpret the results that we obtained by examining the factors that influence the life cycle of high-tech start-ups in India as a whole. In other words, we intended to evaluate and understand whether there are factors in the entrepreneurial, firm-specific, and external environment-specific categories that pervade influence across all the key milestones of a start-up's journey.

To study this objective, we grouped the entire sample into three categories, based on the current status of the life cycle milestone achieved. By conducting MANOVA across these three categories of start-ups, we identified the key factors among the entrepreneurial, firm-specific, and external environment-specific domains that explained the differences prevailing in these three categories. Further, the multinomial logistic regression was conducted on the sample to understand and statistically validate which of the factors have an influence on the entire start-up life cycle.

The results indicated that education of the entrepreneur, financial capitalization of the start-up, and a robust economic climate in the region of operations of the start-ups are the factors that influenced the entire life cycle of high-tech start-ups. The parameter estimates of the multinomial model provides us with more insights on factors contributing to the start-ups to achieve the next step of the milestone in their life cycle. Between the emerged-only and survived-only groups of start-ups, it was observed that an increase in year-on-year SDP growth would benefit the survived group, whereas an increase in VC deals in the region would likely benefit the emerged-only start-ups group. Similarly, in the North Zone, we could likely see more number of start-ups in the emerged phase than the ones in the survived phase.

Between the emerged-only and growth start-up groups, it was found that entrepreneurs with no prior start-up experience and the ones with higher educational pedigree (technical degree or higher) are more likely to be expected in the emerged-only start-ups group. Also, a start-up with no external funding is more likely to belong to the emerged-only group of start-ups, rather than in the grown start-ups group. In the North Zone, we could likely see more number of start-ups in the emerged phase than the ones in the growth phase.

These results provide significant additional knowledge to entrepreneurs, policymakers as well as to start-up ecosystem partners. Our interpretation of these results is as follows. A good educational pedigree can be viewed as a necessary and prerequisite condition for any entrepreneur to set up their ventures in the high-tech sector, whereas this factor may not play a major role in the subsequent life cycle stages of the start-up. Education, particularly technical education, will enable the entrepreneur to identify new entrepreneurial opportunities that can be exploited on account of technological changes. Further, good education also helps the entrepreneur to navigate the challenges of initial days of pre-organization successfully.

Financial capitalization of the start-up has been identified as one of the key factors influencing the activities of the start-up across the entire life cycle. During the initial phases, capitalization via self-funding, support from family and friends will enable the emergence of a high-tech start-up. During the next phase, financial support from seed and angel investors will normally enable the start-up to achieve product-market fit quickly. Further, support from VCs and other strategic investors during the growth phase will propel the start-up to transform itself into a full-fledged enterprise. Throughout our study, we have focused on learning and understanding whether or not, the start-up has been able to get financial support. We have not probed in further detail on whether the nature of funding was through friends or through angel investors and VCs. This finer granularity of detail would have enriched our inferences about the role of financial capabilities influencing the entire high-tech start-up life cycle. We consider this one of the areas to be ripened for further analysis subsequent to our study.

From an external ecosystem perspective, a robust SDP growth and an increase in number of funded VC deals turned out to be the significant influencers across the start-up life cycle. While these parameters did not always come out significant when we analysed the results for each milestone, the results from the life cycle related tests indicated that external environmental support was absolutely critical for the presence of a vibrant and thriving start-up ecosystem. Unlike small businesses, the high-tech start-ups operated in a new space try to offer new products and services, and then try to achieve repeatability and scale-up of operations based on initial acceptability of the new product or service offering. For all these activities to happen, there needs to be a robust external market demand which does not hesitate to try out new offerings. Equally important is the access to financial capital for start-ups that have true potential to scale-up. A region with an increasing number of VC-funded deals indicates access to capital for start-ups with good economically viable ideas. It also serves as an indicator of the quality and maturity of the external ecosystem in terms of capital as well as entrepreneurial ideas.

Policy Implications

The results and inferences drawn out from our study have important implications to start-up entrepreneurs, start-up ecosystem partners, the VC community, and the policymakers in this field.

For the entrepreneurs, especially the prospective and novice entrepreneurs, the key input emanating out of this study is that they need to possess deep skills (technical and business) in order to increase their probability of survival and sustain in the high-tech sector. From our results, we observe that it is easy to set up a new venture, particularly in high-tech sub-sectors such as ICT where entry barriers are very low or nil in many cases. However, to survive and sustain their venture, entrepreneurs need to possess strong R&D and sales skills. Without both of these skills, even if the entrepreneur is able to raise funds or is self-funded, it will be difficult for their start-up to survive. Further, our study indicates that for a successful career in the high-tech sector, the entrepreneurs need to develop the abilities to deal with uncertainty. This is in stark contrast to running and sustaining a small business in an established industry sector. One of the ways to emerge successful in this domain is to possess the mindset of continuous learning and adaptation.

Our results are also useful to the investment community that focuses on the high-tech sector. Our results across the multiple objectives clearly indicated that financial capitalization of the start-up at every stage forms the necessary and sufficient conditions for the start-up to continue its operations and thrive to reach the next milestone in its journey. In this background, our results provide guidance to high net-worth individuals, and friends and family members of prospective entrepreneurs who usually form the first source of capital infusion for new start-ups, on the kind and type of entrepreneurs that they need to support. Second, for seed and angel investors, our results provide the insights on the aspects of the entrepreneur, firm, and external environment that they need to augment to their existing knowledge and competence as they decide to invest and support newly-formed high-tech ventures. Last, for late-stage investors such as VCs, our results complement their understanding and provide additional insights on the type of entrepreneurs that they need to back as well as on the parameters which they need to keep watch on, as they make investment decisions to propel the growth in promising start-ups.

For the start-up ecosystem partners, such as the accelerators and technology business incubators, our results provide a good framework to help them through their entire operations cycle. Armed with our results and complemented by their existing knowledge of the ecosystem, they now can make better informed judgement and decisions on which start-ups to choose for their incubation and acceleration programmes. Further, through our results, they will also now be able to understand and manage the key gaps that they need to fill in among the existing start-up capabilities in order to further move ahead in their life cycle journey. Also, our results and subsequent actions by these ecosystem players will result in the enhancement and availability of the entrepreneurial knowledge in the start-up ecosystem in India.

The results of our study have implications to the policymakers as well. Some of the key recommendations that can be made to policymaking as an outcome of this study are presented here.

Our results point out that in the ICT sector, many novice and prospective entrepreneurs who do not have prior start-up experience are setting up new ventures. This development has two key implications. At one end, it represents the desire and energy of the young workforce in the country to create and operate new ventures. At the other end, the enabling ecosystem to support these activities can be further strengthened. To begin with, policymakers should focus on creating awareness about the necessary and sufficient conditions that are required for novice entrepreneurs to set up new ventures in the high-tech sector. Without appropriate training and skills, and intervention at the start of this cycle, there is a possibility of higher rate of start-up failures, primarily on account of lack of preparedness and awareness of what it takes to create, survive, and sustain a new venture in the high-tech sector. Another policy intervention that could be implemented to enhance this awareness is by channelizing the existing start-up support schemes to those entrepreneurs who have demonstrated prior start-up experiences. This intervention will increase the probability of survival and success of high-tech ventures in our country as well as serve as a pointer to novice entrepreneurs to first work at a start-up and develop the requisite technical and business skills prior to embarking on setting up their own ventures in the high-tech sector.

Results from our study point out that strong sales capabilities relevant to promoting new offerings is a key ingredient along with presence of strong R&D capabilities for start-ups in high-tech sector to survive and sustain their operations. It is observed that most of the current set of entrepreneurs who are setting up new ventures are armed more in technical skills and lack the business, marketing, and sales skills in the proportion that is required for them to survive and sustain their new venture ideas. Interactions with the key ecosystem partners during our data collection exercise revealed that most start-ups fail on account of poor selling and market development capabilities, despite having a very good product offering which had attracted initial customers. In order to overcome this gap, policymakers should undertake awareness creation and training sessions on the importance of possessing business and market development capabilities in the leadership team of start-ups. These measures will help overcome the entrepreneur- and firm-specific gaps that are currently prevalent in the country.

Further, the results from examining the survival of high-tech start-ups clearly bring out the need for existence of a robust economy in order for start-ups to survive. This implies that policymakers need to take cognizance of the fact that they can promote high-tech start-ups only in those regions where there is a good addressable market demand and appetite to consume new product offerings. From our results, a strong year-to-year SDP growth, coupled with an increasing trend in the number of funded VC deals, augurs well for start-ups to survive. Hence, policymakers should ensure that they create a favourable operating environment with the requisite governance structure for the VCs to set up their offices in regions of high macroeconomic growth. These steps will augur well for the creation and sustenance of high-tech start-up ecosystem.

For start-ups that have moved past the survival stage, policymakers can further help in the growth of these start-ups by putting in place policies that will enable these start-ups to new opportunities in the government sector and administration. Opening up the government sector market to high-growth start-ups will result in a win-win situation for the policymakers as well as the government. The policymakers and administrators in the government will gain from the agility and nimbleness of implementation of new, easy mechanisms that eases the stress on government administration by adoption of new technology and offerings provided by the start-ups. Last, of late, it has been observed that start-ups in the growth phase are raising excess capital, beyond what they may need to sustain and grow in the short term. This excess capital, while may be available easily to high-growth Indian start-ups on account of global recessionary trends, is not going to help the start-up growth, unless they are utilized for the right purposes that enable the growth. Suitable policy measures in consultation with the investment community and entrepreneurs will help in the utilization of capital for the right reasons.

These set of policy recommendations have been provided with a view of what measures need to be taken in order to strengthen the achievement of each of the milestones in the high-tech start-up life cycle. If we were to consider the macro aspects of policy recommendations that would augur well across the entire life cycle of high-tech start-ups, then, it would be to strengthen the ecosystem that has been developing along the high-tech start-ups in India. Our study has clearly brought out the key factors that enable or hinder the achievement of particular milestones for high-tech start-ups in India. A closer examination of these factors indicates that they belong to or are part of the larger start-up ecosystem that is prevalent in the country. Bala Subrahmanya (2018) defined the start-up ecosystem as a system comprising prospective as well as currently operating start-up entrepreneurs, their mentors, financiers, trainers, organizations such as universities and institutions, and government policy, and their interrelationships and interactions. When we examined our findings on which factors matter to the entire life cycle of high-tech start-ups, we notice that all of these factors are necessary and vital ingredients that make up the high-tech start-up ecosystem.

Hence, these results indicate that there is a need to strengthen each and every aspect of the high-tech start-up ecosystem in our country in order to enable the creation and sustain the growth of high-tech start-ups. We have already discussed specific policy recommendations around strengthening the external market demand, technical and business skills of the workforce, funding and access to capital, regulatory support from government, and education and training in particular contexts. In addition to these, it maybe also prudent to promote the technology business incubators and start-up accelerators in the country as the mechanism to plug any deficiency or gaps in the abilities or resources of the entrepreneur or the start-up in those areas. Thus, these business incubators and accelerators can be envisioned to play a very significant and important role in enabling the success of high-tech start-ups in India.

Contributions to Existing Literature

This study has made the following contributions to the existing literature.

First, this study has provided an end-to-end empirical evidence of factors that influence and impact the life cycle of high-tech start-ups. Prior studies have either examined the influence of a specific factor or studied a specific milestone in the start-up life cycle. To the best of our knowledge, this study fills the gap of being able to understand the factors that influence all the key milestones of the life cycle of high-tech start-ups.

Second, this study is among the first in the context of emerging economies to examine and understand the key factors contributing to the emergence, survival, and growth of high-tech start-ups, particularly related to India. The results and analysis of this study will pave way for unravelling further insights into the creation of a vibrant start-up ecosystem in India which is poised to turn into a global leader in this domain.

The examination of each milestone event under the lens of target market segment, location of operations, and entrepreneurial background extends the available knowledge in each of the domains. In particular, to the best of our knowledge, there has been no formal evidence on factors impacting the B2B and B2C start-ups in India. This study paves way to further expand on the exploratory results obtained in this study and formulate specific insights to help the growth of start-ups in these sectors. Further, the results of analysis based on the location of operations bring out insights on the specific factors that entrepreneurs and policymakers need to know to set up, survive, and grow their start-ups based on where they locate their start-up in India. Finally, the insight derived on account of entrepreneurial background helps formulation of the right policies that benefit both the local and transnational entrepreneurs.

The categorization of factors into entrepreneurial and firm-specific, during the course of the study, and the empirical analysis of the degree and direction of the contribution of each factor to the phenomenon under study have helped revalidate a few established results in literature in some cases and has provided results different to the existing literature in a few other scenarios. These contributions help in furthering our know-how on the key entrepreneurial and firm-specific factors that influence the high-tech start-up ecosystem.

The adoption of time to event methods in statistical analysis to examine milestone events of the start-up life cycle opens up new ways to interpret and understand the phenomenon. This method could be applied across all the key milestone events to gain further insights due to the statistical merit it has in dealing with information on events of the start-ups that are yet to achieve the milestone under study.

Finally, our results provide key inputs to entrepreneurs, start-up ecosystem partners, and investment community and policymakers working in this sector. We believe that our results will benefit each of these entities as they embark on their respective activities in this high-tech sector.

Limitations and Scope for Future Work

This study has attempted to examine a broad phenomenon at a necessary and sufficient level. However, there is scope for producing further insights and scope for more knowledge to be created by extending this study in several ways. To begin with, this study has primarily focused on examining the factors contributing to the three most important milestone events of the start-up life cycle. While this approach will provide a holistic perspective, future studies may also consider adding to the knowledge by examining the antecedents of high-tech start-up emergence as well as to study the decline or success of start-ups. There have been cross-sectional studies examining these aspects in the past – however, to the best of our knowledge, there are no such studies covering the emerging economy domains.

Further, the scope of this study has been confined to evaluation of the impact and influence of the micro level (firm and entrepreneurial levels) factors and a few macro level (external environment-specific) factors on the life cycle of high-tech start-ups in emerging economies. While there is good insight that this study has produced on account of binding the scope in the discussed fashion, the results of the study would emerge richer if it could incorporate or accommodate a few more variables across each of these dimensions. For example, the inclusion of the contribution of mentors to the start-up life cycle (entrepreneur-specific factor), variables capturing team-level contributions (firm-specific factors), and variables that captured the influence of incubators and/or accelerators (external environment-specific factors) would have further enhanced the insights that could be derived from the study. These factors could not be measured appropriately and incorporated in the study, purely for the lack of willingness on the entrepreneurs' end to disclose these details during the data collection phase. Further, addition of a few more variables specific to the phase of the life cycle being studied and differentiating between product-based and services-based start-ups will provide additional insights.

Finally, there is also scope to extend the current study by way of comparison of the outcomes obtained in this study with other sectors, other economies, and also with developed ecosystems such as of the USA or Europe. This study could be expanded to cover more than one sector in the same geography. This expansion in scope would help understand the sector-agnostic factors that have an influence in the geography of study. A cross-comparative study of the same IT sector-based start-ups with other emerging economies would help understand the regional factors that influence the life cycle of high-tech start-ups in the respective economies. Finally, a comparative study of factors influencing the life cycle of high-tech start-ups across a developed economy versus a developing economy would bring in the knowledge of the key factors that are missing or different in the emerging economies to create a similar impact for the ecosystem.

Bibliography

Aalen, O., O. Borgan, and H. Gjessing (2008). *Survival and Event History Analysis: A Process Point of View*. Springer Science & Business Media.

Acs, Z., J. Audretsch, and D. B. (1987). 'Innovation, Market Structure, and Firm Size'. *The Review of Economics and Statistics* 69(4): 567–574.

Agarwal, R. and M. Gort (1996). 'The Evolution of Markets and Entry, Exit and Survival of Firms'. *The Review of Economics and Statistics* 78(3): 489–498.

Agarwal, R. and D. B. Audretsch (2001). 'Does Entry Size Matter? The Impact of the Life Cycle and Technology on Firm Survival'. *The Journal of Industrial Economics* 49(1): 21–43.

Akaike, H. (1974). 'A New Look at the Statistical Model Identification'. *IEEE Transactions on Automatic Control* 19(6): 716–723.

Aldrich, H. (1980). 'Asian Shopkeepers as a Middleman Minority: A Study of Small Business in Wandsworth'. In *The Inner City: Employment and Industry*, ed. A. Evans and D. Eversley, 389–407. London: Heinemann.

Aldrich, H. and E. R. Auster (1986). 'Even Dwarfs Started Small: Liabilities of Age and Size and Their Strategic Implications', vol. 8., 165–186. Research in Organizational Behavior. San Francisco, CA: JAI Press.

Aldrich, H. E. (1990). 'Using an Ecological Perspective to Study Organizational Founding Rates'. *Entrepreneurship Theory and Practice* 14(3): 7–24.

Aldrich, H., U. Staber, and C. Zimmer (1990). 'Minimalism and Organizational Mortality: Patterns of Disbanding among U. S. Trade Associations, 1900–1983'. In *Organizational Evolution*, ed. J. V. Singh. Newbury Park, CA: Sage Publications.

Aldrich, H. E. (1999). *Organizations Evolving*, 1st edn. London: Sage Publications.

Aldrich, H. E. and M. A. Martinez (2001). 'Many are Called, but Few Are Chosen: An Evolutionary Perspective for the Study of Entrepreneurship'. *Entrepreneurship Theory and Practice* 25(4): 41–56.

Allison, P. D. (1995). *Survival Analysis Using SAS: A Practical Guide*. Cary, NC: SAS Institute.

Almus, M. and E. A. Nerlinger (1999). 'Growth of New Technology-based Firms: Which Factors Matter?', *Small Business Economics* 13(2): 141.

Alvarez, S. and L. Busenitz (2001). 'The Entrepreneurship of Resource-based Theory'. *Journal of Management* 27: 755–775.

Amason, A. C., R. C. Shrader, and G. H. Tompson (2006). 'Newness and Novelty: Relating Top Management Team Composition to New Venture Performance'. *Journal of Business Venturing* 21(1): 125–148.

Amit, R., L. Glosten, and E. Mueller (1993). 'Challenges to Theory Development In Entrepreneurship Research'. *Journal of Management Studies* 30: 815–834.

Andersen, C. (2009). *Free: The Future of a Radical Price*. New York City, NY: Hyperion.

Andries, P. and K. Debackere (2007). 'Adaptation and Performance in New Businesses: Understanding the Moderating Effects of Independence and Industry'. *Small Business Economics* 29(1): 81–99.

Arabsheibani, G., D. De Meza, J. Maloney, and B. Pearson (2000). 'And a Vision Appeared unto Them of a Great Profit: Evidence of Self-deception Among the Self-employed'. *Economics Letters* 67(1): 35–41.

Ardichvili, A., R. Cardozo, R., and S. Ray (2003). 'A Theory of Entrepreneurial Opportunity Identification and Development'. *Journal of Business Venturing* 18(1): 105–123.

Ardishvili, A., S. Cardozo, S. Harmon, and S. Vadakath (1998). 'Towards a Theory of New Venture Growth', *Babson Entrepreneurship Research Conference*, 21–33. Ghent.

Athreye, S. (2010). 'Economic Adversity and Entrepreneurship Led Growth: Lessons from the Indian Software Sector'. UNU-WIDER Working Paper No. 2010/04.

Atkinson, R. D. and R. H. Court (1998). *The New Economy Index: Understanding America's Economic Transformation*, Washington, DC: Progressive Policy Institute.

Audretsch, D. B. (1991) 'New-firm Survival and the Technological Regime', *The Review of Economics and Statistics* 68: 441–450.

——— (1995) 'Innovation, Growth and Survival', *International Journal of Industrial Organization* 13(4): 441–457.

Audretsch, D. B. and T. Mahmood (1995). 'New Firm Survival: New Results Using a Hazard Function'. *The Review of Economics and Statistics* 77(1): 97–103.

Audretsch, D. B. and M. Fritsch (1996). *Creative Destruction: Turbulence and Economic Growth in Germany*, 137–150. Behavioral Norms, Technological Progress, and Economic Dynamics: Studies in Schumpeterian Economics. The University of Michigan Press.

Audretsch, D. B. (1997). 'Technological Regimes, industrial Demography and the Evolution of Industrial Structures'. *Industrial and Corporate Change* 6(1): 49–82.

——— (1998). 'Agglomeration and the Location of Innovative Activity'. *Oxford Review of Economic Policy* 14(2): 18–29.

——— (2001). 'The Role of Small Firms in US Biotechnology Clusters'. *Small Business Economics* 17(1): 3–15.

Audretsch, D. B. and M. Fritsch (2002). 'Growth Regimes over Time and Space'. *Regional Studies* 36(2): 113–124.

Audretsch, D. B., P. Houweling, and A. R. Thurik (2004) 'Industry Evolution: Diversity, Selection and the Role of Learning'. *International Small Business Journal* 22(4): 331–348.

Audretsch, D. B. and E. E. Lehmann (2004). 'Financing High-tech Growth: The Role of Banks and Venture Capitalists'. *Schmalenbach Business Review* 56: 340–357.

Audretsch, D. B. and M. C. Keilbach (2004). 'Entrepreneurship Capital and Economic Performance'. *Regional Studies* 38(8): 949–959.

Audretsch, D. B., M. C. Keilbach, and E. E. Lehmann (2006). *Entrepreneurship and Economic Growth*. Oxford: Oxford University Press.

Bala Subrahmanya, M. H. (2010). *Internet New Ventures in the USA: Winning Venture Capital Support and Going Public (1995–2006)*, report prepared as part of the Fulbright-Nehru Senior Research Fellowship, Davis: University of California.

——— (2015). 'New Generation Start-Ups in India: What Lessons Can We Learn from the Past?' *Economic and Political Weekly* 50(12): 56–63.

——— (2018). 'Graduation from SSIs to SMEs in India: Policies, Performance, and Challenges'. *International Journal of Entrepreneurship and Small Business* 33(2): 241–264.

Barkman, R. (1994). 'Entrepreneurial Characteristics and the Size of the New Firm: A Model and an Econometric Test', *Small Business Economics* 6: 117–125.

Baron, R. A. and G. D. Markman (2003). 'Beyond Social Capital: The Role of Entrepreneurs' Social Competence in Their Financial Success'. *Journal of Business Venturing* 18(1): 41–60.

Baron, R. A. and M. D. Ensley (2006). 'Opportunity Recognition as the Detection of Meaningful Patterns: Evidence from Comparisons of Novice and Experienced Entrepreneurs'. *Management Science* 52(9): 1331–1344.

Barney, J. (1991). 'Firm Resources and Sustained Competitive Advantage'. *Journal of management* 17(1): 99–120.

Barringer, B. R. and A. C. Bluedorn (1999). 'The Relationship between Corporate Entrepreneurship and Strategic Management'. *Strategic Management Journal* 20(5): 421–444.

Barringer, B. R. and J. S. Harrison (2000). 'Walking a Tightrope: Creating Value through Inter-organizational Relationships'. *Journal of Management* 26(3): 367–403.

Barringer, B. R., F. F. Jones, and D. O. Neubaum (2005). 'A Quantitative Content Analysis of the Characteristics of Rapid-growth Firms and Their Founders'. *Journal of Business Venturing* 20: 663–687.

Barringer, B. and R. D. Ireland (2008). *What's Stopping You? Shatter the 9 Most Common Myths Keeping You from Starting Your Own Business*. FT Press.

Barrow, C. (1998). *The Essence of Small Business*. Upper Saddle River, NJ: Pearson Education.

Bartlett, C. A. and S. Ghoshal (1997). 'The Myth of the Generic Manager: New Personal Competencies for New Management Roles'. *California Management Review* 40(1): 92–116.

Bates, T. (1991). 'Commercial Bank Financing of White- and Black-owned Small Business Start-ups'. *Quarterly Review of Economics and Business* 31(1): 64–80.

——— (1997). 'Financing Small Business Creation: The Case of Chinese and Korean Immigrant Entrepreneurs'. *Journal of Business Venturing* 12(2): 109–124.

—— (2005). 'Analysis of Young, Small Firms That Have Closed: Delineating Successful from Unsuccessful Closures'. *Journal of Business Venturing* 20: 343–358.

Baum, J. A. and C. Oliver (1991). 'Institutional Linkages and Organizational Mortality'. *Adm. Sci. Q.* 36(2): 187–219.

Baum, J. A. C. (1996). 'Liabilities of Newness, Adolescence, and Obsolescence: Exploring Age Dependence in the Dissolution of Organizational Relationships and Organizations'. *Proceedings of the Administrative Sciences Association of Canada, Annual Conference.*

Baum, J. A. C., T. Calabrese, and B. S. Silverman (2000). 'Don't Go It Alone: Alliance Network Composition and Startups' Performance in Canadian Biotechnology', *Strategic Management Journal* 21(3): 267–94.

Baumol, W. J. (2002). 'Entrepreneurship, Innovation and Economic Growth: The David–Goliath Symbiosis'. *Journal of Entrepreneurial Finance and Business Ventures* 7(2): 1–10.

Berger, A. N. and G. F. Udell (1998). 'The Economics of Small Business Finance: The Roles of Private Equity and Debt Markets in the Financial Growth Cycle'. *Journal of banking & finance* 22(6) 613–673.

—— (2006). 'A More Complete Conceptual Framework for SME Finance'. *Journal of Banking & Finance* 30(11): 2945–2966.

Beaudry, C. and P. Swann (2001). 'Growth in Industrial Clusters: A Bird's Eye View of the United Kingdom'. Discussion paper 00–38, *Stanford Institute for Economic Policy Research.*

Berman, E., J. Bound, and S. Machin (1998). 'Implications of Skill-biased Technological Change: International Evidence'. *The Quarterly Journal of Economics* 113(4): 1245–1279. Available at https://doi.org/10.1162/003355398555892.

Bianchi, M. (2009). 'Credit Constraints, Entrepreneurial Talent and Economic Development', UNU-WIDER Research Paper No. 2009/20.

Birch, D. L. (1979). *The Job Generation Process: Unpublished Report Prepared by the Massachusetts Institute of Technology Program on Neighborhood and Regional Change for the Economic Development Administration*, Washington, DC: US Department of Commerce.

Bhave, M. P. (1994). 'A Process Model of Entrepreneurial Venture Creation'. *Journal of Business Venturing* 9(3): 223–242.

Bhide, A. (1999). 'Developing Start-up Strategies'. *The Entrepreneurial Venture*, 2ª edn, 121–137. Boston, MA: Harvard Business School Press.

—— (2000). *The Origin and Evolution of New Businesses*, 1st edn. New York City, NY: Oxford Univesity Press.

Blank, S. (2010). 'What's a Startup? First Principles'. Available at https://steveblank.com/2010/01/25/whats-a-startup-first-principles/. Accessed on 30 April 2019.

Blank, S. and B. Dorf (2012). *The Startup Owner's Manual: The Step-by-Step Guide for Building a Great Company.* BookBaby.

Bosma, N., G. de Wit, and M. Carree (2005). 'Modelling Entrepreneurship: Unifying the Equilibrium and Entry/Exit Approach'. *Small Business Economics* 25: 35–48.

Boyacigiller, N. A. and N. J. Adler (1991). 'The Parochial Dinosaur: Organizational Science in a Global Context'. *Academy of Management Review* 16(2): 262–290.

Braggs, S.M. (1999). *Managing Explosive Corporate Growth*, New York: Wiley.

Brenner, M. H. (1987). 'Economic Instability, Unemployment Rates, Behavioral Risks, and Mortality Rates in Scotland, 1952–1983'. *International Journal of Health Services* 17(3): 475–487.

Brockhaus, R. H. (1980). 'Risk Taking Propensity of Entrepreneurs'. *Academy of Management Journal* 23(3): 509–520.

—— (1982). 'The Psychology of the Entrepreneur'. In *Encyclopedia of Entrepreneurship*, ed. C. A. Kent, D. L. Sexton, and K. H. Vesper, 39–56. Englewood Cliffs, NJ: Prentice-Hall. .

Bruce, D. (2002). 'Taxes and Entrepreneurial Endurance: Evidence from the Self-employed'. *National Tax Journal* 55(1): 5–24.

Brüdel, J., P. Preisendörfer, and R. Ziegler (1992). 'Survival Chances of Newly Founded Business Organizations'. *American Sociological Review* 57: 227–242.

—— (1996). *'Der Erfolg neugegruendeter Betriebe: Eine empirische Studie zu den Chancen und Risiken von Unternehmensgruendungen'*, Berlin: Duncker and Humblot.

Bruno, A. V. and T. T. Tyebjee (1985). 'The Entrepreneur's Search for Capital', *Journal of Business Venturing* 1: 61–74.

Brush, C. G., P. G. Greene, and M. M. Hart (2001) 'From Initial Idea to Unique Advantage: The Entrepreneurial Challenge of Constructing a Resource Base'. *The Academy of Management Executive* 15(1): 64–78.

Brush, C. G., T. S. Manolova, and L. F. Edelman (2008). 'Properties of Emerging Organizations: An Empirical Test'. *Journal of Business Venturing* 23(5): 547–566.

Bruton, G. D. and Y. Rubanik (2002) 'Resources of the Firm, Russian High-technology Startups, and Firm Growth'. *Journal of Business Venturing* 17(6): 553–576.

Busenitz, L. W., G. P. West, D. Shepherd, T. Nelson, G. N. Chandler, and A. Zacharakis (2003). 'Entrepreneurship Research in Emergence: Past Trends and Future Directions'. *Journal of Management* 29(3): 285–308.

Buttner, E. H. and B. Rosen (1989). 'Funding New Business Ventures: Are Decision Makers Biased Against Women Entrepreneurs?' *Journal of Business Venturing* 4: 249–261.

Bygrave, W. D. (1989). 'The Entrepreneurship Paradigm (1): A Philosophical Look at Its Research Methodologies'. *Entrepreneurship Theory & Practice* 14(1): 7–26.

Bygrave, W., M. Hay, E. Ng, and P. Reynolds (2003). 'Executive Forum: A Study of Informal Investing in 29 Nations Composing the Global Entrepreneurship Monitor'. *Venture Capital: An International Journal of Entrepreneurial Finance* 5(2): 101–116.

Cader, A. H. and C. J. Leatherman (2011). 'Small Business Survival and Sample Selection Bias', *Small Business Economics* 37: 155–165.

Caliendo, M. and A. S. Kritikos (2010). 'Start-ups by the Unemployed: Characteristics, Survival and Direct Employment Effects'. *Small Business Economics* 35: 71–92.

Callejón, M. and A. Segarra (1999). 'Business Dynamics and Efficiency in Industries and Regions: The Case of Spain'. *Small Business Economics* 13(4): 253–271.

Carey, G. (1998). 'Multivariate Analysis of Variance (MANOVA): I. Theory'. Available at http://ibgwww.colorado.edu/~carey/p7291dir/handouts/manoval.pdf. Accessed on 6 March 2007.

Carland, J. C. and J. W. Carland (2000). 'New Venture Creation Model'. *Journal of Business and Entrepreneurship* 12(3): 29.

Carlsson, B. (1999). 'Small Business, Entrepreneurship, and Industrial Dynamics'. In *Are Small Firms Important? Their Role and Impact*, ed. Z. J. Acs, 99–110. Boston, MA: Springer.

Carlsson, B. and P. Braunerhjelm (1999). '8 Industry Clusters: Biotechnology/Biomedicine and Polymers in Ohio and Sweden'. *Innovation, Industry Evolution and Employment*, 182.

Carroll, G. R. and M. T. Hannan (2000). *The Demography of Corporations and Industries*. Princeton, NJ: Princeton University Press.

Carter, D. A., B. J. Simkins, and W. G. Simpson (2003). 'Corporate Governance, Board Diversity, and Firm Value'. *Financial Review* 38(1): 33–53.

Carter, N. M., W. B. Gartner, W. B., and P. D. Reynolds (1996). 'Exploring Start-up Event Sequences'. *Journal of Business Venturing* 11(3): 151–166.

Cassar, G. (2004). 'The Financing of Business Start-ups'. *Journal of Business Venturing* 19(2): 261–283.

——— (2014). 'Industry and Startup Experience on Entrepreneur Forecast Performance in New Firms'. *Journal of Business Venturing* 29(1): 137–151.

Casson, M. (1982). *The Entrepreneur.* Totowa, NJ: Barnes and Noble Books.

Cefis, E. and O. Marsili (2006). 'Survivor: The Role of Innovation in Firms' Survival'. *Research Policy* 35(5): 626–641.

Certo, S. T. (2003). 'Influencing Initial Public Offering Investors with Prestige: Signaling with Board Structures'. *Academy of Management Review* 28(3): 432–446.

Chakrabarti, A. K. (1990). 'Scientific Output of Small and Medium Size Firms in High-tech Industries'. *IEEE Trans. Eng. Manage.* 37(1): 48–52.

Chan, E. Y., N. Bhargava, and C. T. Street (2006). 'Having Arrived: The Homogeneity of High-growth Small Firms', *Journal of Small Business Management* 44(3): 426–440.

Chandler, A. D. (1977). *The Visible Hand: The Managerial Revolution in American Business.* Cambridge, MA: Taylor and Francis.

——— (1990). *Strategy and Structure: Chapters in the History of the Industrial Enterprise*, 120. Cambridge, MA: MIT Press.

Chatterjee, D. (2010). 'Studies on Some Aspects of Liquidity of Stocks: Limit Order Executions in the Indian Stock Market', PhD thesis, submitted at Indian Institute of Science, Bengaluru.

Choo, F. and K. Trotman (1991). 'The Relationship between Knowledge Structure and Judgments for Experienced and Inexperienced Auditors'. *The Accounting Review* 66(3): 464–485.

Chrisman, J. J., A. Bauerschmidt, and C. W. Hofer (1998). 'The Determinants of New Venture Performance: An Extended Model'. *Entrepreneurship Theory and Practice* 23: 5–30.

Churchill, N. C. and V. L. Lewis (1983). 'The Five Stages of Small Business Growth'. *Harvard Business Review* (May–June): 30–51.

Clement, M. B. (1999). 'Analyst Forecast Accuracy: Do Ability, Resources, and Portfolio Complexity Matter?' *Journal of Accounting and Economics* 27(3): 285–303.

Clement, M., T. Dingermann, Y. Friedman, D. Heisenberg, A. Jahn, M. Keilbach, and R. Seline (2007). *AICGS Policy Report*.

Coase, R. H. (1937). 'The Nature of the Firm'. *Economica* 4(16): 386–405.

Cohen, W. and R. Levin (1989). 'Empirical Studies of Innovation and Market Structure'. In *Handbook of Industrial Organization*, vol. 2, ed. Richard Schmalensee and Robert Willig, 1060–1107. Elsevier.

Coleman, S. (2000). 'Access to Capital and Terms of Credit: A Comparison of Men- and Women-owned Small Businesses'. *Journal of Small Business Management* 38(3): 37.

Coleman, S. and R. Cohn (2000). 'Small Firms' Use of Financial Leverage: Evidence from the 1993 National Survey of Small Business Finances'. *Journal of Business and Entrepreneurship* 12(3): 81.

Coleman, S., C. Cotei, and J. Farhat (2013). 'A Resource-based View of New Firm Survival: New Perspectives on the Role of Industry and Exit Route'. *Journal of Developmental Entrepreneurship* 18(1): 1350002.

Colombo, M. G. and L. Grilli (2005). 'Founders' Human Capital and the Growth of New Technology-based Firms: A Competence-based View'. *Research Policy* 34(6): 795–816.

—— (2010). 'On Growth Drivers of High-tech Startups: Exploring the Role of Founders' Human Capital and Venture Capital'. *Journal of Business Venturing* 25: 610–626.

Cooper, A. C., F. J. Gimeno-Gascon, and C. Y. Woo (1994). 'Initial Human and Financial Capital as Predictors of New Venture Performance'. *Journal of business venturing* 9(5): 371–395.

Cooper, A. C. (2002). 'Networks, Alliances, and Entrepreneurship'. In *Strategic Entrepreneurship: Creating a New Mindset*, ed. M. A. Hitt, R. D. Ireland, S. M. Camp, and D. L. Sexton, 203–222. Oxford: Blackwell.

Cooper, A. and T. Folta (2000). 'Entrepreneurship and High-technology Clusters'. In *The Blackwell Handbook of Entrepreneurship*, ed. Donald L. Sexton and Hans Landström, 348–367. Blackwell Publishers Ltd.

Cooper, R. S. (2003). 'Purpose and Performance of the Small Business Innovation Research (SBIR) Program'. *Small Business Economics* 20(2): 137–151.

Corbett, A. C. (2005). 'Experiential Learning within the Process of Opportunity Identification and Exploitation'. *Entrepreneurship Theory and Practice* 29(4): 473–491.

Covin, J. G. and D. P. Slevin (1991). 'A Conceptual Model of Entrepreneurship as Firm Behavior'. *Entrepreneurship Theory and Practice* 16(1): 7–25.

Cox, D. R. (1972). 'Regression Models and Life-tables'. *Journal of the Royal Statistical Society: Series B (Methodological)* 34(2): 187–202.

Davidsson, P. (2003). 'The Domain of Entrepreneurship Research: Some Suggestions'. In *Advances in Entrepreneurship, Firm Emergence and Growth*, vol. 6, ed. J. A. Katz and D. A. Shepherd, 315–372. Oxford: Elsevier/JAI Press.

———— (2006). 'Nascent Entrepreneurship: Empirical Studies and Developments'. *Foundations and Trends in Entrepreneurship* 2: 1–76.

Davidsson, P. and F. Delmar (1997). High-growth Firms: Characteristics, Job Contribution and Method Observations. RENT XI Conference. Mannheim, Germany. 27 and 28 November. Accessible at https://eprints.qut.edu.au/68083/2/68083.pdf. Accessed on 5 March 2019.

———— (2003). 'Hunting for New Employment: The Role of High-growth Firms'. In *Small Firms and Economic Development in Developed and Transition Economies: A Reader*, ed. D. A. Kirby and A. Watson, 7–20. Hampshire: Ashgate Publishing.

Davidsson, P. and B. Honig (2003). 'The Role of Social and Human Capital among Nascent Entrepreneurs'. *Journal of Business Venturing* 18: 301–331.

Deakins, D. (1999). *Entrepreneurship and Small Firms*. Maidenhead: McGraw-Hill.

Deakins, D. and G. Whittam (2000). 'Business Start-up: Theory, Practice and Policy'. In *Enterprise and Small Business: Principles, Practice and Policy*, ed. S. Carter and D. Jones-Evans. London: Financial Times Prentice Hall.

Dean, T. J. and G. D. Meyer (1996). 'Industry Environments and New Venture Formations in US Manufacturing: A Conceptual and Empirical Analysis of Demand Determinants'. *Journal of Business Venturing* 11(2): 107–132.

Deeds, D. L., D. DeCarolis, and J. Coombs (1999). 'Dynamic Capabilities and New Product Development in High Technology Ventures: An Empirical Analysis of New Biotechnology Firms'. *Journal of Business Venturing* 15(3): 211–229.

Delmar, F. and S. Shane (2003). 'Does Business Planning Facilitate the Development of New Ventures?' *Strategic Management Journal* 24(12): 1165–1185.

———— (2004). 'Legitimating First: Organizing Activities and the Survival of New Ventures'. *Journal of Business Venturing* 19(3): 385–410.

Delmar, F. and S. Shane (2006). 'Does Experience Matter? The Effect of Founding Team Experience on the Survival and Sales of Newly Founded Ventures'. *Strategic Organization* 4(3): 215–247.

Delmar, F., P. Davidsson, and W. B. Gartner (2003). 'Arriving at the High-growth Firm'. *Journal of Business Venturing* 18(2): 189–216.

Department of Commerce, USA (1980). *Benchmark Surveys*. Washington, DC.

Department of IT, BT and S&T, Government of Karnataka (2015). Available at http://bangaloreitbt.in/docs/2015/Startup_Policy.pdf. Accessed on 3 July 2017.

Department of Scientific and Industrial Research, Government of India (2014). Technopreneur Promotion Programme. Available at http://www.dsir.gov.in/tpdup/tepp/tepp.htm. Accessed on 20 February 2013.

Desai N. (2002). 'Venture Capital at Crossroads'. Report by Private Equity Practice Group. Available at www.nishithdesai.com. Accessed on 14 June 2017.

Dew, N., S. Read, S. D. Sarasvathy, and R. Wiltbank (2009). 'Effectual versus Predictive Logics in Entrepreneurial Decision-making: Differences between Experts and Novices'. *Journal of Business Venturing* 24(4): 287–309.

Dhar, R. (2013). 'The Jellyfish Entrepreneur'. Self-published blog. Available at http://blog.priceonomics.com/post/47035579568/the-jellyfish-entrepreneur. Accessed on 16 June 2017.

Dimov, D. (2007). 'From Opportunity Insight to Opportunity Intention: The Importance of Person-Situation Learning Match'. *Entrepreneurship Theory and Practice* 31: 561–583.

—— (2010). 'Nascent Entrepreneurs and Venture Emergence: Opportunity Confidence, Human Capital, and Early Planning'. *Journal of Management Studies* 47(6): 1123–1153.

Djankov, S. and C. McLiesh (2005). *Doing Business in 2005: Removing Obstacles to Growth*. Oxford: Oxford University Press, World Bank, and International Finance Corporation.

Doctors, S. I. and R. E. Wokutch (1979). 'Impact of State and Local Policies'. In *The Status of Small Business in Region 111*, ed. P. W. Houch, 11–17. University Park, PA: Pennsylvania Technical Assistance Program for the SBA.

Drori, I., B. Honig, and M. Wright (2009). 'Transnational Entrepreneurship: An Emergent Field of Study'. *Entrepreneurship Theory and Practice* 33(5): 1001–1022.

Duchesneau, D. A. and W. B. Gartner (1990). 'A Profile of New Venture Success and Failure in an Emerging Industry'. *Journal of business venturing* 5(5): 297–312.

Dumais, G., G. Ellison, and E. Glaeser (2002). 'Geographic Concentration as a Dynamic Process'. *Review of Economics and Statistics* 84(2): 193–204.

Dunne, P. and A. Hughes (1994). 'Age, Size, Growth and Survival: UK Companies in the 1980s'. *Journal of Industrial Economics* 42: 115–140.

Dunne, T., M. J. Robert, and L. Samuelson (1989). 'The Growth and Failure of U.S. Manufacturing Plants'. *Quarterly Journal of Economics* 104: 671–698.

Eisenhardt, K. M. and J. Martin (2000). 'Dynamic Capabilities: What Are They?'. Special issue, *Strategic Management Journal* 21 (October–November): 1105–1121.

Ensley, M. D., A. Pearson, and C. L. Pearce (2003). 'Top Management Team Process, Shared Leadership, and New Venture Performance: A Theoretical Model and Research Agenda'. *Human Resource Management Review* 13: 329–346.

Ensley, M. (2006). 'Family Businesses Can Out-compete: As Long as They Are Willing to Question the Chosen Path'. *Entrepreneurship Theory and Practice* 30(6): 747–754.

Ericson, R. and A. Pakes (1995). 'Markov Perfect Industry Dynamics: A Framework for Empirical Work'. *Review of Economic Studies* 62(1): 53–82.

Estrin, S., K. E. Meyer, and M. Bytchkova (2006). 'Entrepreneurship in Transition Economies'. In *The Oxford Handbook of Entrepreneurship*, ed. M. Casson Yeung, B., A. Basu, and N. Wadeson. Oxford: Oxford University Press.

Eurostat (2007). Available at http://epp.eurostat.ec.europa.eu/statistics_explained/index.php/High-tech_statistics. Accessed on 19 February 2013.

Evans, D. S. (1987). 'The Relationship between Firm Growth, Size, and Age: Estimates for 100 Manufacturing Industries'. *Journal of Industrial Economics* 35: 567–581.

Executive Committee, Commission on Strategic Development, Hong Kong (2007). *Development of High Technology Industries in Hong Kong*, Paper ref: CSD/EC/6/2007.

Feeser, H. R. and G. E. Willard (1990). 'Founding Strategy and Performance: A Comparison of High and Low Growth High Tech Forms'. *Strategic Management Journal* 11(2): 87–98.

Fertala, N. (2008). 'The Shadow of Death: Do Regional Differences Matter for Firm Survival Across Native and Immigrant Entrepreneurs?'. *Empirica* 35: 59–80.

Fish, T. (2009). *My Digital Footprint: A Two-sided Digital Business Model Where Your Privacy Will Be Someone Else's Business!* futuretext.

Folta, T. B., A. C. Cooper, and Y. S. Baik (2006). 'Geographic Cluster Size and Firm Performance'. *Journal of Business Venturing* 21: 217–242.

Forbes, D. P. (2005). 'The Effects of Strategic Decision Making on Entrepreneurial Self-efficacy'. *Entrepreneurship Theory and Practice* 29(5): 599–626.

Freear, J., J. E. Sohl, and W. E. Wetzel Jr (1995). 'Angels: Personal Investors in the Venture Capital Market'. *Entrepreneurship & Regional Development* 7(1): 85–94.

—— (2002). 'Angles on Angels: Financing Technology-based Ventures, A Historical Perspective'. *Venture Capital: An International Journal of Entrepreneurial Finance* 4(4): 275–287.

Freeman, J., G. Carroll, and M. Hannan (1983). 'The Liability of Newness: Age Dependence in Organizational Death Rates'. *American Sociological Review* 48: 692–710.

Fried, J. and D. H. Hansson (2010). *Rework*. New York City, NY: Crown Publishing.

Furdas M. and K. Kohn (2011). 'Why Is Startup Survival Lower among Necessity Entrepreneurs? A Decomposition Approach'. Research paper. Available at https://www.semanticscholar.org/paper/Why-Is-Start-up-Survival-Lower-Among-Necessity-A-Furdas-Kohn/3d9c11d99187b023851cadf54a200ad1af2892ed. Accessed on 5 March 2019.

Gartner, W. B. (1985). 'A Conceptual Framework for Describing the Phenomenon of New Venture Creation'. *Academy of Management Review*, 696–706.

Gartner, W. B., B. J. Bird, and J. A. Starr (1992). 'Acting as if: Differentiating Entrepreneurial from Organizational Behavior'. *Entrepreneurship Theory and Practice* 16(3): 13–31.

Garud, R., A. Kumaraswamy, and P. Nayyar (1998). 'Real Options or Fool's Gold: Perspective Makes the Difference'. Discussion forum, *Academy of Management Review* 3(2): 212–214.

German Federal Ministry of Economics and Technology (1999). *Economic Report '99*. Bonn: Federal Ministry of Economics and Technology.

Geroski, P. A. (1995). 'What Do We Know about Entry?' *International Journal of Industrial Organization* 13: 421–440.

Gilbert, B. A., D. B. Audretsch, and P. P. McDougall (2004). 'The Emergence of Entrepreneurship Policy'. *Small Business Economics* 22(3 and 4): 313–323.

Gilbert, B. A., P. P. McDougall, and D. B. Audretsch (2006). 'New Venture Growth: A Review and Extension'. *Journal of Management* 32(6): 926–950.

Gimeno, J., T. B. Folta, A. C. Cooper, and Woo, C. Y. (1997). 'Survival of the Fittest? Entrepreneurial Human Capital and the Persistence of Underperforming Firms'. *Administrative Science Quarterly*, 750–783.

Gibrat, R. (1931). *Les inégalités économiques* (Economic inequalities). Paris: Bookstore of the Sirey Collection.

Gompers, P. A. and J. Lerner (1999). 'What Drives Venture Capital Fundraising?'. Working Paper 6906, JEL. No. G24, NBER Working Paper Series, Cambridge, MA: National Bureau of Economic Research. Available at https://www.nber.org/papers/w6906.pdf. Accessed on 14 June 2017.

Government of Andhra Pradesh (2014). Available at http://www.ap.gov.in/Other%20
Docs/AP%20Innovation%20and%20Startup%20Policy%202014-2020.pdf. Accessed
on 12 June 2017.

Government of Kerala (2014). Available at https://www.kerala.gov.in/documents/10180/
46696/Kerala%20Technology%20%20Startup%20Policy%202014. Accessed on 12
June 2017.

Government of Rajasthan (2015). Available at http://resurgent.rajasthan.gov.in/resurgent-
policies/rajasthan-startup-policy-2015.pdf. Accessed on 12 June 2017.

Greenberger, D. B. and D. L. Sexton (1988). 'An Interactive Model for New Venture
Creation'. *Journal of Small Business Management* 26(3): 107–118.

Gregoire, D. A., M. X. Noel, R. Dery, and J. P. Bechard (2006). 'Is There Conceptual
Convergence in Entrepreneurship Research? A Co-citation Analysis of FER 1981–
2004'. *Entrepreneurship Theory and Practice* 30(3): 333–373.

Greiner, L. (1972). 'Evolution and Revolution as Organizations Grow'. *Harvard Business
Review* (July–August): 37–46.

Gries, T. and W. Naude (2008). 'Entrepreneurship and Regional Economic Growth:
Towards a General Theory of Start-ups'. UNU-WIDER Research Paper No. 2008/70.

Grimm, C. M. and K. G. Smith (1997). *Strategy as Action: Industry Rivalry and
Coordination*, Cincinnati, OH: Southwestern Advantage.

Gujarati, D. N. (2012). *Basic Econometrics*. New Delhi: Tata McGraw-Hill Education.

Gurley-Calvez, T. and D. Bruce (2008). 'Do Tax Cuts Promote Entrepreneurial
Longevity?' *National Tax Journal* 61(2): 225–250.

Gundry, L. K. and H. P. Welsch (2001). 'The Ambitious Entrepreneur: High Growth
Strategies of Women-owned Enterprises'. *Journal of Business Venturing* 16(5): 453–470.

Gruber, M., I. C. MacMillan, and J. D. Thompson (2008). 'Look before You Leap:
Market Opportunity Identification in Emerging Technology Firms'. *Management
Science* 54(9): 1652–1665.

Haeussler, C., H. Patzelt, and S. A. Zahra (2012). 'Strategic Alliances and Product
Development in High Technology New Firms: The Moderating Effect of
Technological Capabilities'. *Journal of Business Venturing* 27: 217–233.

Hall, H. Bronwyn (1987). 'The Relationship between Firm Size and Firm Growth in
the U.S. Manufacturing Sector'. *Journal of Industrial Economics* 35: 583–605.

Hair, J. F. Jr, R. E. Anderson, R. L. Tatham and W. C. Black (2015). *Multivariate
Data Analysis*, 7th edn. New York City, NY: Macmillan.

Haleblian, J., Kim, J. Y., and N. Rajagopalan (2006). 'The Influence of Acquisition
Experience and Performance on Acquisition Behavior: Evidence from the U.S.
Commercial Banking Industry'. *Academy of Management Journal* 49(2): 357–370.

Hanks, S. H., C. J. Watson, E. Jansen, and G. N. Chandler (1993). 'Tightening the
Life-cycle Construct: A Taxonomical Study of Growth Stage Configurations in
High Technology Organizations'. *Entrepreneurship Theory and Practice* (Winter): 5–29.

Hannan, M. T. and J. Freeman (1984). 'Structural Inertia and Organizational Change'.
American Journal of Sociology 49(2): 149–164.

Harrison, J. and B. Taylor (1997). *Supergrowth Companies*. Oxford: Reed Educational and Professional Publishing.

Hart, M. and E. Hanvey (1995). 'Job Generation and New and Small Firms: Some Evidence from the Late 1980s'. *Small Business Economics* 7(2): 97–109.

Hay, M., P. Verdin, and P. Williamson (1993). 'Successful New Ventures: Lessons for Entrepreneurs and Investors'. *Long Range Planning* 26: 26, 31–41.

Haynes, G. W. and D. C. Haynes (1999). 'The Debt Structure of Small Businesses Owned by Women in 1987 and 1993'. *Journal of Small Business Management* 37(2): 1.

Hayward, M. L. A., D. A. Shepherd, and D. Griffin (2006). 'A Hubris Theory of Entrepreneurship'. *Management Science* 52(2): 160–172.

Hecker, D. E. (1999). 'High-technology Employment: A Broader View'. *Monthly Labor Review* 122(6).

—— (2005). 'High-technology Employment: A NAICS-based Update'. *Monthly Labor Review* 57.

Higgins, M. C. and R. Gulati (2006). 'Stacking the Deck: The Effects of Top Management Backgrounds on Investor Decisions'. *Strategic Management Journal* 27: 1–25.

Highfield, R. and R. Smiley (1987). 'New Business Start-ups and Economic Activity: An Empirical Investigation'. *International Journal of Industrial Organization* 5(1): 51–66.

Hiroyuki, O. and K. Nobuo (2006). 'The Impact of Regional Factors on the Start-up Ratio in Japan'. *Journal of Small Business Management* 44(2): 310.

Hite, J. M. and W. S. Hesterly (2001). 'The Evolution of Firm Networks: From Emergence to Early Growth of the Firm'. *Strategic Management Journal* 22(3): 275–286.

Holtz-Eakin, D. and C. Kao (2003). 'Entrepreneurship and Economic Growth: The Proof is in the Productivity'. Working Paper No. 50. Center for Policy Research, Syracuse University. Available at https://surface.syr.edu/cpr/111. Accessed on 5 March 2019.

Horst, T. (1972). 'Firm and Industry Determinants of the Decision to Invest Abroad: An Empirical Study'. *The Review of Economics and Statistics* 54(3): 258–266.

Hosmer, D. W. and S. Lemeshow (2000). 'Introduction to the Logistic Regression Model'. In *Applied Logistic Regression*, 2nd edn, 1–30. New York City, NY: John Wiley & Sons.

Huyghebaert, N. (2001). 'The Capital Structure of Business Start-ups: Determinants of Initial Financial Structure'. *Tijdschrift voor Bank-en Financiewezen* 3: 84–88.

Huynh, T., D. Aranda, and L. Molina-Fernández (2012). 'Spin-off Performance: Entrepreneurial Capabilities and Social Networks of the Founders in the Creation Period'. *Proceedings of the 7th European Conference on Innovation and Entrepreneurship: ECIE*. 316. Academic Conferences Limited.

Indian Institute of Foreign Trade (2007). 'A Pilot Study on Technology Based Start-ups'. Supported by Department of Scientific and Industrial Research, Government of India. Available at http://www.dsir.gov.in/reports/ittp_citt/Startups.pdf. Accessed on 12 June 2017.

India Venture Capital Association (2012). 'Venture Capital and Private Equity in India'. Available at http://www.indiavca.org/pdf/VCPE_Report2012_Final.pdf. Accessed on 19 February 2013.

iSPIRT (2014). iSPIRT Product Industry Monitor'. Available at https://www.slideshare. net/ProductNation/i-spirt-product-industry-monitor-feb-2014. Accessed on 14 March 2019.

Jacob, J., T. Z. Lys, and M. A. Neale (1999). 'Expertise in Forecasting Performance of Security Analysts'. *Journal of Accounting and Economics* 28(1): 51–82.

Jaffe, A. B., M. Trajtenberg, and R. Henderson (1993). 'Geographic Localization of Knowledge Spillovers as Evidenced by Patent Citations'. *Quarterly Journal of Economics* 63(3): 577–598.

Jim, Collins. and I. Porras Jerry (1994). *Built to Last: Successful Habits of Visionary Companies*. New York City, NY: HarperCollins Publications.

Jo, H., J. Lee (1996). 'The Relationship between an Entrepreneur's Background and Performance in a New Venture'. *Technovation* 16(4): 161–211.

Joshi, K. (2015). 'Economics of Venture Capital Operations in India: Macro Ecosystem and Micro Decision Making'. PhD dissertation, submitted at Indian Institute of Science, Bengaluru.

Johannisson, B. (1990). 'Economies of Overview: Guiding the External Growth of Small Firms'. *International Small Business Journal* 9(1): 32–44.

Johnson, S., J. McMillan, and C. Woodruff (2000). 'Entrepreneurs and the Ordering of Institutional Reform: Poland, Slovakia, Romania, Russia and Ukraine Compared'. *Economics of Transition* 81(1): 1–36.

Jovanovic, B. (1982). 'Selection and Evolution of Industry'. *Econometrica* 50: 649–670.

Kaish, S. and B. Gilad (1991). 'Characteristics of Opportunities Search of Entrepreneurs versus Executives: Sources, Interests, General Alertness'. *Journal of Business Venturing* 6(1): 45–61.

Kane, T. (2010). 'The Importance of Startups in Job Creation and Job Destruction'. *Kauffman Foundation Research Series: Firm Formation and Economic Growth*. Kansas City, MO: The Ewing Marion Kauffman Foundation.

Karnoe, P. (1996). 'The Social Process of Competence Building'. *International Journal of Technology Management* 11(7 and 8): 770–789.

Katz, J. A. (1992). 'A Psychosocial Cognitive Model of Employment Status Choice'. *Entrepreneurship: Theory and Practice* 17(1): 29–37.

Katz, J. and W. B. Gartner (1988). 'Properties of Emerging Organizations'. *Academy of Management Review*, 429–441.

Kazanjian, R. K. (1988). 'Relation of Dominant Problems to Stages of Growth in Technology-based New Ventures'. *Academy of Management Journal* 31: 257–279.

Kim, L. and J. Nugent (1999). 'Korean SMEs and Their Support Mechanisms'. In *Fulfilling the Export Potential of Small and Medium Firms*, ed. Brian Levy, Albert Berry, and Jeffrey B. Nugent, 115–167. Boston, MA: Kluwer Academic Publishers.

Kim, P. H., H. E. Aldrich, and L. A. Keister (2006). 'Access (Not) Denied: The Impact of Financial, Human and Cultural Capital on Entrepreneurial Entry in the United States'. *Small Business Economics* 27: 5–22.

King, A. A. and C. L. Tucci (2002). 'Incumbent Entry into New Market Niches: The Role of Experience and Managerial Choice in the Creation of Dynamic Capabilities'. *Management Science* 48(2): 171–186.

Kirchhoff, B. A. (1994). *Entrepreneurship and Dynamic Capitalism: The Economics of Business Firm Formation and Growth*. Westport, CT: Praeger.

Kirchhoff, B. A. and A. Spencer (2008). 'New High Tech Firm Contributions to Economic Growth'. *Proceedings of International Council for Small Business World Conference, Halifax*. Washington, DC: International Council for Small Business (ICSB).

Kirzner, I. M. (1979) *Perception, Opportunity, and Profit: Studies in the Theory of Entrepreneurship*. Chicago, IL: University of Chicago Press.

—— (1973). *Competition and Entrepreneurship*. Chicago, IL: University of Chicago Press.

—— (1997). 'Entrepreneurial Discovery and the Competitive Market Process: An Austrian Approach'. *Journal of Economic Literature* 35(1), 60–85.

Klein, J. P. and M. L. Moeschberger (1997). *Statistics for Biology and Health: Survival Analysis*. Berlin, Heidelberg, New York, and Tokyo: Springer-Verlag.

Kogut, B. and U. Zander (1992). 'Knowledge of the Firm, Combinative Capabilities, and the Replication of Technology'. *Organization Science* 3(3): 383–397.

Kolb, D. A. (1984). *Experiential Learning: Experience as the Source of Learning and Development*. Englewood Cliffs, NJ: Prentice Hall.

Kolvereid, L., S. Shane, and P. Westhead (1993). 'Is it Equally Difficult for Female Entrepreneurs to Start Businesses in all Countries?' *Journal of Small Business Management* 31(4): 42–51.

Kortum, S. and J. Lerner (1998). *Stronger Protection or Technological Revolution: What is Behind the Recent Surge in Patenting?* Vol. 48, 247–304. Carnegie-Rochester Conference Series on Public Policy. North Holland.

Krasner, O. and M. L. Dubrow (1979). 'The Role of Small Business in Research and Development, Technological Change and Innovation in Region IX'. In *The Environment for Small Business and Entrepreneurship in Region IX*, ed. S. W. Hentzell. Menlo Park, CA: SRI International for the SBA.

Krugman, P. R. (1991). *Geography and Trade*. Cambridge: MIT Press.

Kulicke, M., K. Bayer, G. Bräunling, H. J. Ewers, A. Gerybadze, M. Myer, R. Müller, U. Wein, and U. Wupperweld (1993). *Chancen und risiken junger Technologieunturnehmen: Ergebnisse des Modellversuchs 'Foerderung technologieorientierter Unternehmens gruendungen'*. Heidelberg: Physica.

Lazonick, W. (2005). 'The Innovative Firm'. In *The Oxford Handbook of Innovation*, ed. J. Fagerberg, D. Mowery, and R. Nelson. Oxford: Oxford University Press.

Lee, C., K. Lee, and J. M. Pennings (2001). 'Internal Capabilities, External Networks, and Performance: A Study on Technology-based Ventures'. *Strategic Management Journal* 22(6 and 7): 615–640.

Liao, J., J. R. Kickul, and H. Ma (2009). 'Organizational Dynamic Capability and Innovation: An Empirical Examination of Internet Firms'. *Journal of Small Business Management* 47(3): 263.

Lichtenstein, B. M. B. and C. G. Brush (2001). 'How Do "Resource Bundles" Develop and Change in New Ventures? A Dynamic Model and Longitudinal Exploration'. *Entrepreneurship: Theory and Practice* 25(3): 37.

Lichtenstein, B. B., N. M. Carter, K. J. Dooley, and W. B. Gartner (2007). 'Complexity Dynamics of Nascent Entrepreneurship'. *Journal of Business Venturing* 22(2): 236–261.

Lindholm Dahlstrand, Å. (2004). *Teknikbaserat nyföretagande: tillväxt och affärsutveckling*, Lund: Studentlitteratur.

Lingelbach, D., L. de la Vina, and P. Asel (2005). 'What's Distinctive about Growth-Oriented Entrepreneurship in Developing Countries?' Center for Global Entrepreneurship Working Paper 1. San Antonio, TX: UTSA College of Business.

Lloyd-Ellis, H. and D. Bernhardt (2000). 'Enterprise, Inequality and Economic Development'. *Review of Economic Studies* 67: 147–168.

Low, M. B. and E. Abrahamson (1997). Movements, Bandwagons, and Clones: Industry Evolution and the Entrepreneurial Process. *Journal of Business Venturing* 12(6): 435–457.

Lugar, M. (2001). 'The Research Triangle Experience'. In *Industry-Laboratory Partnerships: A Review of the Sandia Science and Technology Park Initiative*, ed. C. Wessner, 35–38. Washington, DC: National Academy Press.

MacMillan, I. C. and D. L. Day (1987): 'Corporate Ventures into Industrial Markets: Dynamics of Aggressive Entry', *Journal of Business Venturing* 2(1): 29–39.

Magesh, V. and Premnath (2009). 'Government Funding for Technology Startups'. *DARE* 3(2): 26 and27.

Mahadevan, B. (2000). 'Business Models for Internet-based E-commerce: An Anatomy'. *California Management Review* 42(4): 55–69.

Mahmood, T. (1992). 'Does the Hazard Rate for New Plants Vary between Low- and High-tech Industries?' *Small Business Economics* 4(3): 201–209.

Mani, S. (2009). 'The Growth of Knowledge-intensive Entrepreneurship in India, 1991–2007'. UNU-WIDER Research Paper No. 2009/49.

Masurel, E. and K. V. Montfort (2006). 'Lifecycle Characteristics of Small Professional Service Firms'. *Journal of Small Business Management* 44(3): 461–473.

Mata, J. and P. Portugal (1994). 'Life Duration of New Firms'. *The Journal of Industrial Economics* 42(3) September: 227–245.

Matthews, C. H. and S. B. Moser (1995). 'The Impact of Family Background and Gender on Interest in Small Firm Ownership: A Longitudinal Study'. *Proceedings of the ICSB 40th World Conference*, 18–21 June. Sydney, 245–262.

Mazzarol, T., T. Volery, N. Doss, and V. Thein (1999). 'Factors Influencing Small Business Start-ups: A Comparison with Previous Research'. *International Journal of Entrepreneurial Behaviour & Research* 5(2): 48–63.

McClelland, D. C. (1961). *The Achieving Society*. Princeton, NJ: Van Nostrand.

McDougall, P. P., R. B. Robinson, and A. S. DeNisi (1992). 'Modeling New Venture Performance: An Analysis of New Venture Strategy, Industry Structure and Venture Origin'. *Journal of Business Venturing* 7(4): 267–289.

McGee, J. E., M. J. Dowling, and M. J. Megginson (1995). 'Cooperative Strategy and New Venture Performance: The Role of Business Strategy and Management Experience'. *Strategic Management Journal* 16(7): 565–581.

McGrath, M. E. (1994). *Product Strategy for High-Technology Companies: How to Achieve Growth, Competitive Advantage and Increased Profits.* Burr Ridge, IL: Irwin.

McGrath, R. G. and I. C. MacMillan (2000). *The Entrepreneurial Mindset: Strategies for Continuously Creating Opportunity in an Age of Uncertainty*, Vol. 284. Boston, MA: Harvard Business Press.

McKelvey, B. (2004). 'Toward a Complexity Science of Entrepreneurship'. *Journal of Business Venturing* 19(3): 313–341.

McMillan, J. and C. Woodruff (2002). 'The Central Role of Entrepreneurs in Transition Economies'. *Journal of Economic Perspectives* 16(3): 153–170.

McMullen, J. S. and D. A. Shepherd (2006). 'Entrepreneurial Action and the Role of Uncertainty in the Theory of the Entrepreneur'. *Academy of Management Review* 31: 132–152.

Microsoft Accelerator India (2012). *India Tech Startup Starts and Closure.* Report. Available at http://microsoft.com/india/accelerator. Accessed on 12 June 2017.

Millán, J. M., E. Congregado, and C. Román (2012). 'Determinants of Self-employment Survival in Europe'. *Small Business Economics* 38(2): 231–258.

Ministry of Commerce and Industry (2016). 'Startup India Action Plan'. New Delhi: Government of India. Available at http://startupindia.gov.in/actionplan.php. Accessed on 14 June 2017.

Ministry of Finance (2016). *Economic Survey 2014–15.* New Delhi : Government of India.

Ministry of MSMEs, Government of India. (2013). *Recommendations of the Inter-Ministerial Committee for Accelerating Manufacturing in Micro, Small & Medium Enterprises Sector.* New Delhi.

Minniti, M. and W. Bygrave (2001). 'A Dynamic Model of Entrepreneurial Learning'. *Entrepreneurship Theory & Practice* 25(3): 5–16.

Mohr, J., S. Sengupta, and S. Slater (2011). *Marketing of High-Technology Products and Innovations*, 3rd edn. Upper Saddle River, NJ: Prentice Hall.

Monitor, G. E. (1999). *Executive Report.* Kansas City, MO: Kauffman Center for Entrepreneurial Leadership at the Ewing Marion Kauffman Foundation.

Mullins, J. W. (1996). 'Early Growth Decisions of Entrepreneurs: The Influence of Competency and Prior Performance under Changing Market Conditions'. *Journal of Business Venturing* 11(2): 89–105.

Munshi, K. (2007). 'From Farming to International Business: The Social Auspices of Entrepreneurship in a Growing Economy'. Working Paper 13065. Cambridge, MA: National Bureau of Economic Research.

Mutikani, Lucia (2012). 'U.S. Business Startups Rate at Record Low', ed. Lisa Von Ahn. Available at http://www.reuters.com/article/2012/05/02/us-usa-economy-businesses-idUSBRE84113G20120502. Accessed on 5 March 2019.

Nambiar, P. (2011). 'Indian Software Companies like Flipkart, Makemytrip, Inmobi Inching Close to $1 Billion Valuations', *Economic Times,* 9 November.

NASSCOM (2014). *India: The Fastest Growing and 3rd Largest Start-up Ecosystem Globally.* Start-up report. Available at http://www.nasscom.in/india-fastest-growing-and-3rd-largest-startup-ecosystem-globally-nasscom-startup-report-2014. Accessed on 14 June 2017.

———— (2015). *Start-up India: Momentous Rise of the Indian Start-up Ecosystem.*

———— (2018). 'Indian Start-up Ecosystem: Approaching Escape Velocity'. Available at https://www.nasscom.in/knowledge-center/publications/indian-tech-start-ecosystem-2018-approaching-escape-velocity. Accessed on 13 February 2019.

Nelson, R. (1995). 'Recent Evolutionary Theorizing about Economic Change'. *Journal of Economic Literature* 33: 48–90.

Nelson, R. R. and S. G. Winter (1982). 'The Schumpeterian Tradeoff Revisited'. *The American Economic Review* 72(1): 114–132.

———— (2009). *An Evolutionary Theory of Economic Change.* Boston, MA: Harvard University Press.

North, D. C. (1990). *Institutions, Institutional Change and Economic Performance.* Cambridge: Cambridge University Press.

North, D. and D. Smallbone (1993). 'Employment Generation and Small Business Growth in Different Geographical Environment'. Paper presented at the 'National Small Firms Policy and Research Conference', Nottingham.

Nerlinger, E. (1998). *Standorte und Entwicklung junger innovativer Unturnehmen: Empirische ergebnisse fuer West-Deutscheland* 27, Baden-Baden.

Osterwalder, A. and Y. Pigneur (2010). *Business Model Generation: A Handbook for Visionaries, Game Changers, and Challengers.* John Wiley & Sons.

Oxford English Dictionary (2016). 'start-up'. Available at https://en.oxforddictionaries.com/definition/start-up. Accessed on 16 June 2017.

Parker, S. C. (2006). Learning about the Unknown: How Fast Do Entrepreneurs Adjust Their Beliefs?' *Journal of Business Venturing* 21(1): 1–26.

Pavia, T. M. (1990). 'Product Growth Strategies in Young High-technology Firms'. *Journal of Product Innovation Management* 7: 297–309.

Paulraj, A. S. (2012). 'Does India Need a High Technology Industry?' *The Hindu, Business Line*, 21 November.

Paulson, A., R. Townsend, and A. Karaivanov (2006). 'Distinguished Limited Liability from Moral Hazard in a Model of Entrepreneurship'. *Journal of Political Economy* 114(1): 100–145.

Pe'er, A. and I. Vertinsky (2006). 'The Determinants of Survival of De Novo Entrants in Clusters and Dispersal'. Working paper, Darthmouth College, Tuck School of Business.

Penrose, E. (1959). *The Theory of the Firm.* NY: John Wiley & Sons.

Pinchot, G. III (1985). *Intrapreneurs*, 32–64. New York City, NY: Harper & Row, .

Politis, D. (2005). 'The Process of Entrepreneurial Learning: A Conceptual Framework'. *Entrepreneurship Theory & Practice* 29(4): 399–424.

Politis, D. and J. Gabrielsson (2005). 'Exploring the Role of Experience in the Process of Entrepreneurial Learning'. Working paper series. Lund: Lund Institute of Economic Research.

Politis, D. (2008). 'Does Prior Start-up Experience Matter for Entrepreneurs' Learning? A Comparison between Novice and Habitual Entrepreneurs'. *Journal of Small Business and Enterprise Development* 15(3): 472–489.

Porter, M. (1980). *Competitive Strategy: Techniques for Analyzing Industries and Competitors*. New York City, NY: Free Press.

Porter, M. E. (1998). *Competitive Advantage: Creating and Sustaining Superior Performance*. New York City, NY: Free press.

Pullen, J. P. (2013). 'Emerging Tech: 9 International Start-up Hubs to Watch, Entrepreneur'. 7 May. Irvine, CA: *Business Daily*.

Purrington, C. and K. E. Bettcher (2001). 'From the Garage to the Boardroom: The Entrepreneurial Roots of America's Largest Corporations'. *SSRN* 1260383.

Quinn, R. E. and K. Cameron (1983). 'Organizational Life Cycles and Shifting Criteria of Effectiveness: Some Preliminary Evidence'. *Management Science* 29(1): 33–51.

Read, S., M. Song, and W. Smit (2009). 'A Meta-analytic View of Effectuation and Venture Performance'. *Journal of Business Venturing* 24: 573–587.

Rees, J. and H. Stafford (1986). 'Theories of Regional Growth and Industrial Location: Their Relevance in Understanding High-technology Complexes'. In *Technology Regions and Policy*, ed. J. Rees. Totawa, NJ: Rowman and Littlefield.

Reese, P. R. and H. E. Aldrich (1995). *Entrepreneurial Networks and Business Performance: A Panel Study of Small and Medium-sized Firms in the Research Triangle*. London: Routledge.

Reuber, A. R., L. S. Dyke, and E. M. Fischer (1990). 'Experientially Acquired Knowledge and Entrepreneurial Venture Success'. *Academy of Management Proceedings*, vol. 1990, no. 1, 69–73. Academy of Management.

Reuber, A. R. and Fischer (1994). 'Entrepreneurs' Experience, Expertise, and the Performance of Technology-based Firms'. *IEEE Transactions on Engineering Management* 41(4): 365–374.

Ruef, M., H. E. Aldrich, and N. M. Carter (2003). 'The Structure of Founding Teams: Homophily, Strong Ties, and Isolation among US Entrepreneurs'. *American Sociological Review* 68(2): 195–222.

Reynolds, P. D. (1992). 'Predicting New-Firm Births: Interactions of Organizational and Human Populations'. In *Entrepreneurship in the 1990s*, ed. D. Sexton and J. Kasarda. Boston, MA: PWS-Kent Publishing.

Reynolds, P. D. (1993a). 'High Performance Entrepreneurship: What Makes It Different?' Paper presented at the Babson Entrepreneurial Conference. Houston: University of Houston.

——— (1993b). 'The Role of Entrepreneurship in Economic Systems: Developed Market and Post-socialist Economies'. Paper presented at the Second Freiberg Symposium on Economics. Freiberg. 9–11 September.

Reynolds, P. D. and B. Miller (1988). *Minnesota New Firms Study: An Exploration of New Firms and Their Economic Contribution*. Minneapolis, MN: Centre for Urban and Regional Affairs.

Reynolds, P. and B. Miller (1992). 'New Firm Gestation: Conception, Birth, and Implications for Research'. *Journal of Business Venturing* 7(5): 405–417.

Reynolds, P. D. And D. J. Storey (1993). *Local and Regional Characteristics Affecting Small Business Formation: A Cross-national Comparison*. Paris: OECD.

Reynolds, P. D., M. Hay, S. M. Camp (1999). *Global Entrepreneurship Monitor*, 3. Kansas City, MO: Kauffman Center for Entrepreneurial Leadership.

Reynolds, P. D. and S. White (1997). *The Entrepreneurial Process*. Westport, CT: Quorum Books.

Ries, E. (2011). *The Lean Startup: How Today's Entrepreneurs Use Continuous Innovation to Create Radically Successful Businesses*. Crown Books.

———— (2014). *A Startup Enxuta*. Sao Paulo: Leya.

Robinson, K. C. (1998). 'An Examination of the Influence of Industry Structure on Eight Alternative Measures of New Venture Performance for High Potential Independent New Ventures'. *Journal of Business Venturing* 16: 165–187.

Roininen, S. and H. Ylinenpää (2009). 'Schumpeterian versus Kirznerian Entrepreneurship: A Comparison of Academic and Non-academic New Venturing'. *Journal of Small Business and Enterprise Development* 16(3): 504–520.

Romer, P. M. (1986). 'Increasing Returns and Long-run Growth'. *The Journal of Political Economy*: 1002–1037.

Ronstadt, R. (1988). 'The Corridor Principle'. *Journal of Small Business Venturing* 3(1): 31–40.

Rose, R. C., N. Kumar, and L. L. Yen (2006). '"The Dynamics of Entrepreneurs" Success Factors in Influencing Venture Growth'. *Journal of Asia Entrepreneurship and Sustainability* 2(3).

Rosenthal, S. S. and W. C. Strange (2005). 'The Geography of Entrepreneurship in the New York Metropolitan Area'. *Federal Reserve Bank of New York Economic Policy Review* 11: 29–53.

Roure, J. B. and R. H. Keeley (1990). 'Predictors of Success in New Technology-based Ventures'. *Journal of Business Venturing* 5(4): 201–220.

Sandberg, W. R. (1986). *New Venture Performance: The Role of Strategy and Industry Strurture*. Lexington, MA: Lexington Books.

Samuelsson, M. and P. Davidsson, P. (2009). 'Does Venture Opportunity Variation Matter? Investigating Systematic Process Differences between Innovative and Imitative New Ventures'. *Small Business Economics* 33(2): 229–255.

Sapienza, H. and C. Grimm (1997). 'Founder Characteristics, Start-up Process and Strategy/Structure Variables as Predictors of Shortline Railroad Performance'. *Entrepreneurship Theory and Practice* 22(1): 5–24.

Sarasvathy, S. (2004). 'The Questions We Ask and the Questions We Care about: Reformulating Some Problems in Entrepreneurship Research'. *Journal of Business Venturing* 19: 707–717

Sarasvathy, S. D. (2001). 'Causation and Effectuation: Toward a Theoretical Shift from Economic Inevitability to Entrepreneurial Contingency'. *The Academy of Management Review* 26(2): 243–263.

Saxenian, A. (2002). 'Transnational Communities and the Evolution of Global Production Networks: The Cases of Taiwan, China and India'. *Industry and Innovation* 9: 183–202.

——— (2003). 'Transnational Technical Communities and Regional Growth in the Periphery'. *Institutions, Innovation and Growth: Selected Economic Papers.*

Saxenian, A. and C. Y. Li (2003). 'Bay-to-Bay Strategic Alliances: The Network Linkages between Taiwan and the US Venture Capital Industries'. *International Journal of Technology Management* 25(1 and 2): 136–150.

Schere, J. (1982). 'Tolerance of Ambiguity as a Discriminating Variable between Entrepreneurs and Managers'. *Proceeding of the Academy of Management Conference.* New York City, NY, 404–408.

Scherer, F. M. (1980). *Industrial Market Structure and Economic Performance*, 2nd edn. Chicago: Rand McNally College Pub. Co.

——— (1984). *Innovation and Growth: Schumpeterian Perspectives.* Cambridge, MA: MIT Press.

Scherer, F. M., and D. Ross (1990). *Industrial Market Structure and Economic Performance*, 3rd edn. Boston, MA: Houghton Mifflin.

Scherer, F. M. and D. Harhoff (2000). 'Technology Policy for a World of Skew-distributed Outcomes'. *Research Policy* 29(4): 559–566.

Schoonhoven, C. B. and K. M. Eisenhardt (1990). 'Speeding Products to Market: Waiting Time to First Production Introduction in New Firms'. Special issue, *Technology, Organizations and Innovation. Administrative Science Quarterly* 35(1): 177–207.

Schreyer, P. (2000). *The Contribution of Information and Communication Technology to Output Growth: A Study of the G7 Countries.* Working Paper No. 2000/2. Paris: OECD Publishing.

Schumpeter, J., A. (1934). *The Theory of Economic Development: An Inquiry into Profits, Capital, Credit, Interest, and the Business Cycle.* New Brunswick, NJ: Transaction Books.

Scott, M. and R. Bruce (1987). 'Five Stages of Growth in Small Business'. *Long Range Planning* 20: 45–52.

Scott, M. G. and D. F. Twomey (1988). 'The Long-term Supply of Entrepreneurs: Students' Career Aspirations in Relation to Entrepreneurship'. *Journal of Small Business Management* (October): 5–13.

Securities and Exchange Board of India (2012). 'List of Registered Venture Capital Funds'. Available at http://www.sebi.gov.in/investor/venturecap.html, accessed on 14 June 2017; and http://www.sebi.gov.in/investor/forventure.html, accessed on 14 June 2017.

——— (2015). 'Alternate Capital Raising Platform'. Available at http://www.sebi.gov.in/cms/sebi_data/attachdocs/1427713523817.pdf. Accessed on 14 June 2017.

Shane, S. (1995). 'Is the Independent Entrepreneurial Firm a Valuable Organizational Form?' *Academy of Management Journal* (Best paper proceedings): 110–113.

——— (2000). 'Prior Knowledge and the Discovery of Entrepreneurial Opportunities'. *Organizational Science* 11(4): 448–469.

Shane, S. and S. Venkataraman (2000). 'The Promise of Entrepreneurship as a Field of Research'. *Academy of Management Review* 25: 217–226.

Shane, S. and R. Khurana (2003). 'Bringing Individuals Back in the Effects of Career Experience on New Firm Founding'. *Industrial and Corporate Change* 12(2): 519–544.

Shepherd, D. A. and M. Shanley (1998). *New Venture Strategy: Timing, Environmental Uncertainty, and Performance.* Thousand Oaks, CA: SAGE Publications.

Shepherd, D. A., J. E. Douglas, and M. Shanley (2000). 'New Venture Survival: Ignorance, External Shocks and Risk Reduction Strategies'. *Journal of Business Venturing* 15: 393–410.

Shepherd, D. A., J. S. McMullen, and P. D. Jennings (2007). 'The Formation of Opportunity Beliefs: Overcoming Ignorance and Reducing Doubt'. *Strategic Entrepreneurship Journal* 1: 75–95.

Shook, C. L., R. L. Priem, and J. E. McGee (2003). 'Venture Creation and the Enterprising Individual: A Review and Synthesis'. *Journal of Management* 29(3): 379–399.

Singer, B. (1995). 'Contours of Development'. *Journal of Business Venturing* 10(4): 303–329.

Singh, J. V., R. J. House, and D. J. Tucker (1986). 'Organizational Change and Organizational Mortality'. *Administrative Science Quarterly* 31: 587–611.

Smollen, L. E. and M. A. Levin (1979). 'The Role of Small Business in Research and Development, Technological Change and Innovation in Region IX'. In *A Region's Struggling Savior: Small Business in New England*, ed. J. A. Timmons. Waltham, MA: SBANE Foundation.

Solow, R. M. (1956). 'A Contribution to the Theory of Economic Growth'. *The Quarterly Journal of Economics*: 65–94.

——— (1957). 'Technical Change and the Aggregate Production Function'. *Review of Economics & Statistics* 39(3): 312–320.

Song, M., K. Podoynitsyna, H. van der Bij, and J. I. M. Halman (2008). 'Success Factors in New Ventures: A Meta-analysis'. *Product Development & Management Association* 25: 7–27.

de Soto, H. D. (2000). *The Mystery of Capital: Why Capitalism Triumphs in the West and Fails Everywhere Else.* New York: Basic Books.

Starr, J. and I. MacMillan 1990. 'Resource Cooptation via Social Contracting: Resource Acquisition Strategies for New Ventures'. *Strategic Management Journal* 11(5): 79–92.

Startup Genome (2012). *Start-up Ecosystem Report 2012.* USA.

——— (2015). *Start-up Ecosystem Report 2015.* USA.

Sternberg, R. (1996). 'Technology Policies and the Growth of Regions: Evidence from Four Countries'. *Small Business Economics* 8(2): 75–86.

Stevens, J. P., ed. (2002). 'K-group MANOVA: A Priori and Post Hoc Procedures'. In *Applied Multivariate Statistics for the Social Sciences*, 4th edn, 208–255. London: Lawrence Erlbaum Associates Publishers.

Stevenson, H. H. and J. C. Jarillo (1990). 'A Paradigm of Entrepreneurship: Entrepreneurial Management'. *Strategic Management Journal* 11: 17–27.

Stinchcombe, A. L. (1965). 'Social Structure and Organizations'. In *Handbook of Organizations*, ed. G. James, 142–193. Chicago, IL: Rand McNally.

Storey, D. J. (1982). *Entrepreneurship and the New Firm.* Beckenham: Kent.

——— (1983). *The Small Firm on International Survey.* London: Croom Helm.

——— (1985). 'Manufacturing Employment Changes in Northern England 1965–78: The Role of Small Business'. In *Small Firms in Regional Economic Development,* ed. D. J. Storey. Cambridge: Cambridge University Press.

——— (1994). *Understanding the Small Business Sector.* London: Routledge.

Stough, R. R., K. E. Haynes, and H. S. Campbell (1998). 'Small Business Entrepreneurship in the High Technology Services Sector: An Assessment for the Edge Cities of the U.S. National Capital Region'. *Small Business Economics* 10: 61–74.

Strotmann, H. (2007). 'Entrepreneurial Survival'. *Small Business Economics* 28: 87–104.

Suarez, F. F. and J. M. Utterback (1995). 'Dominant Designs and the Survival of Firms'. *Strategic Management Journal* 16(6): 415–430.

Suchman, M. C. (1995). 'Managing Legitimacy: Strategic and Institutional Approaches'. *Academy of Management Review* 20(3): 571–610.

Sullivan, M. K. and A. Miller (1990). 'Applying Theory of Finance to Informal Risk Capital Research: Promise and Problems'. *Frontiers of Entrepreneurship Research* 14: 296–310.

Sutton, J. (1997). 'Gibrat's Legacy'. *Journal of Economic Literature* 35(1): 40–59.

Taube, F. (2009). 'Diversity and the Geography of Technology Entrepreneurship: Evidence from the Indian IT Industry'. In *Sustaining Entrepreneurship and Economic Growth–Lessons in Policy and Industry Innovations from Germany and India,* ed. M. Keilbach, J. Pawan Tamvada, and D. B. Audretsch. New York City, NY: Springer.

Teece, D. (1986). 'Profiting from Technological Innovations: Implications for Integration, Collaboration, Licensing, and Public Policy'. *Research Policy* 15: 286–305.

Teece, D. J., G. Pisano, and A. Shuen (1997). 'Dynamic Capabilities and Strategic Management'. *Strategic Management Journal* 18(7): 509–533.

Thakur, S. P. (1999). 'Size of Investment, Opportunity Choice and Human Resources in New Venture Growth: Some Topologies'. *Journal of Business Venturing* 14: 283–309.

Thurik, A. R. (1999). 'Entrepreneurship, Industrial Transformation and Growth'. *The Sources of Entrepreneurial Activity* 11: 29–65.

Times of India (2015). 'Bengaluru Is Home to 5 of India's 8 Unicorn Start-ups'. 12 October. Bengaluru.

Timmons, J. A. and S. Spinelli (1999). *New Venture Creation: Entrepreneurship for the 21st Century,* vol. 6. New York City, NY: McGraw-Hill and Irwin.

Tornikoski, E. T. and S. L. Newbert (2007). 'Exploring the Determinants of Organizational Emergence: A Legitimacy Perspective'. *Journal of Business Venturing* 22(2): 311–335.

Tushman, M. and P. Anderson (1986). 'Technological Discontinuities and Organizational Environments'. *Administrative Science Quarterly* 31: 439–465

UNESCO Science Report (2010). *The Current State of Science around the World: Chapter 17, India.* Available at http://www.unesco.org/new/fileadmin/MULTIMEDIA/HQ/SC/pdf/sc_usr10_india_EN.pdf. Accessed on 12 June 2017.

US Small Business Administration (2016). *SBA Rules and Regulations.* Washington, DC.

Van de Ven, A. H., R. Hudson, and D. M. Schroeder (1984). 'Designing New Business Start-ups: Entrepreneurial, Organizational, and Ecological Considerations'. *Journal of Management* 10: 87–107.

Van de Ven, A. H. and R. M. Engleman (2004). 'Event- and Outcome-driven Explanations of Entrepreneurship'. *Journal of Business Venturing* 19(3): 343–358.

Van Gelderen, M., R. Thurik, and N. Bosma (2006). 'Success and Risk Factors in the Pre-startup Phase'. *Small Business Economics* 26(4): 319–335.

Venkataraman, S. (1997). 'The Distinctive Domain of Entrepreneurship Research'. In *Advances in Entrepreneurship: Firm Emergence and Growth*, ed. J. Katz. Greenwich, CT: JAI Press.

Venture Intelligence (2013, 2014, 2015, and 2016). 'Database on Private Company Financials, Transactions & Valuations for India'. Available at http://www.ventureintelligence.com. Accessed on 12 June 2017.

Venture Pulse (2015). *Global Analysis of Venture Funding, Q2, 2015*. KPMG–CBInsights quarterly report.

Vernon, R. (1970). *The Technology Factor in International Trade*. Cambridge, MA: *NBER Books*.

Vesper, K. H. (1980): *New Venture Strategies*. Englewood Cliffs, NJ: Prentice Hall.

——— (1990). 'New Venture Strategies'. *University of Illinois at Urbana-Champaign's Academy for Entrepreneurial Leadership Historical Research Reference in Entrepreneurship*.

Wang, S. (2006). 'Determinants of New Firm Formation in Taiwan'. *Small Business Economics* 27(4 and 5): 313–323.

Warne, R. T. (2014). 'A Primer on Multivariate Analysis of Variance (MANOVA) for Behavioral Scientists'. *Practical Assessment, Research & Evaluation* 19(17).

Weber, M. (1930). *The Protestant Ethic and the Spirit of Capitalism*, trans. T. Parsons. New York City, NY: Scribner (1904).

Wennberg, K. and G. Lindqvist (2010). 'The Effect of Clusters on Survival and Performance of New Firms'. *Small Business Economics* 34: 221–241.

Wennekers, S., A. Van Stel, R. Thurik, and P. Reynolds (2005). 'Nascent Entrepreneurship and the Level of Economic Development'. *Small Business Economics* 24: 293–309.

Westhead, P., D. Ucbasaran, M. Wright, and M. Binks (2005). 'Novice, Serial and Portfolio Entrepreneur Behaviour and Contributions'. *Small Business Economics* 25: 109–132.

Wiewel, W. and A. Hunter (1985). 'The Interorganizational Network as a Resource: A Comparative Case Study on Organizational Genesis'. *Administrative Science Quarterly* 30(4): 482– 499.

Wiklund, J. and D. Shepherd (2003). 'Aspiring for, and Achieving Growth: The Moderating Role of Resources and Opportunities'. *Journal of Management Studies* 40(8): 1919–1941.

Wiklund J., H. Patzelt, and D. A. Shepherd (2009). 'Building an Integrative Model of Small Business Growth'. *Small Business Economics* 32: 351–374.

Williamson, I.O., 2000. 'Employer Legitimacy and Recruitment Success in Small Businesses'. *Entrepreneurship Theory and Practice* 27–42 (Fall).

Wincent, J. and M. Westerberg (2006). 'Resource Contribution from Entrepreneurial Firms in Strategic SME Networks'. *Journal of Entrepreneurship and Innovation* 7(1): 23–31.

World Intellectual Property Organization (2007). *International Patent Classification*, vol. 5, 8th edn. Publication No. 560E.5/8.

Woywode, M. (1998). *Determinanten der Ueberlebenswahrscheinlichkeit von Unternehmen: Eine empirishe Ueberpruefung organizationstheoretischer und industrieoekonomischer Erklaerungsansaetze*. Baden-Baden: Nomos.

Wright, W. F. (2001). 'Task Experience as a Predictor of Superior Loan Loss Judgments'. *Auditing* 20(1): 147–156.

Zahra, S. A. (1993). 'A Conceptual Model of Entrepreneurship as Firm Behavior: A Critique and Extension'. *Entrepreneurship: Theory and Practice* 17(4): 5–22.

——— (1996). 'Technology Strategy and New Venture Performance: A Study of Corporate-sponsored and Independent Biotechnology Ventures'. *Journal of Business venturing* 11(4): 289–321.

Zahra, S. A., R. D. Ireland, and M. A. Hitt (2000). 'International Expansion by New Venture Firms: International Diversity, Mode of Market Entry, Technological Learning, and Performance'. *Academy of Management Journal* 43(5): 925–950.

Zahra, S. A. and G. George (2002a). 'Absorptive Capacity: A Review, Reconceptualization, and Extension'. *Academy of Management Review* 27(2): 185–203.

——— (2002b). 'The Net-enabled Business Innovation Cycle and the Evolution of Dynamic Capabilities'. *Information Systems Research* 13(2): 147–150.

Zimmerman, M. A. and G. J. Zeitz (2002). 'Beyond Survival: Achieving New Venture Growth by Building Legitimacy'. *Academy of Management Review* 27(3): 414–431.

Zingales, L. (1998). 'Survival of the Fittest or the Fattest? Exit and Financing in the Trucking Industry'. *The Journal of Finance* 53(3): 905–938.

Index